W9-CFV-551

5-7 studio beg

Secrecy & Cultural Reality

XJ-31

Secrecy & Cultural Reality

UTOPIAN IDEOLOGIES

OF THE

NEW GUINEA MEN'S HOUSE

※

Gilbert Herdt

University of Michigan Press
Ann Arbor

Copyright © by the University of Michigan 2003
All rights reserved
Published in the United States of America by
The University of Michigan Press
Manufactured in the United States of America
⊗ Printed on acid-free paper

2006   2005   2004   2003   4   3   2   1

No part of this publication may be reproduced, stored
in a retrieval system, or transmitted in any form
or by any means, electronic, mechanical, or otherwise,
without the written permission of the publisher.

A CIP catalog record for this book is available from the British Library.

Library of Congress Cataloging-in-Publication Data

Herdt, Gilbert H., 1949–
    Secrecy and cultural reality : utopian ideologies of the New
Guinea men's house / Gilbert Herdt.
        p.   cm.
    Includes bibliographical references and index.
    ISBN 0-472-09761-x (Cloth : alk. paper) — ISBN 0-472-06761-3
(Paper : alk. paper)
    1. Sambia (Papua New Guinea people)—Rites and ceremonies.
2. Sambia (Papua New Guinea people)—Sexual behavior.   3. Secret
societies—Papua New Guinea.   4. Initiation rites—Papua New Guinea.
5. Sex customs—Papua New Guinea.   6. Homosexuality, Male—Papua
New Guinea.   7. Papua New Guinea—Social life and customs.
I. Title.

DU740.42 .H464   2003
305.8'89912—dc21   2003001358

Dedicated to my sister,
Cindy Brown,
for her courage and wisdom.

In the secret societies we seem to have guardians of this unconscious experience who only allow its content to reach the general public in some disguised form. *—W. H. R. Rivers*

※

The man who lays his secrets before the world shows his rivals how to become his enemies. *—Gola proverb*

※

If the anthropological study of religious commitment is underdeveloped, the anthropological study of religious non-commitment is nonexistent. The anthropology of religion will have come of age when some more subtle Malinowski writes a book called, "Belief and Unbelief" (or even "Faith and Hypocrisy") in a Savage Society. *—Clifford Geertz*

※

Women are the bane of a peaceful society, and as long as men never compromise their masculine unity, they will hold the secret to a paradisiacal world devoid of women and full of life's pleasures. *—Donald F. Tuzin*

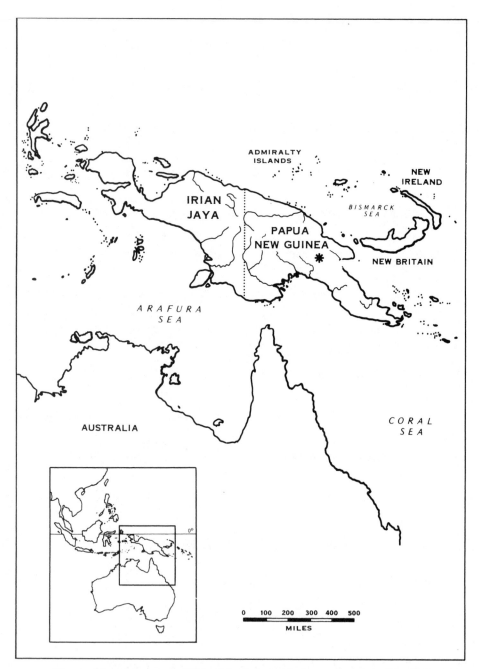

Map 1. New Guinea and off-lying islands (asterisk denotes location of Sambia)

Contents

�粦

Preface & Acknowledgments

A BOOK IS A CHAPTER from one's life, at least it is for me, and like all liminal markers, it foreshadows endings as well as beginnings. The invitation to give the Lewis Henry Morgan Lectures in 1991 was no different in this way, though it took far longer, a decade longer, than I imagined to sort the chaff and save the wheat.[1]

The present book is a greatly revised version of the original lectures. In it, I have proposed a general theory of the conditions that foster secrecy, especially among men, who, in dealing with social anxiety and mistrust, deploy rituals of conditional masculinity to gain purpose and agency, achieve homosociality and trust, imposing hierarchy and rule over younger males and women. The personal and institutional outcome is to create an alternative, hidden cultural reality in society. While previous theorists in Melanesian ethnography and anthropological study in general have paid little attention to the role of sexuality in these processes, this book demonstrates the significance of sexuality in homosociality and relationships between the genders. This historical formation is especially interesting in view of the fact that in Melanesia it precedes the development of "homosexuality" as a category or homosexual subjects in the cultural meaning system. I draw upon Victorian studies to contextualize the social career of Lewis Henry Morgan (chap. 1), showing how homosociality and ritual secrecy existed as a means of achieving intimacy before homosexuality stepped onto the stage of modernity.

I should have been cautioned against the pitfalls of investigating secrecy by the famous example of the German sociologist Georg Simmel, who spent years on this construct in the human imagination early in the twentieth century (see chap. 2). The key to studying secrecy is to allow the passage of at least a decade, maybe even two, in order to say something new about the subject. My own research into secrecy has led me to define two distinctive types, which I term *ritual secrecy* and *contractual secrecy;* this book is about the former. Though ritual secrecy is a compact between persons (unlike contractual secrecy, as between lawyer and client), it is closer to the category of the gift, the order of things which can neither be sold or given, but must be kept (Godelier 1999). Eventually, I hope to publish a larger study focused on understanding contractual secrets formed between individual agents in the modern and postmodern eras, especially the way that hidden contractual relations were historically productive of sexual subjectivity and private selfhood since the time of the French Revolution.

Beginning with my own historical society and moving outward to Papua New Guinea, I deconstruct the exoticism inherent in secrecy and the tendency to transform members of social out-groups into marginalized Others typical of the way in which secrecy is treated in the academy and popular culture today. I encourage my readers to question the dominant misunderstandings and prejudices against secrecy that prevail in anthropology and the social sciences: that secrecy is generally a sham or hoax, rather than a valid means of establishing trust and interdependence in times of social and political instability, and that secrecy is a cursory social practice rather than providing the impetus for creating utopian cultural reality. Such views conflate the individual or private secrecy of late modern life with the more complex, collective secrecy that was a product of myth and ritual ceremonies in areas such as Melanesia and New Guinea. We should be skeptical of the idea that secrecy always works "against" society; instead, it can be viewed as an alternative method of constructing and legitimating hegemonic control of the social order by one particular group—or one gender, as in the case studied here—over another, a view close to Simmel's. Such a critique inevitably challenges the received worldview that secrecy is a force that disrupts interpersonal relations and works to undermine human potential. An alternative approach is to view secrecy as one of the desperate tools of the human imagination for managing highly complicated—if not at times seemingly impossible—social relations. I must admit to my concern at being seen as an apologist for secrecy in taking such an approach.

Being a Westerner (furthermore, an American), a lifelong academic, and a neoliberal who abhors institutional secrecy places me in an awkward position. As an anthropologist who values cultural relativism, I subscribe to the ideology that transparency of intent through social action is the most preferable means of creating a positive social climate and promoting the ideals of democracy. On the other hand, as an anthropologist, I am aware of the middle-class privileges and liberal democratic tradition implied by this ethnocentric suspicion of collective secrecy. More than two decades of work in New Guinea have convinced me that secrecy is but one of the many cultural and political devices employed by societies that hover desperately near the edge of cultural overthrow, often due to the forces of war.

The tenacity of secrecy in human society can never be taken for granted. The Western liberal democracies thought that they had left the culture of secrecy behind with the cold war (Moynihan 1998). During the cold war, especially in the 1950s and 1960s, these concerns were intensely focused upon East versus West rhetoric, gender segregation based on exaggerated perceptions of gender role differences, and the cultural imaginal of international espionage. But James Bond and his adolescent boy's world of sexual reveries and more-or-less clearly defined enemies have been retired. Present-day fears of corporate spying and sabotage, coverups and denials of wrongdoing at the highest levels of the government and military, and allegations of scandal in the White House have further blurred the boundary between the rights of an individual to a private life where he or she may pursue a number of personal interests and the right of the public to know of treason and public threat.

Indeed, just as we thought secrecy was about to disappear from the national consciousness, at least as a signifier of state security and patriotic nationalism, the events of September 11, 2001, shattered the present. Amid the worldwide hunt for those terrorists responsible for the attack against America and the effort to bring down the ruling Taliban in Afghanistan, the U.S. government deployed new and virtually unprecedented measures of secrecy. These efforts have subsequently caused a variety of retrospective examinations of the relationships between war and secrecy, and hence, masculinity, as, for example, the question of how much Franklin D. Roosevelt engaged the United States in a secret war leading up to the Allied effort early in World War II (Persico 2001). Secrecy refuses to go away and may become more contested than ever in the life of civil societies.

My own introduction to ritual secrecy was among the Sambia, a group of hunters and gardeners numbering two thousand people inhabiting the southeastern fringe of the Central New Guinea Highlands. I was able to observe—through a total of sixteen different male initiation ceremonies over a number of years—the systematic way in which secrecy permeated every aspect of male subjectivity, social relationships, and sexual activity. Secrecy was a part of female ritual and secular life in Sambia culture as well, albeit separate from males. Sambia boys, beginning anywhere from age seven to ten, were initiated into two fundamental secret structures of knowing and being: ritual practices of boy-insemination that continued for many years until marriage and fatherhood, and a concomitant structure of nose-bleeding rites begun in first-stage initiation and perpetuated until the individual's death later in life (Herdt 1982b). Here, one is constantly impressed by how ritual secrecy serves as a structure of subjectivity in the production of cultural reality. Of course there are a variety of additional forms of hidden power embracing religious practice—shamanism, spiritual healing, sorcery, dream divination, and soothsaying among them (Herdt and Stephen 1989)—but it is ritual secrecy that dominates male Sambia mental life and the creation of their particular sociality.

Cultural communities like those of the Sambia in precolonial Melanesia, and Highlands Papua New Guinea especially, lacked the necessary resources and political consensus to establish sufficient trust or unity between the genders and across generations to ensure social reproduction. The solution to this problem was thereby sought after in several domains, most notably ceremonial exchange and secret initiation cults. Of these two paradigms, I believe that ritual secrecy was the more difficult and tenuous to maintain, but also the most effective in dealing with the challenges of living in armed societies requiring social cooperation (cf. the ancient Greeks; Dover 1978). This may seem a bold claim, but I believe that is warranted in the light of the accumulating evidence to be reviewed below.

What is distinctive of the Sambia and other kindred groups in New Guinea is not that men attempted to dominate women as well as younger males with the appeal to readiness for warfare as their ultimate justification, for that is surely common. Men's rhetoric here was anchored in reality and was not merely a matter of rationalizing their tenuous domination; however, their claim was neither innocent, smooth, nor seamless. As I have stated from the beginning of my anthropological work, the boys resisted initiation (Herdt 1981), but what I did not emphasize was how Sambia men also resisted initiating their own sons and grandsons (chap. 3). Could they entrust their own sons with ritual secrets? The primary fear was that the boys might betray them to their mothers, that is, the wives of the men, and thus undermine the entire foundation of ritual secrecy. But the men's anxiety revealed a deeper problem: the very nature of this shared secret reality, its legitimacy, its utopian flavor, and its social construction (chap. 4). It is hard to know the extent to which these political and psychological dynamics were present in precolonial societies; however, a careful examination of ethnographies and deconstruction of several critical ethnographic cases suggests that New Guinea men have faced the issue of sensing that ritual is their own invention, and they needed somehow to hide this fact from themselves (chap. 5).

Ritual secrecy before the Pax Australiana was an epic project of gender politics, a kind of endless reclamation of the male body with a utopian goal: reclassifying boys as men and transferring their subjectivities from the women's house to the men's house. Rebirth is the primary metaphor in Melanesian communities, "rebirth through ritual," including the sanitization of the young boy's body and the resocialization of the contents of his mind, knowing, and being. According to local male belief, these changes in social status for the boy—who had been formerly categorized with women—were the royal road to his physical growth and maturation. The "ideologies" involved in this dietetics rationalized and motivated a variety of complex "encompassments," of claims and counterclaims about what ritual does for each gender, as Marilyn Strathern has adequately demonstrated (1988: 115).

This study will carefully examine how the boy's own subjectivities were altered in order for him to become a secret-sharer and to test his loyalties and trustworthiness among the community of men. This requires that we study ritual secrecy as the embodiment of subjectivities, aesthetics, and energetics through the staging of social performances in public and private, or secret, relationships. Anthropologists have long doubted what constitutes the "truth" and "illusion" of male-dominated traditions (Keesing 1982a), and for good reason. However, I am reminded of Malinowski's reaction to the critics of his theory of Trobriander magic: "The natives understand that magic, however efficient, will not make up for bad workmanship" (1922: 115). The warning is applicable pari passu to the romantic-cynical view of ritual secrecy. The Sambia understand all too well that while ritual secrecy is a way of generating social relations under complicated political circumstances, the deployment of secret rites cannot make up for bad faith or incompetent gender relations.

I have referred to skeptics of these traditions as being in the "cynical-romantic" tradition of anthropology's romantic rebellion against the Enlightenment (Shweder 1984). By this, I mean that anthropologists who subscribe to the tenets of cultural relativism have often viewed the cultures of Melanesia as integrated systems of meaning, coherent and worthy in their own separate contexts, both following in the Malinowski tradition of functionalism and in keeping with Boas's principles of descriptive relativism (Geertz 1984a; Spiro 1989). Ethnographers' romantic regard for these cultures, however, had its limitations; for instance, when it came to the arena of ritual secrecy in male-female relationships, the romanticism turned into cynicism. Many ethnographers have followed the lead of K. E. Read (1952) in describing the relevant ritual performances of men as a hoax, or even worse, as a lie. This is the principal aspect of these ethnographic interpretations that I will argue against in this book.

It is wrong empirically (at least) to claim that ritual secrecy was primarily a deception, fraud, or hoax—as it was typically depicted by the ethnographers just mentioned. Such accounts presented ritual secrecy as an empty exercise used to cover up the presumptuous desires of men who wanted to dominate their society or the nonconstructive efforts that make for vast edifices of cultural production, such as the Sepik River Tambaran men's cult house complex (Tuzin 1980). To the extent that such perspectives render a worldview differently, they seriously distort and misrepresent the local ontologies or cultural realities of these complicated and fragile symbolic structures (Harrison 1993). Such interpretations refuse to accept the legitimacy of the cultural reality endorsed by these people. I believe that this refusal on the part of anthropologists is linked to the trouble that secrecy posed for the personal circumstances of male ethnographers, as well as with the difficulty of truly comprehending the life and death stakes that were involved with these regimes of ritual secrecy in the men's house.

The basis of the ontological theory on secrecy featured in this work was originally published as the article "Secret Societies and Secret Collectives" in the sixtieth anniversary issue of the journal *Oceania* (1990). Certain ideas and fragments from that article have been used herein, and permission to reprint the material by Oceania Publications is gratefully acknowledged. Thanks go to Francesca Merlan and Les Hiatt for their comments and assistance. A study of the coming-out process among lesbian and gay youth in Chicago that I worked on in the late 1980s provided me with another perspective, although that material is not directly applicable here. The time I have spent teaching in higher education has provided me with another source of inspiration and insight on this topic. At Stanford University in 1981–82, I taught my first seminar on New Guinea secret societies. My students there were of great help in reconceptualizing theories and ethnographies in the literature at the time. In particular, I would like to recognize the significant contributions of Eytan Bercovitch in this regard and direct attention to his own later work among the Atbalman of New Guinea, which has been a pleasing and much needed addition to the literature. Another seminar on secrecy and culture, taught at the University of Chicago in 1994–95, provided additional critical ground. Finally, presentations to the faculty seminar at Vanderbilt University during my sabbatical in 1997–98 were of help in bringing the work to its present form.

The Department of Anthropology at the University of Rochester served as my host for the Morgan Lectures, and I am ever grateful for their invitation. In particular, I am indebted to Professor Alfred Harris, then editor and coordinator of the Morgan series. Equally helpful was the kind personal and intellectual exchange I experienced with Professors Grace Harris and Al Harris at their home and in many other settings over the course of my visit. I would also like to thank the other faculty of the university for their hospitality, especially Robert and Nancy Foster. It is a pity that the retirement of Al Harris and change in the management and publisher of the Morgan series resulted in this book being printed elsewhere.

This work relied upon the insights of several notable scholars, in particular the German sociologist Georg Simmel and my dear teacher and friend, the late Kenneth E. "Mick" Read. I am indebted to my friend and colleague, Ray Fogelson, for introducing me to the ethnography of Lewis Henry Morgan. At this point, I would like to acknowledge a large intellectual debt to several scholars whose works on secrecy have been influential in my thinking: Fredrik Barth, Maurice Godelier, Erving Goffman, Robert Murphy, Simon Ottenberg, Marilyn Strathern, and Donald Tuzin.

I would also like to offer deepest gratitude to my colleagues and friends Eytan Bercovitch, Bruce Knauft, Michele Stephen, and Donald Tuzin, whose work has taught me about the cultural production of secrecy. For comments and critical feedback on the original lectures or subsequent texts, I am indebted to Eytan Bercovitch, Caroline Bledsoe, Andy Boxer, Volney Gay, Tom Gregor, Gert Hekma, Gregg Horowitz, Bruce Knauft, Bill Murphy, Niels F. Teunis, and the late Robert J. Stoller. Although I have not always agreed with all of the criticisms and suggestions, their influence upon me (both conscious and unconscious) is profound, and I hope this work repays their rich heritage in some measure.

The book was begun on sabbatical in Amsterdam, the Netherlands, where I was Visiting Professor of Anthropology at the University of Amsterdam in 1992–93. I am grateful to the University of Chicago for its sabbatical support. Seminars in Dutch, French, and German universities during the time afforded important opportunities for exchanging ideas about this book, and I should like to thank Han ten Brummelhuis, Maurice Godelier, Brigitta Hauser-Schaublin, Pierre Lemonnier, Ton Otto, and H. U. E. Thoden van Velsen for their hospitality. I would also like to thank Professors Johannes Fabian, Frans Husken, and Willy Jansen for their kindness. The completion of this book was also funded by an award of the William Simon Henry Guggenheim Memorial Fellowship, the support from which is gratefully acknowledged.

And let me recognize the support of Ingrid Erikson and Susan Whitlock for their editorial work at the University of Michigan Press.

Finally, this book is dedicated to my dear sister, Cindy Brown, kin and friend to me in this equally strange and marvelous world. To her I offer this small tribute of my love and respect.

CHAPTER I

Lewis Henry Morgan &
Victorian Secret Societies

IT IS NOT COMMONLY KNOWN THAT, as a young man, Lewis Henry Morgan enjoyed the intimacy of male secrecy at a time when the ground between public and private cultural spaces was unstable and secret societies produced trust and mistrust between the men who occupied their reality. Morgan—the nineteenth-century lawyer whose investigation of Iroquois social organization in upstate New York is critical to the development of anthropology in the United States—created, occupied, and subsequently abandoned men's secret societies. Secrecy was a condition of Morgan's masculinity, sexuality, and sociality, as it was for other men of his time; however, unlike his peers, he was instrumental in founding a number of secret societies, in addition to participating in several within Native American culture. Morgan's story, recounted here, provides insight in understanding ritual secrecy and the role of anthropology in the more exotic New Guinea men's clubhouse societies.

In detailing this little-known theme in the life of Morgan, it is not my intention to suggest that he "caused" anthropology to handle the subject of secrecy in a particular way. Nor am I interested in tracing the impact of Morgan's work upon ensuing theories of secrecy; that is the subject of an entirely different book. Morgan's life and work—so ordinary, yet so remarkable—shows that ritual secrecy was an uncommonly popular solution to collective problems of nineteenth-century society, especially in men's lives.

Examining the role of clandestine men's clubs and secret fraternities in Morgan's time not only disproves the historically dubious idea that secrecy is a sham, it also clarifies how secrecy was once at the forefront of public concern in regard to changing gender roles and religious beliefs, rather than being caught up in the domain of individual rights and confessions, as it is in the tabloid culture of today. The men of Victorian-era America lived with their own personal and political concerns about secret societies, which share almost nothing in common with our late-modern prejudices, as we shall see. A study of Morgan's participation in men's secret clubs reveals the basis of how anthropology and the social sciences have viewed ritual secrecy in non-Western societies. Moreover, it deepens our understanding of the complexity of the subject, since Morgan and his contemporaries were themselves skeptical toward and uncomfortable with these pervasive men's secret societies, even as they became fashionable among Victorian men. Secrecy in the Victorian age was not purely concerned with political activities, as it was during the cold war. In the latter case, outcry against secrecy was based on the fear of infiltration by "communists" and their agents in international espionage networks. At the same time, secrecy was not restricted to the realm of the purely personal, as in present-day tabloid scandals, Twelve Step programs and encounter groups, or television talk shows where the narrative of self-revelation identifies stories of secrecy, personal growth, and individual failure or success. Instead, the Victorians were preoccupied by social anxieties that were as much political as personal when it came to secrecy. In this respect, Morgan was not unique in his cultural experience of ritual secrecy; rather, his life experience embodied the principles of ritual secrecy and reflected the problems of his historical era.

This revisionist view necessitates an experience-near theory of how secrecy is formulated and reflected back into sociocultural theory and methodology in the present day. Rarely, if ever, have social scientists—those who have had the most to say about secrecy in cultural studies—either experienced secrecy as a profound (not trivial) way of being or lived with the presence of institutional secrecy pervading their adult lives, unless it has been in the context of fieldwork or some other kind of research study. In historical context, secrecy and passing were problems related to outgroup stigma and impression management, as famously outlined by Erving Goffman (1963), and tended to be limited to institutionalized populations—both criminal and medical—and, of course, closeted homosexuals, whose sexual desires were silenced and punished by their society. However, these experiences were largely ignored or dismissed by academics and never brought into the process of theory formation, at least not openly. Today, a number of lesbian and gay anthropologists who grew up concealing their desires and living under a veil of silence and secrecy—many of whom passed as heteronormal in their university careers (Lewin and Leap 1996; Weston 1993)—directly employ their resistance to heteronormativity as a means of theoretical insight into cultural dynamics (Herdt 1997a).

Early ethnographers' experiences with secrecy—whether personal or political, at home or in the field—would be treated as shameful and brushed aside as something of an embarrassment, much as other men treat the subject of locker-room jokes or late-night drinking party conversations. This dislocation of subjectivity, a system of secrecy in itself, resulted in social scientists coming to disown their own experiences so that they could never be compared to the quaint and exotic forms of Otherness they had discovered in the men's houses of non-Western societies. In short, what had once seemed strange about ritual secrecy to previous generations of anthropologists in the twentieth century was both familiar and indispensable to the cultural reality experienced by nineteenth-century Victorians such as Lewis Henry Morgan.

Morgan and Victorian Male Cultural Reality

Particularly in the first half of his life, Morgan was deeply involved in idealistic male secret orders and fraternal lodges, beginning with his early initiation into Greek-admiring societies and culminating with the purchase of ritual initiation among the Iroquois of New York. His admiration for the Greeks and the American Indian was the basis of his creative effort to build bonds of ritual and secret friendship with other men. Morgan's romantic belief in the unity of the human species and his belief in progress, though seemingly at odds with one another, were ultimately reconciled by his view that "the rise of civilization had, in fact, destroyed something valuable" (Patterson 2001: 30): "Democracy in government, brotherhood in society, equality in rights and privileges" (Morgan 1877: 562). As the years passed, the meaning and role of secrecy in social life changed for Morgan as he became cynical. Only later, following his unexplained disillusionment and abandonment of the last of his involvements with secrecy, did Morgan remove himself from the company of the Iroquois and withdraw into scholarly circles, thereafter consistently refusing to join his former colleagues.

Lewis Henry Morgan's romantic yearning for an alternative social reality of homosocial secrecy locates his life and work squarely in the tradition of American expressive individualism. Among this new generation of democratic voices—following after Washington, Jefferson, and other founders of the United States of America—many notable figures come to mind: Emerson and Thoreau, already celebrated in Morgan's day, as well as Hawthorne, Melville, and Whitman—a contemporary of Morgan throughout his long life, who, like Morgan, honored freedom, learning, and justice, favoring less the search for material ends than a "deeper cultivation of the self" (Bellah et al. 1985: 33). Unlike Morgan, Whitman never married, but instead became a lover of men. As his literary fame increased, these passionate affairs were treated with increasing openness and detailed in his most significant work, *Leaves of Grass*, remarkable for its time. Far more common in the lives of other men, however, is male homosociality— an intimate, exclusionary, bumping-elbows kind of masculinity—distinct from sex with men and the construct of homosexuality. We now understand the tension between these forms of sociality to be the product of a moment in middle-class gender role formation and the crisis of masculinity (D'Emilio and Freedman 1988; Kimmel 1996; Lane 1999; Sedgwick 1990).

Whatever their basis in Eros, the desires at the center of these secret homosocial fraternities were neither pure nor simple. Power and hierarchy coexisted with ideals of innocence and equality. As is often characteristic of periods that frame rapid social changes, anxiety—mostly reflected in the fear of losing one's social position, reputation, and ability to provide for one's family—was prevalent in the Victorian era. The most significant problem faced by the middle class and aspiring workers was managing the conflict between the capitalist ideal of competition in the marketplace and the implicit need for shared intimacy, including sexual intimacy, which, of course, existed before the creation of "homosexuality" in modernity (Bech 1997). The expression of these desires among working-class men found its way into the pubs and dance-halls, taking a different form than traditional heterosexual interaction given that these spaces were host to members of both sexes and featured performances of conspicuous consumption and production. By contrast, secret brotherhoods brought aspiring middle-class and professional men into sympathetic fraternity with others of their own social status. While homosexuality was not a part of Morgan's life (as far as is known), homosocial male cloisters in premodern societies, such as those to which he belonged, struck a balance in the relationship between the desire by men to subscribe to these homosocial male disciplines and the erotic energy created within the participants at the liminal border of their public and private lives.

To understand men's secret societies during this period of history is to open a Pandora's box of contentious political and social movements that competed for the interests and attentions of the American people, particularly progressive and enlightened men and women, who were burdened by the demands of countervailing desires and contradictory gender relations. The social order of the time was beset with challenges posed by the early women's suffrage movement, which itself developed in a parallel fashion out of the objectives put forth by vocal abolitionist and antislavery organizations and, in turn, contributed to the formation of the staunch temperance movement. The demand for women's rights inspired other groups to advocate for social reform in an environment that was becoming increasingly hostile and repressive toward sexuality—despite the reactions to this trend in relations between the genders in the Victorian age (Foucault 1980; Gay 1986; Smith-Rosenberg 1975). "It was an age of golden hypocrisies, a great time for masks and secrets, public lies and private truths. But a private truth can be quite fragile when neither part can name it in public, and you are both too shy to name it even when you're alone" (Bram 2000: 81).

This period of American postrevolutionary society is informed by three cultural concerns: "forging a national identity, territorial expansion, and justifying a slave-based economy in southern states" (Patterson 2001: 32). As a "frontier" (at least from the perspective of the early nineteenth century) positioned at the forefront of the Industrial Revolution that was spreading through the New England area at the time, western and upstate New York played host to many of these secret or semisecret movements. Simultaneously, as the historians have shown, a series of metaphysical "attacks" and spiritualist happenings also emerged in that particular location and continued for a number of years (Braude 1989). Reports and testimonies of the period might remind the anthropologist of ecstatic religions, characterized by the struggle between orthodoxy or patriarchy and symbolic rebellions of the oppressed and disenfranchised projected to the cosmic level (Lewis 1971).

Upstate New York and the Finger Lake communities had, for years, been renowned as the birthplace of esoteric and millenarian sects. The region was an epicenter of the late-eighteenth-century and early-nineteenth-century millenarianism ideology endorsed by a Native American prophet named Handsome Lake, whose religion is presently centered on the Seneca Reservation that Morgan first visited in 1845 (Wallace 1972). Otherwise unaccountable religious happenings were common; the whole area was described as "a section of the country 'burned over' by repeated outpourings of the spirit and auspicious millennial tidings during the evangelical revivals of the Second Great Awakening" (Braude 1989: 10). Coincident with the rise of feminism in the national consciousness, spiritualism and séances became popular throughout the local towns and villages. The role of women was highly conflictual and was probably a matter of personal and philosophical discord for Morgan, too. Theosophy championed the use of occultism, "the belief that secret or hidden knowledge can give access to magical powers" (Braude 1989: 178). The birth of Mormonism and Millerism in 1827, which paved the way for the Jehovah's Witnesses in the 1840s, demonstrates the degree to which prophecy and other metaphysical activities were at work in producing new religions and populist zealots. It was a time in which social networks among individuals were created from similarity of beliefs. Indeed, the city of Rochester itself—in which Morgan himself was to reside—gained renown as a hotbed of feminism, abolitionism, and psychic and religious cultism from the 1840s (Braude 1989: 10ff.) until well after the mid-century.

When Morgan set up a law practice in Rochester in the 1840s, inexplicable religious and spiritual visitations were a significant part of the folklore of upstate New York (Resek 1960: 11–15). To take but one example from the town, unnamable spirits and visitations from the dead seemingly haunted the house of Quaker abolitionists Amy and Isaak Post. In this form of materialization, the mediums could raise the spirits and make the ghosts appear. Notice, moreover, that the same house served as Rochester headquarters for reform activities of many kinds, including lectures by visitors from far and wide, not to mention fugitive slaves (Braude 1989: 10–11). The Underground Railroad was active here, and no less a dignitary than Frederick Douglass hailed from Rochester. In time, the religious formations gave refuge to the female voice, as "spiritualism and woman's rights spread simultaneously through the network of Quaker abolitionists who produced the first supporters for both movements" (Braude 1989: 59). Susan B. Anthony was herself the daughter of a Rochester Quaker family. A few years later, Amy Post, whose house was haunted by mysterious powers, went on to found the Rochester Equal Suffrage Association, and so on. In other words, this mid-nineteenth-century cultural scene was home to a society of dualities that presaged a revolutionary period of changing reali-

feminist movements

ties and social movements, especially feminism. Certainly these "spiritual attacks" reflected gender transformations in a society that had hitherto typified women either as objects of Victorian motherhood, domesticity, and spiritual grace, or, on the other side of the tracks, "fallen women" to be shunned and vilified (Smith-Rosenberg 1975).

The rising position of women in the middle class was beginning to break through these dualities and thus impinge upon masculinity. Intimacy between women was a new arena; creative bonds of friendship and camaraderie among both married and single women were taking hold (Smith-Rosenberg 1975). A deeper kind of ritual and friendship became evident in the intimate relations of unrelated women, sometimes involving erotic feelings (Faderman 1981). Through the construction of new ways of being and forms of discourse about democratic social involvement—including reformist politics, moral purity, and spiritual cleansing—women's influence upon men was greater than ever before in the premodern era (Trumbach 1994). Indeed, Victorian women could be described as "proto-lesbians"—a new and "modern" class of social women (Faderman 1999).

The enlargement of women's lives created unprecedented and sometimes unwanted challenges to men, especially to young middle-class males in search of social achievement and domestic security (Carnes 1990). How were they to get ahead in society? How were they to combine successful jobs and careers with social climbing and "traditional" marriages, or with "untraditional" women? Some individuals no doubt stumbled over the problem of competing with peers, of finding women competing with them in the domestic sphere. How were these men to dominate their kin, boys with whom they grew up, and school chums, when this meant establishing themselves as superior to the others and sacrificing camaraderie? After the Civil War, men were increasingly challenged by the early feminist movement and took refuge in ideas of progress that drew from Lamarck and Spencer, such as notions of "survival of the fittest" supporting traditional male social bonds (D'Emilio and Freedman 1988; Lane 1999). Morgan's generation was to recognize the "increasing importance of the monogamous patrilineal family and the diminished status of women" (Patterson 2001: 30). Aspiring males faced the prospect of migration—of giving up their patriarchal communities and social intimacies without the clear prospect of successful marriage and financial security. In short, during a period in which the rights of women were growing, the perception (not reality) of greater solidarity among women at the expense of male control

summary

traditional gender roles disturbed

was also increasing, and men's anxiety with each other was precipitating a crisis in the previously accepted forms of male homosociality.

The gendered differences so evident in the social economy of the prior age, which traditionally divided women between family hearth and the public marketplace, were being disrupted. The notion of "gendered traits" gains currency as a result of the emerging political economy of work and home in the middle class. Whereas premodern society did not clearly differentiate gender role from self or sexual identity, the Victorian age gave rise to the increasingly popular representation of an autonomous social self (Giddens 1990). It is no wonder that spiritual attacks and séances brought a new texture and creative narratives for the emerging "social self" in such an age, especially the subaltern Woman. Overlapping or contradictory moral expectations of men and women were carried over into all manner of domestic and social relations. A social structure of shifting and uncertain moralities complicated personhood, not unlike the situational morality of precolonial New Guinea (Read 1955). The creation of sexual relations, of intimate citizenship (Weeks 1985) across these domains became tense and contested. Men's attitudes about women's sexual nature were changing, and women's expectations about marriage and demands for a voice in public life were controversial. Such changes also exposed women to new definitions of religious virtue and moral purity. In time, these cultural ideals associated maleness with sexual aggression and economic competition, and they divided the image of woman between motherhood and grace, on the one hand, and prostitution and fallen grace, on the other. The latter became a cultural fetish; to borrow the phrase of Emily Apter (1991), the "cabinet secrets" of the prostitute became one of the obsessions of medicine and the modernization of moral genders.

However, already in the mid–nineteenth century, the claims for emancipation and women's rights were coming under fire. The cultural spaces of gender uncertainty exerted new pressures, and sometimes contradictions, about who could do what—both in public affairs and in the confines of domestic family life. Men had to do something, we might say, because women were doing something new. The activist and intellectual woman, particularly in the upper middle class and upper class, were likely to have been involved in social activism in the urban centers, or in the towns and vicinities of places such as Rochester, New York. What seems likely is that the loss of male rule—or rather the perception of declining male authority—generated increasing anxiety in individual men, and hence new social formations of collective male secrecy as a diffuse technology of power (Foucault 1980). The crisis in masculinity, much touted by historians, seems to have precipitated a slew of male reactions, panic formations, and "masculine protest," at the level of personal meaning (Carnes 1989). However, we must be cautious about the source of this reaction, resisting the temptation to reduce the change to individual psyches or their unconscious defenses as denoted by the construct of "protest masculinity" (Herdt 1989c), since all of these changes were predictive of much that was to follow—the modernization of men's and women's roles and the transformation of male intimacy. This is the forgotten chapter of the male secret society.

Beginning around the time of Morgan, a whole new set of secret societies began to take shape, notably in the homosociality of upwardly mobile middle-class men. The regime of male secret organizations and fraternal orders, such as the Grand Order of the Red Man, formed around new and widening cliques of such men. The older secret orders, especially the Freemasons, were regarded as threatening, even politically dangerous (Robinson 1989). However, these secret societies had long claimed some of the most illustrious figures in Western liberal democratic history among their followers, including the Revolutionary heroes Washington and Jefferson, and they were strongholds of voluntary male social and political association. As a social movement, these groups reflected the changing features of masculinity and male social mobility, particularly the challenges of feminism. The female rights movement and spiritualist cults were to arise at the center of public/private dualities, mediating male/female relations and certain gendered traits (nurturing for women, aggression among men) and relationships (especially middle-class marriage), while exaggerating others (e.g., homosociality). The men who sought this new secretive homosociality in gender-segregated secret associations were at sea in the social change, as their desire for secrecy negotiated "the conflict between ardent individualism and the longing for fellowship" (Braude 1989: 164). The women's increasing social activism and the men's increasing secret associations form complementary parts of a common social field across historical time.

In the nineteenth century, aspiring workers or middle-class men (including lower-status professionals—the merchant, lawyer, doctor, educator, and cleric) were more likely than not to have joined a secret male society (Carnes 1989, 1990). The increasing number of male fraternal orders and the swelling of their ranks during this period are impressive, even by the standards of contemporary society. Millions of American men had undergone at least one initiation into a secret order of this kind during the last third of the nineteenth century—which seems remarkable today, and not simply because secrecy has gotten a bad name.

Ritual secrecy was popular but controversial, even feared, in Victorian society: hidden homosocial networks that depended upon ritual practices of initiation and secret ceremonies of status began to flourish, much as they were common to contemporary Melanesia and other areas of the non-Western world at the time. As Carnes (1989) has shown in his thoughtful book *Secret Ritual and Manhood in Victorian America*,[1] the scope and range of these nascent organizations is astounding. Dozens of them flourished, sometimes self-consciously and romantically created in imitation of Oriental and American Indian images of ceremonial secret societies or, more likely, the imaginal of exoticism in Victorian popular culture. With mysterious and arcane names such as the Odd Fellows, Red Men, Knights of Pythias, Grand Army of the Republic, and later, after Morgan, the Grand Order of the Red Men, they were indeed all the rage among men. The Freemasons in particular were widely associated with subversive practices that extolled the values of expressive individualism, mythically identified with George Washington and other Revolutionary war figures up through the time of Morgan, whose own father was a prominent Mason. Indeed, the quasi-secret cult Masons, once created as a counterhegemonic formation in reaction to the control of religious worship by the feudal Church, provides a link between Renaissance and contemporary forms of ritual secrecy (Robinson 1989). Though implicitly antisocial in their day, the meanings of such organizations are long gone. They largely petered out in the first decades of the twentieth century, as the Great War mobilized men and hastened new waves of feminism and sexual reform movements (D'Emilio 1983). Surely it is no coincidence that as homosexuality became increasingly visible, between 1870 and 1900, homosocial male groups of heterosexuals, including secret societies, declined.

A new idea of male "human nature" was growing popular among the aspiring middle class—that it was "normal and natural" to join segregated secret clubs and to be initiated through special or esoteric rites. A new cultural reality was created—albeit hidden from the public, and particularly those public or domestic spaces trafficked by women. How can we imagine a reality created collectively in culture that is not public? This is the enigma that we face in the case of Lewis Henry Morgan—and, in general, with respect to the problem of ritual secrecy at large. The emerging secret reality commandeered social relations, requiring that a man pledge loyalty through "Adoption Degrees" to newfound socially fictive brothers and fathers. Their loyalties and fictive kinship supported male-admiring practices in a space entirely apart from women. [These new secret orders solidified the political and economic interests of aspiring middle-class men as much as they kept the women at a safe distance.] "As young men, they were drawn to the male secret orders, where they repeatedly practiced rituals that effaced the religious values and emotional ties associated with women" (Carnes 1990: 48).

Victorian ideals among men such as Morgan did not encourage expressive emotional confessions or sexual stories of the self, as known to us from the age of television (Plummer 1995). Men did not join these groups in a self-reflexive manner to discover or express deep feelings; that was neither their social purpose nor their psychological intention. But apparently a good many of these men were troubled enough to seek a separate shared reality in which to build confidence and trust in their social and personal strivings. Rituals of solidarity hidden from women were a key to this end. Aspiring middle-class actors who had the resources to join secret associations thus sought a homosocial atmosphere of male camaraderie amid the romantic idealism of mythic rites and nature worship. In short, the popular men's secret societies provided a safe refuge that gave men a divergent cultural reality removed from the domestic hearth and immune to the claims for new rights by women and other vocal dissenters who contested men's traditional authority, moral and sexual superiority.

But this brings up the great puzzle of ritual secrecy—indeed, it is the same puzzle that has long perplexed the anthropological literature on small societies. For anthropology it begins with Morgan (1901) and Parker (1909); for sociology it began with the work of the great Georg Simmel (reviewed in chap. 2). "If the rituals reaffirmed the values of Victorian America, why did the orders take pains to keep them secret?" (Carnes 1989: 3). Writers such as Lionel Tiger (1970) and, before him, Freud (1923) once appealed to a biologically innatist position that men are attached to each other libidinally; that is, males have an intrinsic desire to form circles or havens of same-gender attachment and intimate security to shelter their masculinity (Tuzin 1997: 178ff.). Such an ultimate cause, however, is insufficient to explain the historical variations and cross-cultural conditions observed in ritual secrecy in such places as Victorian

America or New Guinea. Moreover, it obscures whether such an intrinsic drive includes homoeroticism, an important question to which we must return in the study of secret social groups in Melanesia.

We are dealing here, in the remarkable arena of male ritual secrecy, with the mixture of rule and power. To be socially superior, to rule in public relations, does not provide power in all domains. Public and domestic tensions abound. Obviously, power plays an important role in the mixture, which may destabilize all social relations in a particular society. The particular idea of "power" to which we appeal is significant, whether formal or informal. For Foucault's (1973) model of power as discursive and omnipresent, a part of the very norms internalized by the individual, the link between rule and power typically occurs through technologies of power and formations of the State, such as the public health apparatus and bureaucracies. Such an approach may well apply to Victorian America, but it encounters many difficulties when transplanted into precolonial communities such as those of Melanesia (Herdt 1992).

In Morgan's day it seems likely that the rise of the women's movement and other social upheavals introduced by opposition to slavery, alcohol abuse, and heterosexism opened new and deeper fears and schisms than previously existed between husbands and wives, fathers and daughters, brothers and sisters. Perhaps this void motivated men's participation in a club of misogyny and the splitting of Woman's image into Mother and Whore (Chodorow 1978). This posed an unprecedented challenge to the received meanings and privileges of masculinity, prompting the creation of secret men's groups like those founded by Morgan.

Morgan, Secret-Maker

Born in 1818 in Aurora, New York, Lewis Henry Morgan was the son of a wealthy farmer, Jedidiah, who was prominent in local politics and community affairs. Jedidiah was morally upright, a staunch Presbyterian who paid for the erection of the local Masonic Lodge. His father's official title in the temple must have seemed grand to a small boy: Worshipful Master of the Scipio Masonic Lodge and High Priest of the Aurora Chapter of the Royal Arch Masons (Carnes 1989: 96). Jedidiah held the post until his premature death in 1826. However, he was also a practical man with worldly ambitions, who got himself elected to the state senate and became a friend of Governor DeWitt Clinton. The governor, New York's best-known

Mason, laid the cornerstone of the elder Morgan's Masonic temple, an important show of local political theater. This religious secret and political nexus is significant, for it shows the interface between secret Masonic activities and the production of public power and wealth. Indeed, its political connection would haunt the family in the years to come. Long afterward, rumors of political patronage shadowed the governor and tainted the Masons. Secrecy, in this connection, was a source of suspicion and corruption. For decades after, the name of the Masons was mired in scandal, tainted by the "expose of Masonic secrets" throughout western New York (Carnes 1989: 97).

Lewis Henry was eight years old at the time of his father's death. The death was a great blow to the boy, and as so often happens in childhood loss, the grief exerted a lifelong influence on Morgan, a theme ignored in the better-known biographies of Morgan (see White 1959). Carnes's account of these events relies upon the overdetermined notion of unconscious compensation for the early and traumatic loss of Morgan's father through the search for and investment in secret ritual bonding with other men. Carnes remarks that as a boy, Morgan was "shaken by the loss" and was reared by his mother after his father's death.

Some readers may be skeptical of such a Freudian reading. However, paternal loss appears as a definite symbolic theme at critical junctures throughout Morgan's life, as is stressed in Carnes's historical biography. For example, the context in which Morgan initiated his first secret association was the moment of his return home from the study of law. He had been living at college and immersed in a homosocial academic atmosphere. His return was to an all-female household, ruled by a powerful woman:

> When he returned home after graduating from Utica (now Union) College in 1840 as a twenty-two year old attorney without prospects of a practice, secret societies became his regular escape from domestic duties and from the affectionate vigilance of the women in the family. (Carnes 1989: 96)

Moreover, shortly before his marriage in 1850–51, Morgan curiously drew up a will stipulating that after death he was to be buried near his father. The timing suggests the sudden desire to conjure the presence of his father on the eve of matrimony.

In fact, the loss of a parent was common during these times, and the issue of "paternal neglect" on the frontier was of such widespread social interest that one observer complained in 1842 that it "had become epidemic" (Carnes 1990: 47). Concomitantly, historical documents of the era, such as autobiographies and diaries, revealed how the "symbolic importance of motherhood" exerted a feminine pressure on Victorian men (38). As if to echo the theme of the age, Morgan was to remark years later that the loss of a parent could never be overcome, in an apparent reference to his own loss. The language and practices created by the organizations with which Morgan was involved reflect a symbolic focus on fathering, which supports Carnes's general claim about the compensatory psyche of these clubs.

Growing up on the frontier after the Revolution and during the time of America's "invasion" of Indian lands, Morgan's development must have been riddled by many of the conflicting influences reviewed previously. Certainly he was exposed to populist ideas and movements, whose politics must have involved not only his natal family but later his own position as an aspiring attorney, too. The encroachment of white settlers and land-grabbers upon Indian lands, abolitionism and militant antislavery activism, the budding women's movement, the conflict between science and religion, and vehement temperance activities were all heatedly debated. We can be reasonably sure that Morgan interacted with some of the key players in Rochester surrounding these debates, since he supported antislavery activities and Native American revivalism. Clearly Morgan was committed to the emancipation of the slaves and the unity of North and South. Morgan's support of Native American land reform was particularly critical later in his life (Resek 1960), for as White (1959) has noted, Morgan later devoted much of his time and political effort to the protection of Native American rights and their empowerment through congressional legislation. However, his attitudes about women and feminism, spiritualism and the occult, are obscure. Morgan's character suggests that if he felt antipathy toward early feminism, it would have been intellectualized, and perhaps subordinated to his liberal views that all people should be equal in rights and privileges. Whether he flirted with spiritualism, a popular form of romantic entertainment, remains unknown.

Morgan attended Cayuga Academy in Aurora. Through his socialization and formal education, he was introduced to classical ideas and texts, and took to reading Plato and Socrates in Greek and Latin. The student lawyer at this point was uninterested in ethnology or the American Indians; he was immersed in the great philosophers and no doubt in the male idealization of Greek culture common to the period (Halperin 1990: 56ff.).

Like other American and British middle-class men, Morgan's imagination was captivated by classical romanticism, signified by his first involvement in a secret society. By contrast, his second secret organization not only provided his introduction to anthropology (Stern 1931: 16ff.) but also inspired him to be initiated into the secret society of the Indians. These intellectual, social, and political activities, coupled with his activism as a self-righteous partisan lawyer, suggest an enlightened thinker and social idealist working to improve himself and society—the historical principles of middle-class American expressive individualism (Bellah et al. 1985). Whatever the unconscious sources of Morgan's attraction to secret fraternities, they rapidly gained a foothold in the larger cultural imagination of the times.

The first of the men's societies in Morgan's development was a social and classical literary club for young men known as the Order of the Gordian Knot, or simply the Gordian Knot, a Greek-admiring semisecret fraternity in Aurora, New York.[2] This emerged during the hard years of Morgan's early law practice when work was scarce. He had a lot of time on his hands, and much of it went into the secret club. The order convened in the local Masonic Temple near Rochester, New York, and eventually grew to 500 members. From what little is known, it had the characteristics of a voluntary association of upwardly mobile men, bound by common interests of social class, locale, and perhaps the need for mutual support in their commercial dealings with one another. After the Gordian Knot was disbanded, Morgan's idealization of the Greeks carried over into later life. In his famous *League of the Iroquois*, for example, he openly admires Greek ethics for "the acumen and inspiration of their marvelous intellect" (1901: 142). He waxes poetic in his discussion of the virtues of their religion, stating that "they perfected and beautified that stupendous production of genius and credulity, the polytheism of the ancient world" (143).

The second secret order was modeled on the Indians, closer to home, and was perhaps influenced by the romanticism of Washington Irving's far-flung literary ideas about Indians (and romantic writings on Moorish Alhambra in Spain) and an emerging image of "primitive society" in human evolution. This club also marked his transition into revivalist traditions of Native Americans in the Finger Lakes area of New York. Morgan began his study of the Iroquois in 1841 (Fenton 1941: 148), with a variety of meetings that resembled fieldwork. In 1843 he decided to change the Order of the Gordian Knot into an Iroquois-admiring society (later known as the Order of the Iroquois).

Early on, Morgan met Ely Parker, the son of a Seneca chief, at the New

York State archives in Albany (Carnes 1989: 95). This fortuitous meeting began a long and fruitful collaboration, one of the most profound partnerships in the history of American anthropology. Parker's association was critical to Morgan's eventual introduction, not only to Iroquois culture, but also to their controversial secret formations (the False Face Society). The two men also "became fast friends" and comrades, as testified by Morgan's dedication of *The League of the Iroquois* to Parker in the same year that Morgan married (White 1959: 4–5).

About the same time, but independent of Morgan, a group of former Masons in 1843 formed a wholly new society called the Improved Order of Red Men. This other group employed certain rites similar to those of Morgan's secret order, but the ceremonies more closely resembled those of the Odd Fellows, both in their socially esoteric and political functions. This society would eventually number in the hundreds of thousands throughout the United States and outlive Morgan. However, the budding popularity of these movements failed to inspire Morgan's praise; indeed it seemed to repel him. This negative reaction was the start of an emotional and then physical withdrawal from the secret groups. Morgan's increasing attitude of cynicism was a harbinger of later cultural sentiment.

Even before his first visit to the Seneca at the Tonawanda Reservation, on October 1, 1845, Morgan was already fascinated by Iroquois initiation rites and secret societies, having journeyed with George Ripley of Rochester to attend the Six Nations Council to see the installation of a new chieftain or Sachem. Shortly thereafter, "Jimmy Johnson, successor to Handsome Lake, recited the prophet's message on October 12 and 13, and Ely Parker sent Morgan an English Synopsis" (Fenton 1941: 148, n. 1). This made a deep impression on Morgan.

What Morgan was to create had a strong undercurrent of spiritualism and relativism in its understanding of the Indians and ideals of secrecy. The role of Parker was important in fostering this spiritual dimension. Parker's work on the False Face Society of the Iroquois was highly "respected" and valued, even over Morgan's. According to one authority, though, it was "deeply involved with the Masonic mysteries" (Fenton 1987: 140). In other words, Parker was not only an intellectual partner in secrecy, but also a cocreator of the Order of the Iroquois. When Morgan convened the first meeting of this new Order, "it was composed of members of the local Freemasons and a few New York Indian scholars" (Fenton 1987: 140). We can assume that Parker was among them, since he was known to admire and support Native American customs. Certainly Morgan strongly believed in the role of spiritual beliefs as a source of human understanding; Book II of *The League* starts, "The mind is, by nature, full of religious tendencies" (1851: 141).

Morgan called his local secret chapter The Grand Order of the Cayuaga Tribe. In time other secret chapters dispersed across New York and were given other "tribal" names. His fellows voted Morgan their Grand Sachem or Chief, bestowing upon him the proper name Skenandoak (apparently in commemoration of the famous Iroquois friend of the American Revolutionaries). Morgan led his fellows into the new order by imitating all kinds of Iroquois customs, manners, dress, history, and, especially, initiation ceremonies. The change in Morgan's identity suggested at least a partial desire to "go native" in certain idyllic interludes with local Iroquois. Morgan's writings make it clear that he saw in Indian society the hallmarks of a higher civilization—prior to the "distortions" of private property and profit motives (1877: 561–62). His behavior at times was odd enough that the Iroquois were mystified and a bit frightened by him (Carnes 1989: 98).

Morgan reasoned that the best way to share in the romantic meaning of Indian life was to experience Indian rituals. Even before he had set foot on a reservation, he superintended the creation of the order's first induction ceremony, which he called an "indianation." The ceremony bore no relation to any Seneca ritual (Carnes 1989: 95). Nonetheless, Morgan's ingenious use of Iroquois symbolism anchors Victorian "identity work" in his remarkable anthropology. It also links what is distinctive of Victorian manhood to ritual secrecy—that it depends upon embodiment for its physical, and subjective, dimensions. Embodiment is a basis of ritual secrecy; while knowledge is involved in the creation of its totality, neither rational teaching nor abstract knowledge is sufficient to produce cultural reality (identity). For that, separation and submersion of the person in ritual praxis is required.

What role did such a secret "religious formation" play in an area renowned for the emergence of protest religions? An initiation ceremony dreamed up by Morgan provides clues. As written in the "Constitution of the Grand Order of the Iroquois Organized at Aurora, New York, by Morgan," we find this preamble:

> Believing that the institution of an Indian Order—having for its
> object a literary social confederation of the young men of our State,

for the purpose of making such Order the repository of all that remains to us of the Indian,—their manners, customs, and history; their mythology, government and literature; and for the further purpose of creating and encouraging a kinder feeling toward the Red Man, founded upon a true knowledge of the Virtues and blemishes of the Indian character; and finally to make up an institution that shall mutually cast the broad shield of its protection and the mantle of its benevolence over these declining races; and lastly our own intellectual and moral improvement. (Morgan 1917: 17)

Within Morgan's own secret group, itself reminiscent of the famous medicine societies of the Iroquois (Parker 1909), some spiritualism and revivalist connection seem certain. Though directed by Morgan, other noted scholars such as Henry Schoolcraft and of course Ely Parker later joined the Order, attracting the attention of local reformers and neighboring Iroquois tribesmen. It is no doubt true that the spirit of the times was individualistic, even antiauthoritarian. Morgan promoted social change in the spirit of the era and thereby tested the very limits of the expansionist white society's tolerance of his expressive ideal that glorified Indian life. Indeed, one cannot help but wonder if his activism created a site of cultural resistance to white hegemony, within the secret fraternity, in alliance with the Indians. In these and other matters, including his own bodily experiences, I have the impression that Morgan was engaged in personal, as well as political, development.

As its prestige grew, and Morgan's "head was filled with notions about primitive society" (Resek 1960: 23), he changed the name of the secret society to the Grand Order of the Iroquois. The rituals constructed by Morgan and his colleagues are a fascinating amalgam of the romantics' search for a Garden of Eden and the naive trumpeting of a boy's club, with a striking number of references to the "Great Spirit" (translated as "Father"). The key seems to have been that the men being initiated into the Grand Order had "lost their fathers" and needed a Great Spirit to protect them. Astonishingly, Morgan "advised initiates to rediscover their lost fathers" in his personal counsel to them:

When Sachem Lewis Henry Morgan pleaded with the Great Spirit to "receive us as your children," and to "save from the grave" the memory of departed fathers, he was "regenerating" the paternal bonds of which he had been deprived as a boy. (Carnes 1989: 96–97)

The appeal and invocation of the name of the Father was the signature of the times. It became iconic of these Victorian movements and masculine secret formations throughout the remainder of the nineteenth century. For that matter, its appeal to Christian iconography and homosocial haven imagery is not so far distant from the Iron John mythology alive today (Kimmel 1996). The implied purity of male work, identity, and secret commitment, emotions of collective grief, the renewal of spiritual purity, and the intense intimacy briefly shared by Morgan and his comrades are all akin to what anthropologists have long known as a rite de passage (Van Gennep 1960). In such a masculine movement, we might guess, the sign of the Father is being substituted for conscious homoerotic attachment; their ritual rebirth need not displace the heterosocial domestic order with a homosexual one (Herdt 1989c, 1990). This particular contrast, as we shall later see, is informative of what is distinctively Melanesian about ritual secrecy, since it is the male and not the female body that is desired among New Guinea peoples such as the Baruya and Sambia (Godelier 1986).

Ever restless, Lewis Henry Morgan's long romance with Native American culture was to shift, and then recede. He soon tired of imitations of the Iroquois rites: he wanted to experience the realness of the thing. While his fellow initiates were content with what he had created, "Morgan came to doubt whether they could vicariously share in the deeper impulse of Indian life through experiencing spurious rituals" (Carnes 1989: 95). This yearning led to Morgan's petition in 1846 to undergo the ceremony of adoption into the Iroquois tribe. One can imagine the curious response of the Iroquois to this unparalleled request. They consented, but only if Morgan would pay for the necessary feast (to which he agreed). The "Adoption Degree" was made through the Hawk clan and the ritual consummated in due order. Jimmy Johnson, by then over seventy years old and among the famous dignitaries living in that area of the country, became Morgan's new "father." It is not clear how much of a mark the initiation left upon Morgan, but it certainly made a queer impression on the Iroquois. (Some of the texts and rites are set down in Morgan's work and writings: see Fenton 1987; Parker 1909.) Morgan's "adoption" into the Iroquois tribe through the Corn Harvest Festival signaled a desire for a deeper immersion into their culture, including its mysteries and medicinal powers. This is where he had parted company with his contemporaries, who were content to taste the imitation, not the original; but the original was ultimately to disappoint Morgan too.

The flavor of Morgan's interests in the esoteric and the secret rites emerges to some extent in his later writings on the False Face and Wooden Face Societies, their medicine lodges, and other exclusive or secretive associations. Though facilitated by Ely Parker and other native consultants, these ethnographic accounts are written as if Morgan were an insider, and some of them reveal the fresh sensitivity of a member of the elect, especially in volume I of the *League of the Iroquois* (Morgan 1851). A variety of arguments have questioned whether Morgan's account was consistent with secret practice. For example, Morgan claimed that the False Face Societies helped to continue the practice of witchcraft: "Belief in witches is to this day, and always has been, one of the most deeply-seated notions in the minds of the Iroquois" (156–57). Because of the "terror" with which the Iroquois regarded their witches, the accused was put to death. This helps explain the cultural sources of the secrecy of witchcraft and membership in the secret societies. These practices were nearly unbelievable to Morgan's mind, given the charitable attitude he attributed to the Indians. Anyone could be possessed of an "evil spirit" and assume for "nefarious" purposes animal or spirit form, he noted. "When one became a witch, one ceased to be himself." To subvert and to further their aims, the witches collected in "a secret and systematic organization, which has subsisted for ages" (157). "These meetings were held at night, and the fee of the neophyte was the life of his nearest and dearest friend, to be taken with poison, on the eve of his admission." To combat these malevolent forces, a special Falseface Band was created whose chief purpose was to "propitiate those demons called False-faces, and among other good results to arrest pestilence and disease" (159). The Band reportedly wore "hideous masks," could appear in dreams, and had flutes and other sacred instruments that accompanied their rituals and through which they could "propitiate those demons" (Morgan 1901: 158–59; Parker 1909). One suspects that these descriptions coming into Morgan's hands must have deeply disturbed his idealism about the Indians, especially in the light of his own Christian beliefs, and may perhaps have permanently damaged his identification with their culture. The real no longer lived up to the ideal.

Iroquois specialists later challenged some of these interpretations of the secret societies, and I leave those debates to them. Nevertheless, we see now how Morgan had tried to puzzle out the inner workings and meanings of secret societies among the Iroquois and how his work forms and informs the genealogy of all the anthropology of secrecy that followed. Certainly these beliefs and practices are the stuff from which secret societies are made in many places, including Papua New Guinea. In fact, there are remarkable resemblances between the Iroquois False Face Society and the famed Tambaran societies of the Sepik River, especially the Ilahita Arapesh (Tuzin 1980; see chap. 5).

In any case, all this was to end. The events of his adoption marked a developmental watershed in Morgan's life. He appeared to tire of his engagements with the Iroquois, with the Hawk clan, and with his ties to the Iroquois people. Concurrently he lost interest in the social functions of the second secret society he had founded, just as it was reaching its zenith. His initial enchantment with the rites—with their ability to generate the deeper spiritual feeling he had once admired and longed for among the Iroquois—seemed to go sour on him, as Morgan seems to have turned cynical. "Within a year he lost interest in the Order of the Iroquois and its 'boyish' rituals; it disbanded shortly thereafter" (Carnes 1989: 98). By 1847, then, after four years' involvement with the secret societies and a fairly long stretch of "fieldwork," Morgan's desire for all these associations dissipated. What had precipitated such a dramatic change?

Although we can never be certain of the actual chain of events, it seems likely that Morgan's growing domesticity, his social and financial success, culminating in his marriage, are at the heart of this radical change. Morgan was—to capture the proverbial sense of things in the American idiom—about to "settle down." And to "settle down" meant to leave the adventuresome forays into Indian country behind, just as the evenings would be taken up with domestic activities, rather than secret fraternities. The identity crisis indicates a transformation of sociality and selfhood, a dissociation of the subject from the once desired object: the rituals and secret societies, as embodied in the Iroquois. The evidence suggests that just as his interest in ritual secrecy was flagging, Morgan's interest in Christianity was on the rise. It will not surprise the reader, much less the anthropologist, to know that it was precisely this moment when Morgan began to write his great work, *The League of the Iroquois*. He had removed himself from direct experience of intimate homosocial spaces in the field; the secret societies had given way to domestic places next to his study.

Morgan's early political activism seems at odds with his later philosophy of social evolution, but only in part. Intellectually, his later life was spent in elucidating the principles of social progress and of the development of civilization, which increasingly preoccupied his search for the unity of human kind and universals of social structure (Stocking 1987). This is but a developmental difference: between the younger Morgan, engaged in romantic idealizations of the Indians through the molding of the admiring secret society, versus the older, more skeptical, scholar, who quit the secret fraternities, removed himself from all intimate contact with the Iroquois, and finally refused to join anything at all. The tension in Morgan's development in the middle decades of the nineteenth century aptly mirrors the Janus of anthropology in the twentieth: the relativistic field-worker who lives with the locals and is actively pro-nativist; versus the philosophical and skeptical academic don, who has ceased fieldwork and conceptualizes the Human Condition, a necessary tribute to modernity.

Morgan's admiration for Iroquois culture was not to decline but to grow over the years, as if his emotional distance permitted him to create, in the private experience of his library, the famous Iroquois texts—a utopian objectification thwarted by the actual encounter. Still, there can be no doubt that Morgan believed that Iroquois religion surpassed our own cultural ancestors. He thought that the Iroquois were "more wise" than the Greeks and Romans, and more "confiding in the People" than the Egyptians. Morgan thus concluded of the Indians, "The fruits of their religious sentiments, among themselves, were peace, brotherly kindness, charity, hospitality, integrity, truth, and friendship; and towards the Great Spirit, reverence, thankfulness, and faith" (1901: 224). Such a Garden of Eden emerged in his later portrayal of the Iroquois.

As a younger man, however, Morgan and other men of his time wanted something more inclusive of their identities: a closeness and camaraderie, homosocially trusting in and being trusted by their fellows, with the blessings of a paternal spirit, pursued through ritual secrecy.[5] The secret fraternities were a means to this utopian end, albeit a failed one.

Morgan After Secrecy

As Morgan ended his active field study among the Iroquois he began to write his treatise, *The League of the Iroquois* (1847). By about 1850, Morgan had married his cousin Mary Elizabeth Steele, of Albany, New York. He was thirty-two. By the time of his marriage, he had ceased his field activities with the Indians; the divergent cultural reality of the secret societies was replaced by matrimonial life. Why did he marry his cousin? What was involved in the decision to marry inside a family already very close-knit, and heavily dominated by strong women? At the very least, we can infer a desire on Morgan's part to confine his trust, as well as his romantic and sexual life, to the restricted security circle of his extended family, who had helped to arrange the marriage. It was as if the outside world posed anxieties, which the eligible bachelor chose not to take on. In this way, through the creation of a restricted circle, Morgan was a perfect Victorian, and his domestic life illustrates the tendency to cloying domesticity that was to usher in a subsequent historical crisis of masculinity at the end of the century.

Morgan entered the bourgeois conventions of Rochester life. In 1851 the newlyweds "moved into a house on South Fitzhugh Street in Rochester, and Morgan devoted himself wholly to his professional and domestic life" (White 1959: 5). Indeed, in his account of Morgan's work, Leslie White states that "from the close of 1850 until the summer of 1857, Indian affairs were laid entirely aside" (262). While his law practice was not so successful, Morgan became a highly successful capitalist and entrepreneur in financial ventures, especially in railroad companies. In fact, Morgan ran one of these railroads during the time in which he was writing his treatises on the evolution of society. During this time his active collaboration with Ely Parker continued, from which were written a series of significant scholarly papers. Increasingly, Morgan dedicated himself to the legal and political reform of Indian land rights in New York state.

Morgan was certainly not alone in his desire to join secret fraternities that would take him away, however temporarily, from the tense or disconcerting or drab conventionality of domestic life to seek idyllic or romantic homosociality. What is common to Morgan's and his fellows' involvement in secret societies is the escape into another, parallel, or utopian cultural world. The cultural reality of the Victorian age is reflected in, but also refracted by, the curious creation of these men's secret clubs. Both the social and political links between the men, as much as their personal friendships and needs, are captured in the story of Morgan. These practices were so widespread in later nineteenth century society that upward of 40 percent of all American men may have participated in them, including the majority of middle-class men (Carnes 1989: 2). Some groups numbered in the hundreds of thousands. By 1896, we are told, out of "a total adult male population of nineteen million," secret societies made up "five and a half million members" within the United States (Carnes 1989: 1). The Grand Lodge of the Red Men was particularly successful: "By 1900 hundreds of thousands of Red Men were finding their way into wigwams of the order each week. Annual receipts exceeded a million dollars" (Carnes 1990: 40). These circles of hygiene and masculine or Christian purity are evident throughout American history, up to the present (D'Emilio and Freedman 1988; Kimmel 1996; Moran 2000). Unique to Morgan's story, however, is the romantic joining of American Indian cultural renditions with male desires and contradictions in Victorian America.

The many strands of these secret societies suggest a problematic for anthropology's treatment of men's secret clubs as exotic and alien from daily life in the twentieth century. The history of secrecy is far closer to home in anthropology than we would have imagined, and the story of Morgan is mirrored in other quarters in the history of our civilization, if only we care to look. This idea objectifies a long-standing ambivalence in Western thought, and hence in its social science, regarding the good and bad sides of secrecy. Just as Morgan's life illuminates Victorian masculinity and its conditional character, so too secrecy impacted upon the public and domestic domains, sexuality and marriage, so that profession and friendship—once so separate—were reconstructed. These arenas of male agency were fragmented and not of a piece (nor were they *at* peace) within Morgan. Like other men of his time he sought alternative realities through which to create greater trust, or fraternity, with others, the mystical, and the Indians.

Religion was one of the prime sources of pressure in Morgan's life, as for many other Victorians of his era. The Reverend Joshua Hall McIlvaine, D.D. (1815–97), "pastor of the First Presbyterian Church in Rochester for many years and a close friend of Morgan" (White 1959: 202), was especially important. In Adam Kuper's account of Morgan, much is made of the influence of McIlvaine, who was "intimately associated with Morgan's research," being a philologist and Sanskritist (1991: 43). "He did his best—with the support of Morgan's wife—to ignite Morgan's Christian faith, but with only partial success, though he claimed that Morgan's heart lay in the end with the Christian religion" (43). The pastoral connection is also important to Morgan's domestic life, since the two men were close; the Reverend was both his senior and the keeper of his father, Jedidiah's, faith. The intellectual influence of McIlvaine was repressive as well, for he apparently deleted from Morgan's manuscripts prior to publication key passages that endorsed evolutionary thought, or that went against the Scriptures. Once more, a fascinating mixture of both conservative (i.e., religious) and progressive (i.e., women's emancipation) attitudes is apparent in one of Morgan's close friends.[6] That this man was of immense import to Morgan can be shown by that fact that Morgan dedicated his general treatise, *Ancient Society*, to McIlvaine.

It is interesting that Morgan created one last fraternal organization during his later years of domesticity. The Pundit Club, or simply "The Club," as it came to be known, "was organized on the evening of July 13, 1854, at Morgan's home" (White 1959: 202). The Reverend McIlvaine was also a prominent member. But Morgan was its "prime mover" and was voted "secretary." Between 1854 and 1880, Morgan read thirty-two papers before the Club. (In 1856, Morgan was elected to a far more elite scientific establishment, the American Association for the Advancement of Science, which motivated him to prepare his celebrated paper on the "Laws of Descent of the Iroquois.") The Club was a scholarly, intellectual, and scientific circle, and while we cannot be certain of it, we may surmise that women were excluded. Perhaps in this sonorous little utopia we see not a secret society—though it could have become that in another time and place—but rather the cozy gentleman's club of Victorian scholars, linked by their common privilege and modernist regard for letters and science that set them apart from the domestic family—and excluded women as colleagues. Nevertheless, the presence of their women was as close as the next sitting room in Morgan's house. Indeed, the scholars depended upon the existence of that parallel parlor for the meaning of their own existence, as well as for the food and service supplied by their wives. The conventions of the day justified their separation and allowed for this special scholastic intimacy, precisely because of the beliefs and roles that relegated men and women to different homosocial spaces. Some of these developments, including the secret history, may have been typical of middle-class men in Morgan's era. But it was less typical to found secret clubs, and perhaps even more unusual to found and then leave them, as Morgan did.

What truly set Morgan apart, however, was his other desire—the one we have come to think of as prototypical of the anthropological experience in this century: to enter another culture, and even ideally to be initiated into its secret circle. Nothing could be more symbolic of the dawning of anthropology's romantic rebellion against the Enlightenment project of science and rationality (Shweder 1984). What was the source of this interest in Morgan's life? The answer may lie in the same sources that motivated his secrecy. During the peak of his involvement in the secret rites around 1845–46, Morgan may have experienced a kind of delayed grief reaction and symbolic mourning. We do not have to be Freud to reconstruct the challenges before him. He lacked a father, brothers, and apparently close male friends after returning from college. Perhaps he sought male friendship and confidence in the earlier literary society; but like most literary groups, its ability to address emotional challenges, as well as mortality, was no doubt limited. Was this the source of the motivation driving his secret associations? "Morgan's fascination with initiatory ritual may have reflected an unconscious wish to follow in his father's steps" (Carnes 1989: 96). Morgan's appeal that men be received by the Great Father Spirit as "children" and to have them save the memory of their fathers "from the grave" is nationalistic, nostalgic, and notational of an unconscious wish. I would draw attention, moreover, to the anxieties facing Morgan, and to the shared anxieties—real and imagined—which he dealt with by the construction of secret societies. Suffice it to say that when relationships are badly fettered by anxiety and mistrust, men who value social and political cohesion with like-minded others erect utopias, either to gain control or to create a better society than the one in which they live. That is the Janus of secrecy.

Iroquois tradition has changed since Morgan's time. Though the followers of Handsome Lake attempted to eliminate the medicine societies, Parker's (1909) later account suggests that the effort failed. The groups lived on in secret, though the medicine societies are no longer a relaxed subject of discussion; the kind of cynical scrutiny characteristic of Western social science, and even anthropology, is no longer welcome. As with other "tribal" groups in the United States and abroad, social rights to reclamation and cultural preservation are being asserted: "Today, secrecy and sacredness are watchwords of the militants who spurn ethnologists and insist that museums remove all masks from exhibit and return them" (Fenton 1987: 140).

While Morgan's romanticism ended in cynicism, it gave birth to Iroquois cultural analysis—perhaps the hallmark of anthropology's invention of the other, the creation of the object of culture through the subject that studies it. Today, it is commonly argued, and not without reason (Lévi-Strauss 1974; Stocking 1997), that we should date anthropological epistemology from the time of Malinowski's *Diary* (1967). But the narrative of

Morgan's odyssey suggests that we may historically move back the date of this intellectual transformation by two generations and spatially move it across the Atlantic. Hence with Morgan was born what we might call the role of the anthropologist as cryptographer of secrecy and the hidden codes in social life (see chap. 5). To recall the opinion of Stocking: "The true founder of British social anthropology was the American Lewis Henry Morgan" (1987: 301)—whose rediscovery by Rivers was the beginning of a method and a theory of fieldwork. Now let us add that Morgan founded the anthropology of secrecy.

During the period of the nineteenth-century transition to modernity, anthropology has pioneered the description of what we might call ritual secrecy as a particular and privileged mode of practice in small-scale societies. Lewis Henry Morgan's romantic Iroquois studies, revolutionary and clever as they were, ended in his intellectual remove from the Other through the construction of universal frameworks, which did not challenge in any respect Western cultural stereotypes of secrecy in the last century. Is it not supremely ironic that Morgan—a mystic, romantic, and religious Christian—produced an authoritative text on social evolutionism that became a mythic charter for Marxist theory? Anthropological science, born in the discovery by Morgan of classificatory kinship terminology among the Iroquois (1877), as lauded by Fortes (1969), formed the basis of Engels's work on the political economy of gift exchange in small societies (Gregory 1982: 15–18). Engels was fascinated by the claim that the earliest stage of human society was the "matriarchal gens" that preceded patriarchal forms, as he misconstrued Iroquois society. Even more, Engels thought that he had found, within the domestic sphere itself, the very hotbed of competing claims negotiated by secret clubs and spiritual séances in Morgan's time—a class war, with the husband as bourgeois ruler, and the wife as the proletariat that would rise up against him (Engels 1972: 128; see also Kuper 1991: 73). The image hardly fits the social reality of the Iroquois; but it certainly comes closer to the hidden reality not far from the smoky den of cigars in Morgan's Club. When we reflect upon the secrets of sex hidden by the now failed Soviet regime (Kon 1995), including the fact that the Soviets outlawed homosexuality and made abortion the means of birth control, we come even closer to Engels's oppression perpetuated not only against women, but against homosexuals and minorities as well.

Morgan's submersion in Iroquois culture suggests the kind of dialectic between extreme idealization and romantic anticipation of "going native" that is sometimes followed by cynical detachment; the "reverse culture shock" and removal of the self from the field into the text, a not uncommon pattern (Herdt and Stoller 1990)—especially in the Victorian era, when the colonies were believed to hold the secret to a deep and darker side of the human condition. Because these male fraternities were largely unknown to later generations and Morgan was silent on the experience, especially the secretive aspects—much as late Victorian anthropology was largely silent on the legacy of religion and spiritualism, no less than the discussion of sexuality (Herdt and Stoller 1990; Tuzin 1994)—the field experiences of Morgan were never informative or "transformative" (to use Kuper's [1991] sense of the legacy of Morgan's syncretic) for the field. Indeed, Morgan's writings on the False Face Society of the Iroquois seem only to have reinforced preconceptions regarding the structure, function, and meanings of the culture-bound category of "secrecy" in Native American groups.

Studying Secrecy

Secrecy as a collective force in human societies typically emerges in historical situations in which humans suffer deeply unstable relationships. Faith is insufficient in such a world; trust is required to create alliances against an uncertain world. But what is the means of creating this trust? Personal coherence is increasingly problematic, as the failure to achieve trust becomes intolerable. Perhaps it might be objected that all societies are unstable, blemished by incoherence and the difficulty of achieving trust; I will not deny the general assertion. But I will answer that men and women—and especially men—attempt to make themselves "strong" through hierarchies that promote this trust within a disorderly social world. Their way is to make their masculinity invincible; to stake claims for their immortality; they want to believe that the empire will last a thousand years, defeat its enemies, raise the gods, and create an eternal utopia. All the while their masculinity is conditioned on the existence of this utopian world. Perhaps one of the essential characteristics of modernity and the middle class is the yearning for a safe and stable private space that promises to last forever and eschews special conditions for the creation of gender. Men in particular, but women as well, promote this audacity through ritual secrecy in all of its hidden ways of embodiment: being, knowing, and doing that ensure their perpetuation. In their utopia they must not fear that they will fail—that is the condition of their masculinity. Boys are initiated with the promise of agency based upon condition. What they desire and believe are built up through body rituals and dietetics of a kind that differs fundamentally from rational knowledge and cannot be tested against the canons of language or Cartesian epistemology (Whitehouse 1995). Ritual secrecy is thus its own means to its own end.

Practicing this kind of ritual secrecy is tumultuous and historically shaky. Where actors require an additional social leverage or political advantage, they can turn to secrecy: not, as often imagined, to grab for power, but rather to hold on to the tenuous power they already claim. Of course, secret practice is a "weapon" and "resource," depending upon one's perspective within the local system of power relations; a kind of omnibus means of promoting social affairs—mysterious, diffuse, a matter less of faith than of initiation into secret practice, often esoteric or sacred in character, but also fragile in its hold upon the cultural imagination of a people. Make no mistake: ritual secrecy is about (among other things) the *male imagination*, and without that imagination, and the messy prerequisites of masculinity in a particular land, there can be no secrecy. The cynic might like to think that material-historical conditions or the subversion of power are sufficient to explain the existence of this archaic and peculiar form of embodied ritual, secrecy. But that is not so, and one purpose of this book is to demonstrate why.

Of all the ingenuous solutions to the problem of agency and dependency in human life, this kind of secrecy reigns supreme in the human imagination. Morgan's creation in his own Victorian society and his discovery among the Iroquois of something he thought to be kindred were to presage what anthropologists were to discover in the most surprising places in the century that followed. It is true that anthropologists have sometimes made these secret groups appear quaint or silly; even more sadly we have sometimes contributed to the demise of these extraordinary systems of the imagination. However, anthropology has also preserved these hidden realities and strained to make them a part of the human variation—and this surely has furthered understanding of the human condition, which is, after all, one of the aims of anthropology.

By the early part of the twentieth century and the establishment of modern anthropology, this history of Morgan's secret societies would be forgotten, and an awareness of Victorian men's secrecy would also be lost to coming generations of anthropologists. Anthropology's love affair with postmodernism would kindle a fire of self-absorption that would have been unimaginable to Morgan, and certainly vulgar and objectionable to Malinowski. The work of Geertz (1988: 78) is a source of this ennui but not the source of its excess, as his objection to the postmodern ethnographer's confessional makes clear: "When the subject so expands does not the object shrink?" Secrecy is virtually gone, or erased, from these burgeoning confessional accounts. Even today, I think, to admit of participation in secret associations, especially for males, goes too far. Anthropologists are not so far removed from the conditional masculinity of the last century in that respect. If agency requires secrecy, as I suggest for the men's house in New Guinea, then perhaps the mystique of fieldwork has secured the same effect. Ritual secrecy waits to be rediscovered as if it were another country awaiting colonization.

Some colleagues fear that exoticism is the new sin of anthropology. Indeed, it is easy to sensationalize the strange and ignore the familiar, leading to further bouts of attack against and defense of relativism (Geertz 1984a; Spiro 1986), a matter to which we must return at the end of this book. Nevertheless, one must search long and hard to find a body of cultural traditions as strange and variegated as those of American culture today. Is not this warning against exoticism enigmatic in view of how little anthropology has been dedicated to the interpretation of secret forms of our own sociality? Indeed, the forms of secrecy known to us—from James Bond to monster movies, the Oprah Show, and the ever-popular Twelve Step programs that transform self-help problems from alcoholism to sexual compulsions into a new religion of healing—let alone the ones our imaginations imagine but have not yet located—beg for cultural analysis in this New Age of fundamentalism. In this popular view still, "We are only as sick as our secrets." Anthropology has just begun to look closer to home to investigate secrecy. Be forewarned, then, that what is hidden in other times and places is susceptible to exoticization, and nowhere more so than in New Guinea. In fact, the familiar looks very strange upon examination at home (Herdt 1999a).

This prelude on nineteenth-century origins of anthropology and secrecy opens a general lesson about a particular secrecy, one that Lewis Henry Morgan may have glimpsed but never voiced—indeed, could never be fully conscious of—in his work. And this we must think on: In these traditions ritual secrecy is received as "natural," as elementary as the body, more virtuous than the gift. It accommodates the desires of the actor to the conventions of <u>power and meaning</u>; the ritual knowing gradually becomes a part and parcel of being, protecting the self from the anxieties and doubts of a messy, even polluted, public world; and this secret reality satisfies in one stroke the historical yearning of an era with the self-interest purveyed by performance of a common rite. Hence in secret praxis, social behavior and hidden reality merge; the ritual secret *becomes* personal subjectivity; culture and ontology are one.

CHAPTER 2

Why Secrecy?

THAT CULTURAL SYSTEMS OF SECRECY occur unevenly across societies ancient and modern, large and small, is certain; they are surely not universal in the social life of human groups. Nor must we confound the existence of secrets in the lives of individual actors—whether via the concept of Freud's unconscious wishes, or the phenomenological social self of Lewis Henry Morgan, Georg Simmel, George Herbert Mead, and Erving Goffman, among the many distinguished scholars who have considered this topic—with that form of secret knowledge and ontological being constitutive of the cultural reality of secret societies. Surely in the experience of privacy and individualism in the West the secret is a universal possibility, perhaps even likelihood, its vicissitudes contingent upon the desires and life experiences of individuals—the "accidental" series of the individual life history, in Freud's sense. Indeed, it is precisely the contingent nature of human existence—its dependence upon shared symbolic reality, and the uses of secrecy to make and break consensual reality within the same society—that continues to make secrecy an enduring interest of social study.

However, the elaboration of these potentials into a full-blown "culture" or sociality of hidden practices and knowledge is quite another matter. Whatever the sources of such a historical formation, what is needed is not the psychoanalyst but the hand of the anthropologist and sociologist to provide both a lens and a method for understanding this phenomenon. For those of us privileged enough to reside in North American or Western European societies early in the twenty-first century, it is hard to imagine how reality could be divided between a public world and another so divergent that exit from one and entry into the other requires secret initiation. Most of us, scholars included, react in disbelief or with cynicism when confronted with stories of ritual cults and exotic practices that supposedly kept outsiders in the dark; in a sense this skepticism is no different than the nineteenth-century view that gave rise to the antisocial theory of secrecy (see chap. 1 on Lewis Henry Morgan). We might call this the "missing discourse" on secrecy in the experience of anthropologists.

It is this book's premise that in certain times and places—and here we shall focus on Melanesia—the unstable character of social relations creates such anxiety and mistrust that it is impossible to make mutual plans and goals for social adaptation between male compatriots. Profound disruptions across generations of males made social relations conditional. In times of war and violence, the inability to predict allies or to trust colleagues led to great misfortunes and social disasters in which entire villages were destroyed. This social chaos and human calamity led to the use of secret ritual initiation practices and the founding of an institutional complex called the men's house as the cultural and psychological solution to an otherwise intolerable and perhaps ultimately unsuccessful sociality. The creation of "masculinity" as a social product and masculine performances as the main production of the men's house became the sine qua non of its existence. In such a social and psychological world, a huge gulf exists between the women's relational practices and social spaces, and those of the men. Prior to initiation, children are folded into their mother's world. The creation of agency in boys in such a world is problematical, contingent, and fragile. Indeed, *secret masculinity* is an apt term to describe the myriad processes that result in the adult outcome of marriage and fatherhood expected in the life course of young men.

But the contingency of their masculinity was not the only price Melanesian societies had to pay for this secret pact: secrecy in intimate social relations is a radical breach or hiatus that generates its own chronic dilemmas and human tragedy. In my own analysis of precolonial societies in Melanesia, I believe that much of the reason for this historical conundrum stems from warfare, as you shall see. No society was immune to its terrible consequences, but New Guinea Highland groups in particular, lacking the mechanism for redress and motivated by the value of blood revenge, were severely disrupted by virulent and seemingly endless deadly war. The images of New Guinea warfare popularized in the film *Dead Birds*, about the Dani people of West New Guinea, are misleading for the culture area as a whole. The film paints a far too simple picture of "ritualized" violence, of tit-for-tat, which, however true it may have been for the

Dani, does not begin to explore the cruelty and ravages of war raiding and violence among the peoples who will be studied closely in this book. The brunt of war was the responsibility of the men's house. The men's house was by definition a homosocial and male-privileged space, one given over to the stories of war and to the socialization of recruits who needed to survive it. This is the subtext of male ritual, violence, and sexuality as seen in the fine ethnographies of Kenneth Read, Fredrik Barth, Maurice Godelier, and Donald Tuzin, to be reviewed herein. Access through initiation was thus age-graded and hierarchical: first by gender; second by age; third by the commitment to emulate and aspire to be a Great Man; and finally, toward the end of life, by that die-hard's sense of clinging to power and hence to utopian immortality.

To excuse individual human actors and men as a category for their part played in the necessary social tragedy of secret masculinity is too simple as well, and probably misleading. Within the guise of secret ritual practice there can be no doubt in my mind that social abuses and such terrible, unseemly tragedies as murders and rape have occurred, and far more frequently than we probably would like to know. To call the initiations into the secret men's house "rites of terror" (Whitehouse 2000: 21) is not far from the mark. Thus, the following account raises but cannot ultimately satisfy the ethical questions with which I conclude this study. Anthropology, as we have seen time and again, most recently in the debate over the accusation of ethical abuses by the scientists and journalists among the Yanomami people of the Amazon, remains ill prepared to deal with the quandaries of such devastation (Geertz 2001). In the conclusion I shall examine the positionality of (primarily) male anthropologists who have typically misrepresented ritual secrecy as a game or a sham in the men's houses of New Guinea, essentially evading the moral and ethical problems posed for social study across time and space.

Lewis Henry Morgan's own use of secrecy reveals a tension about the cultural uses and potential abuses of ritual secrecy (see chap. 1). The secret orders that Morgan founded were not for selfish purposes in any narrow sense of the term, but neither, in the end, were they for the creation of a larger social purpose; Morgan himself grew disenchanted and ultimately withdrew from his creations. In fact, the story of secrecy in Morgan's life is illustrative of ambivalent individualism and conditional masculinity—of how the desire for male solidarity could be found in the men's secret societies, or not at all—among nineteenth-century men. Living in a time of radically changing social roles and gender customs, when a crisis in religion was sweeping away simple faith and the crisis in gender was destabilizing the hierarchy of relations between men and women, male secrecy represented a secure homosocial space without a necessary homosexuality, a search for the eternal and a generative ritual, but without the spiritualism of women or the rejection of reproductive mothering.

In short, this cynical and romantic view of secrecy as antisocial is very old but flawed in Western social thought, and we shall inquire into its sources in the history of anthropology. Secrecy goes against the grain of civil society and the higher good in public affairs, it is still believed; but seldom has it been studied by anthropologists in Western nations, with the exception of such remarkable and fine works as those on Mafia secrecy in nineteenth-century Sicily (Blok 1974), antisocial sorcery fears and accusations in rural France (Favret-Saada 1980), and British contemporary witches for whom witchcraft is a part-time occupation (Luhrman 1989a).

This is a book about a particular historical form of secret masculinity and the cultural reality it produced: a pervasive ritual secrecy laced throughout social life. No doubt similar social forms are to be found in Western history, particularly before the modern period—a subject too large and complex to study here. However, in the modern period, it was common to regard Western European and North American social formations as relegating women in the nineteenth century to domestic spaces, while Victorian men were expected to enter the public spaces of the marketplace in order to compete and achieve male solidarity. Subsequent scholarship in the study of public/private domains in civil society has modified such a view. Masculinity, once seen as a "trait," has come to be regarded as a social product and a performative structure, which stipulates particular social needs and norms (Connell 1995). The risk was failure to achieve the necessary performance in intimate relations and social work, and male secret sociality arose to meet the challenge of this conditional masculinity. It bears a family resemblance to a special order of secret masculinity, long known from parts of the non-Western world, that is constitutive of male initiation rites and secret ceremonies. The zenith of these could be found in the precolonial societies of Melanesia and the island of New Guinea in particular.

Only through ritual initiation can New Guinea boys in these precolonial societies achieve the agency necessary to be full partners with men and women—the ability to be regarded as moral agents and full persons. The foundation of the men's secret society is a social contract to resocialize boys into masculine agents. But in order to attain this adult agency they must submit to being an object of desire and, among particular groups such as the Sambia of the New Guinea Highlands, to sexual objectification by older males who are themselves in the process of becoming agents. Prior to marriage, then, this process of becoming agents extends both to young initiates and older bachelors, who form a symbolic "marriage" set within the context of the men's society. By accommodating themselves to their respective secret roles in this symbolic play, the boys are promised eventual transformation from objects to subjects and the ability later to perform sexually as masculine agents with women and to serve as masculine warriors in the eyes of other men. This transformation reproduces inequality in male/male relations, which is hidden inside the secrecy of the men's house.

Why Secrecy in New Guinea?

One of the critical issues of Melanesian study over the past century has been whether men's secret organizations are the center of these precolonial cultures or the marginal decentering locus of society. The anthropological view, often cynical toward the role played by men's ritual secrecy, has been strongly influenced not only by modernist theories of secrecy but also by the reaction of colonial powers to secret societies (chap. 5).

It was once speculated, by Simmel (1950) and Foucault (1980), among others, that for certain historical individuals or groups, secrecy is a necessary protective device in the effort to avoid oppression. In the modern period there is good evidence in support of this idea, at least in the historical formation of sexual cultures (Herdt 1997a). However, such a view cannot explain the phenomenon of ritual secrecy in precolonial New Guinea, where the very people who were dominant and in power—adult senior men—were the ones who created and then reproduced the secret society. The difficulty with all such formulations of "culture" and "power" as applied to ritual secrecy is that they subscribe to an implicit homogeneous system of cultural meanings, a unitary form of reality performed on the stage of society. As Barth once noted, "Anthropologists are strong on using conceptions from the other cultural traditions we are studying as a means to transcend our own categories—but we tend subsequently to domesticate these ideas by re-integrating them through abstraction into our pre-established anthropology" (1987: 86).

Conversely, it has long has been suggested by cultural critics of these practices that while other areas of a society were necessary or adaptive, the mere existence of secrecy suggested a lack of authenticity—duplicity, lying, cheating, hoaxes, and the effort to dominate or control others through deceptive means (reviewed in Schwimmer 1980). If we therefore assume, as did earlier scholars in the Melanesian literature, that ritual secrecy was for male domination of women and children, we are faced with a striking paradox. If the men are in power, why do they need secrecy to attain what they already possess? But if we deny that adult men are in power, we are then led to the enigmatic position that either the man's performance of authority is a sham, or else these acephalous societies have no legitimate authority or leadership at all. Clearly, the latter position is extreme and unsupported by the literature for a very long time (Berndt and Lawrence 1971; Godelier and Strathern 1991; Read 1959). Furthermore, if we agree with the sociobiologists, who typically insinuate that men physically or socially have the advantage over women (Tiger 1970), then we do not elucidate the matter of "power" nor problematize the relationships among power, ritual, and warfare for men at all. These prior lines of reasoning have avoided deeper questions. Where does male power come from? How are men's ontology and subjectivity socially created to support this power? By rethinking these questions we are led back to challenge the widespread assumption that "male power" is already present in personality, culture, or society, and thus to analyze the cultural basis for the cynical views of ritual secrecy in our own tradition of knowledge and understanding regarding such matters.

This bring us back to the question, Why study secrecy, and why is secrecy the solution to certain social problems? This book argues that a historically particularistic process of the development of male sexual subjectivity occurs in the men's house, without which boys would not occupy their adult positionality in these communities. I will argue this for the Sambia in chapter 3, and while others may question the relevance of the Sambia case for understanding these processes (see also Herdt 1993), several critical points provoke comparison. At the time of initiation rituals, Sambia boys are symbolically treated as proxies for women (their mothers and sisters) (see Herdt 1982a). Because of the binary quality of secrecy—its powerful tendencies to essentialize and objectify insiders versus outsiders, and then to treat outsiders as Other—the entry of boys is highly disruptive, because they are classed with their mothers as outsiders before initiation.

The bodies of the boys are not male bodies and do not have the utopian qualities of mind, body, and spirit associated with initiated men. Thus in their initiation performances, (the initiates *stand in* for women symbolically in all relevant ritual actions) (Herdt 1982b). These concepts apply to the ideology. On the practice side, however, the boys have existed within the women's culture, which has no concept of male discipline or ritual discipline per se. It also lacked the subjective imagery of men's secrecy or the embodiment of ritual discipline, as in nose-bleeding purification (Herdt 1982c). Other New Guinea peoples who practice "boy-inseminating" practices also symbolize the desire on the part of men both to "grow" prepubertal boys and sometimes to "play" with them erotically (Herdt 1984a; 1999a). Once purged of pollution from the contaminated world of the women's houses, the boy's body is treated as a pure anlage of maleness but without sexual maturity or social masculinity. Temporarily the boy is perceived as, and also substituted for, the excluded women.

Now we can ask: What is the internal aim (what Foucault would have called the internal discourse, not available to those on the outside of the men's house institution, and certainly not available to women and children) of relationships created through ritual secrecy? In general, it is for the provision of social regulation through the creation of hierarchy and a code of honor in the men's house: a special trust, loyalty, and belongingness. Why is this badge of honor necessary for the men? After all, are they not members of the same patriclans, great clans, phratries, and tribes? Aren't their fraternal and filial ties to one another sufficient to create loyalty and trust? The answer is clearly "no." As a long line of scholars have suggested, particularly for New Guinea Highland societies (reviewed in Berndt and Berndt 1962; Brown 1995; Harrison 1993; Herdt 1981; Knauft 1985; Mead 1935; Meggitt 1964, 1979; Reay 1959), male/male relations are unstable and given to fracture. Fraternal competition and implicit age-peer rivalry are constantly mentioned as divisive forces throughout the literature (Forge 1972; Godelier 1986; Knauft 1993; Read 1965; A. J. Strathern 1974). The most notable of these forces in precolonial Melanesian societies was the threat of murder, rape, and pillage by external enemies. However, the threat to life and property by assault from neighbors, even affines, was ever present; intervillage relations were chronically unruly and unpredictable) Therefore, marital arrangements between kin groups (e.g., clans) were contingent and, without the presence of other mediating factors, such as the existence of ceremonial exchange systems (Feil 1978), tended to deteriorate. Delayed exchange marriage through such practices as infant-betrothal was notoriously difficult to consummate (Godelier 1982), making social order, especially intervillage relationships, unpredictable.

The perceived threat, however, did not stop at the boundaries of the village: men routinely asserted that women, imported as wives from neighboring communities, were given to sorcery and the use of their vaginal or menstrual fluids to weaken and kill their husbands. That the sons of these same women were expected to be the next generation of warriors suggests the depth of mistrust in the daily life and politics of village communities.

The intergenerational schism was potentially explosive. The problem was that the older men did not trust boys prior to initiation. This statement is complex and needs unpacking, being a composite of political economy, oedipal dynamics, and spousal conflict, among other factors. However much grandfathers, fathers, and older brothers cared for the boys, they could not trust in them—either in their bodies or in their minds. If we were to say that this was "because of their mothers' influence over the lads," we would be partially right, since the account that men give in their own secret internal discourse at ritual initiation includes such testimonials. After all, the boys' bodies are saturated with pollution from the women's houses, and their bodies are thus unwitting agents of the transmission of pollution (Herdt 1982c). However, these prior accounts typically omitted the intentionality and agency of the boys themselves (and my own work only begins to address the gap; see Herdt 1987b). That is, the older men did not trust in the desires and intentions of the boys either; and it was the fear of betrayal and mistrust, as much as the boys' polluted bodies, that vexed the elders (Godelier 1989). Yet, of necessity, the men had to socialize the boys to protect the village from external attack, and to do this, they had to transmit power to the boys. This was no mean task: the men had to overcome their own doubt about the loyalty and trustworthiness of the boys.

However, whatever their own trepidation regarding this oedipal dilemma, the men were faced with an equally daunting force on the side of the boys themselves; they had to overcome the resistance of the boys to initiation. This was sometimes open, naked, and hostile. I have observed boys who hid or ran away into the forest in order to avoid being initiated, and the efforts and the countermeasures taken by the men to overcome them were a regular part of the social consciousness brought to these events (Herdt 1987a). Perhaps it seems obvious that boys would want to avoid the pain and ordeals of these rites de passage, as the late Roger Keesing (1982a) once suggested. The matter is not as simple as that in retrospect, as Maurice Godelier (1986) has hinted in his accounts of the Baruya and the notable film series *Toward Baruya Manhood*, which documents their initiations. The boys admired the men; they loved their fathers and grandfathers; they wanted to emulate and be like the Great Man—that mythological concoction of sexy and swashbuckling virtue that was the pride of the men. But in these speculative images notice how I have taken liberties with the putative social sophistication of the boy as a subject, and indeed, such imagery construes the boy as an agent. But that is too facile.

While there is a wide degree of individual variation in this area of social entry into the men's house and secret reality, with differences in the subjectivities of males, a consistent line of evidence supports the idea that prepubertal boys in New Guinea precolonial societies were ambivalent and even hostile to being initiated by the men (reviewed in Gewertz 1982; Herdt 1987a; Read 1952; Tuzin 1982). When we ask why the (obviously ambivalent) prepubertal boys are inclined to the role dictated for them, the answer seems to be: "Because of the culture" (Mead 1935: 282). But such a view imagines a singular cultural reality, even though the boys could not know what hidden reality lay beyond the doors of the men's house.

This fractured view of the political economy of secrecy reveals the importance of separating culturally sanctioned rule and authority from power, while recognizing that in precolonial Melanesian societies, at least, there was no singular cultural reality or means for the achievement of power and control over public affairs. Power, as a variety of diffuse means of seeking and attaining regulation, was realized through diverse "technologies" and "devices" of social control (Foucault 1980), among them the significant but largely alien form (in the Western view) of ritual secrecy. Initiation into ritual secrecy created gender-distinctive worldviews. The habitus of these views were based in spatially segregated living arrangements throughout Melanesia. This in turn produced social actions and developmental subjectivities akin to full-blown ontologies (I say "akin" to but not the same as, since to essentialize these gendered worldviews as "ontologies," particularly in the Platonic sense, would make the men's hegemonic position inherently superior, and thus displace women from higher reality-making sociality, a notion that is unfaithful to the ethnography of the area). There were competing interests in these communities, which gave rise to distinct social and historical productions, including ritual practices. The divergent realities connected to these rituals differed by gender: they were productive of, associated with, and created effects in individual awareness that concomitantly rationalized and motivated the rituals.

Initiation secrecy, in this model, is a strategic sacred and sexual system, a means of overcoming ambivalence, of creating eventual trust and loyalty between males. Trust, however, involves inclusion in a circle, and ritual initiation does this the hard way: by moving a boy inside the circle, all others are shut out. Conceptualizing ritual secrecy as relations that separate the genders and that make boys "mediatory objects produced by the men's transactions" (M. Strathern 1988: 214) provides the theoretical space for understanding both the divergent aims of the genders and the means by which boys become objects (including erotic objects) of the men. Initiation is not of course the only social means for promoting the development of physical and moral "maturity" in the production of social "masculinity," even in Melanesia. Nor is sexual objectification typical of this process, as I have noted elsewhere (Herdt 1984a). To make "whole" and to "complete" the person is a symbolic process (Read 1952) involving a variety of "forms that propagate" (Strathern 1988), among them the sexual—though few anthropologists have said so, Marilyn Strathern being one. And fewer male anthropologists have studied this aspect, or at least not belittled it—a curious point to which we shall return in the Conclusion.

But this is key: to create loyalty and trust the men of many of these communities had to overcome their own ambivalent attitudes about initiating their sons—not in terms of affection, but in terms of politics. Their ambivalence does not of course mean that these fathers failed to love and protect their sons, or failed to regard them affectionately in their domestic moments (see Langness 1990). The distinction is vital and the cause of much misunderstanding, as in the recent distortion of these issues by Langness (1999, esp. 63ff.), who trivializes the erotic component of male ritual secrecy. The men's emotional ambivalence ought to be interpreted not only as a matter of personal experience (as Langness does) but of political psychology.

During my initial fieldwork among the Sambia in 1974 and 1976, for example, elders would not let the uninitiated boys come near the men's house. Uninitiated boys were excluded because they were agents of pollution who shared in women's bodies, fluids, and clothing. What the men failed to articulate—simply because it was tacit knowledge (Polanyi 1966;

also see Barth 1987; Lewis 1980)—was that these boys shared in the women's culture and worldview. The men feared this relatedness and secretly dreaded that the boy's intimacies with his mother might somehow usurp male rule. Was this a rational fear? The question must be answered not in terms of individual differences but in terms of cultural reasoning. Surely the men dreaded pollution and depletion (Herdt 1982c); even more they feared the betrayal of boys and the undermining of their tenuous hold. In short, prior to initiation a boy was not a trusted agent, and this very difference conditioned the emotions with which the boy was regarded and his sexual classification in a system of secrecy.

Observers of these men's cults have sometimes conflated the public face of men's actions with the private and secret experience, as I long ago complained (Herdt 1981). But the paradox of power in societies such as the Gahuku-Gama, Baktaman, Ilahita Arapesh, Sambia, Baruya, and others studied in this book suggests male rhetoric and related public discursive practices assert supremacy; while secret ritual and the internal discourse of the men's house express anxiety, fearfulness, nostalgia, and inferiority. Both sides of male discourse are troubling and have never been satisfactorily explained. (The closest account, though not a totalizing one, has been to see these as variable elements of morality; see Read 1955.) I think the key lies in analyzing how ritual secrecy builds status empowerment and sexual subjectivity through rituals of embodiment in the developmental subjectivity of the boy.

In a prior generation, the paradoxical nature of the men's reality was referred to in terms of the Freudian defensive device "protest masculinity" (reviewed in Herdt 1981, 1987a, 1989c; Herdt and Stoller 1990). This notion asserted that the men were using masculinity and aggression as defenses against their own anxieties about women, especially to counter feelings of dependence upon women (Langness 1967). But as Godelier (1986) has skillfully shown, the paradoxical reality of men is a bit more complicated: publicly treating women as polluted, degraded, crafty and manipulative, alternately shy and sexually lascivious, and perhaps most paradoxical of all, *harmless to the men;* while secretly regarding women as threatening, disloyal and mutinous, even lethal (able to infect and deplete the male body) to male personhood. Like other scholars from an earlier period I once used the notion of defensive or protest masculinity (Herdt 1981, 1989c). But I now think that this concept is inadequate, not because it is Freudian, but because the process implied by Freud does not explain the developmental subjectivity. Protest masculinity appeals to a reductive aspect, the conscious and unconscious fear of women through defensive thoughts and actions that attempt to create triumph out of trauma (Stoller and Herdt 1985). The construct already takes for granted or grants "power" as an intrinsic sense of superiority to male reality. What the Freudian concept cannot explain, because it does not deconstruct its assumptive identity state (masculinity), is where the power in maleness comes from. (Freud [1925], of course, took it for granted that males were superior to females, certainly anatomically and psychically.)

The paradox remains intriguing and requires ritual secrecy as a solution because in New Guinea it is not assumed that males are intrinsically superior to females—quite the contrary. Femaleness is, if anything, an inherently more vital and fertile principle in the world (Gillison 1993; Herdt 1981; Mead 1949). By interrogating the symbolic meanings of secrecy, one questions the basis on which male power and authority exist and are represented in the scheme of things, which questions the sources of male reality. Thus, we begin to reflect upon how male rule is created through social means such as ritual and how it is threatened or at risk because it is not inherently present in the beginning of the cosmos. This insight frees cultural analysis to examine the influence of the men's house in producing male subjectivity, linking social life to the development of male sexual subjectivity and adult male rule.

This approach now exposes an untruth in male ideology: that all males are equal. The system of Great Men, with its mythological imagery previously described as reliant upon an ideology of solidarity and equality in small social groups of men (Allen 1967), actually underscores this flaw (Godelier 1986). As Melanesianists have long suggested, relations among males were complicated, not egalitarian (Read 1959; M. Strathern 1992), just as relations between women and men were inherently unequal (see chap. 4). Ritual secrecy, then, seen from the life-course perspective—beginning with the boy's entry into the men's house before puberty, and following his growth and social development into old age—was a means of securing inequalities between males in these precolonial New Guinea societies.

The Divergent Desires of Men and Boys

Stated simply: the social, political, and erotic desires of men and boys differ—reflecting a variety of formative influences on their being or ontology, most notably warfare and the binaries of secret (vs. public) life and gender (male vs. female). Boys lack agency in the men's world because they are occupants of the women's house. Their masculinity is nil. In fact, boys actually have negative social status positions in the men's world due to their being classified with women. Thus, the boys are not subjects and cannot be agents of their own desires. Their positionality can only be that of objects.

The boys are unable to express their aims and desires, and are not accepted as full moral agents by men—or for that matter, by women, either. In order to become agentic in the men's world, the boys must be transformed from being "children" or "female-like" things, to "initiates" or "male-like things"—a notion so commonplace now as to occupy the status of cliché (Herdt 1982a). Typically this transformation requires a change in the bodily essences of the boys in some way; and typically, it is only the same gender—men for boys, and women for girls—who are believed capable and competent to complete this transformation (M. Strathern 1988). Among the Sambia, as is well known, this transformation in subjectivity and agency from child to initiate requires that the boys become recipients of semen.

Generally, there was a historical pattern surrounding this transformation in male reality and gender status in New Guinea societies, as implied before. The boy was initiated with mistrust, perhaps to overcome the suspicion of disloyalty on the part of the older men. Therefore, as the liminal way station en route to permanent residence in the men's house, the boy's initiation was a coerced or semi-involuntary compact, in which the boy serves as a subordinate (a woman-proxy, at first, due to his sociosexual classification with women) to certain older males. This subordination was political and social everywhere; among a few of the so-called ritual homosexuality societies, it was also sexual (Read 1984; Schwimmer 1984). The boy was transferred jurally forever from being under the authority of the women and his mother, and placed in the men's house, both of which structural changes immediately ameliorated the boy's social status in the men's house. These structural changes also made possible the defensive use of ritual secrecy thereafter as a means of screening the inner thoughts and desires of the boy from his mother and later his wife, the only other woman with whom he would have an intimate relationship. By accepting his subordination to the men, the boy began the advance of his own social career—a small but growing ability to enact his desires in secret and public.

Acceptance of his subordinate position therefore accomplishes three aims: First, it enables the boy to be socialized (actually resocialized) by men, in the direction of secret masculine codes and social and moral goals. Second, it enables the boy to develop the awareness of how to dominate and manipulate his future wife and other women, as dictated by the men's society. Third, it provides "role distance" (Goffman 1959) from the part the boy plays in being subordinated or dominated, which is generative of fantasies and desires—developmental sexual subjectivity—all constitutive of the receptive ritual secret masculinity being engendered in him by his seniors in order to perform in public as an adult manly agent. The puzzling qualities of this intricate process have been best summarized by Simon Ottenberg from his West African study:

> In this sense secrecy, which by its nature appears to have an isolating and withdrawing quality (Bellman 1984), creates inquiry and assertiveness in the young child in response to it, and this process helps move the child along in maturation—paradoxically, to a clearer understanding of the larger world of which secrecy forms only a part. (1989: 56)

Again, however, initiation was resisted both by senior men and by boys, so the secrecy was transformative of the resistance on both sides. Preinitiated Sambia boys typically resisted assuming the powers of the senior men, and they did not want their childhood sociality and cultural reality, shared with their mothers and other women, usurped (see chap. 3). More strongly, the boys did not want access to the ritual secrets, most commonly because they associated the privilege of the secrets with the pain of rituals. Moreover, the majority of Sambia boys at their commencement of initiation did not desire the hidden homosociality of the men's house. They already had a comfortable domicile: the women's house, with the moral agency of meanings of the women's world. Of course many boys were curious about the secret doings in the men's house, but in most cases, their curiosity was not sufficient to overcome their fear and anxiety toward it (Tuzin 1997). Only later, as the initiates approached manhood, did their attitudes fundamentally change. As they came closer to marrying, they adopted the alternative cultural reality of the men's house—which they had long shared in and were soon to inherit. But it was not until they were faced with the prospect of forming intimate relations with a woman in the person of their assigned bride that they became more highly motivated to actualize and implement the secret reality of the men's house. In short, at the moment they were to commence sexual relations with wives from potentially or actually hostile neighboring hamlets, then their desire to master ritual secrecy was matched by and energized through their sexual desire for women.

This kind of social developmental regime of ritual secrecy is thus a mutual compact between the generations to secure the commitment of boys to take on the rule of the older men by first securing their trust and proving their loyalty to the men's house. The boys' acceptance of their positionality—being at first objects, not subjects, of desire—facilitates their authority. By accepting their position as passive recipients of ritual action (for the Sambia, ritual insemination; for others, bodily treatment and decoration) the boys-become-youths prove their loyalty and earn acceptance in the inner sanctum of male secret power.

Secrecy as Antisocial: Historical Views

Is not the mere existence of secrecy, the critic asks, indicative of the duality of human existence, a proof of conflict within a society, no less than for an individual? Many authorities before the creation of anthropology thought in this way, and the great social theorists—including Durkheim, Freud, Simmel, and others—have generally subscribed to a negative view of secrecy that emptied it of social and cultural meaning.

A significant impetus of this romantic-cynical attitude about secrecy in anthropology comes from the great French sociologist Emile Durkheim, who argued that no human institution could rest upon lie or error. Society must be grounded in "reality" itself, Durkheim thought; "social facts" must present a singular and totalizing social subjectivity sufficient to describe this as "collective consciousness." This rational and Platonic truth has been the basis for social theory and anthropology since the turn of the century (Durkheim 1915: 14).

Of course, the advent of postmodernism has altered features of this epistemology. Theory has moved in recent years from regarding culture as an "acted document," the discursive knowledge and practices of which are identified with public social life, its exchanges and seemingly transparent lives (Geertz 1973, 1988), to practice theories that blur the boundaries of texts, persons, and communities (Knauft 1995). However, this epistemic change has not entered much into how sociologists and anthropologists interpret secrecy. In its most fundamental sense, society is still regarded as a public phenomenon, its institutions grounded in "the nature of things," that is, constituted by consensual "social and cultural reality" (Geertz 1984b; Giddens 1990). Many anthropologists continue to suggest that ritual secret meanings signify collective signifiers and codes (Barth 1975; Wagner 1972, 1975) in the public domain, though some scholars of secrecy, such as Schwimmer (1980), have long suggested the shortcomings of such theory. The signs of ritual secrecy appeal to something hidden, a force contra society, against culture. Secrecy does not match "reality" in this Western public/secular sense, which has led to problematic readings by social and cultural theorists who assumed that secrecy is either groundless or fraudulent, a "false consciousness" that deceived its own practitioners, in which case it cannot serve as a Durkheimian social fact (Whitehouse 1995).

This is the sense in which I will refer to many earlier ethnographic accounts from around the world as cynical-romantic views of ritual practices of small societies since the Victorian era. As we have seen, such a negative attitude was absent from the story of Lewis Henry Morgan, though Morgan's peers were suspicious of secrecy, and his own feelings about secret societies obviously changed after he married and became famous.

Many of the dualistic qualities of secrecy previewed in Western history—individual/society, public/private, and so on—are the source of perennial debates about the meaning of what Durkheim (1914) called the "duality of human existence," the social view that humans are individuals and members of groups. But secrecy also goes against the grain of some of the most cherished Western notions of "human nature," which fear the "nature" or "animal" side of people, in favor of the "social contract" in neoliberal democracies. I think these sentiments are historically very old manifestations of a Western Protestant and Calvinist tendency that valued public sociality and mistrusted all things clandestine or secret.

Psychoanalysts have contributed strongly to the cynical attitude about ritual secrecy, mistakenly conflating it with the individual or what I have called contractual secrecy, as reflected in the following prominent passage from Bruno Bettelheim:

Rites that claim occurrences contrary to nature, but that cannot demonstrate such events, must be secret if the participants are to be able to maintain to themselves that the occurrences did in fact take place. Moreover, secrecy protects the belief against the doubts of skeptics, who, because of the secrecy, cannot collect evidence detrimental to the belief. . . . The fact that all these are fictions must be hidden if the devotees are to be able fully to enjoy the psychological advantages gained by symbolic achievement. Secrecy thus is necessary for the continuing satisfaction of the needs of the believers. (1955: 228–29)

I think that this view, quite close to Freud's general evaluation of religion as an "illusion" that fulfills the needs of the worshipper who regresses to an infantile state when confronted with anxiety, mirrors the psychoanalytic interpretations of ritual secrecy in New Guinea (Lidz and Lidz 1989). Secrets, as in the popular culture notion of "family secrets," may be quite harmful to the lives and aspirations of individuals (Bok 1962); and cultural myths may motivate the use of secrets within families to suppress the revelation of difference, including sexual difference (Herdt and Koff 2000). Surely the culture of secrecy surrounding the Church and the publicity surrounding accusations of sexual coercion by priests and cover-up by the Church in 2002 have accentuated the deep mistrust of sexual secrets. However, another strand of thought sees the potential in secrecy for creativity (Pincus and Dare 1978), and, going back further, protection of individual liberty through secrecy (Simmel 1950).

Simmel on Secrecy

The writing of Georg Simmel on secrecy, as much as anyone's, drew attention to secrecy as an important paradigm for critical social theory, and no text in the social study of this area is better known than his influential essay "The Secret Society," written around 1900 (reprinted in his collected works [1950]). In his remarkable essay, Simmel advances the main theme of an ontological theory of secrecy in understanding the creation of cultural reality, and I regard this as the precursor to the approach taken here. While Simmel does not explicitly contrast ritual versus nonritual secrecy, his reference to ritual opens the way for an ontological view:

The striking feature in the treatment of ritual is not only the rigor of its observance but, above all, the anxiousness with which it is guarded a secret. Its disclosure appears to be as detrimental as that of the purposes and actions or perhaps of the very existence of the society. . . . Under its characteristic categories, the secret society must seek to create a sort of life totality. (1950: 359)

Simmel's suggestion that ritual secrecy creates a "life totality," or what I will call a secret ontology (shared reality), is illustrated in the case studies that follow.

Simmel stressed the fundamental insight that secrecy is, as we might say today, a form of cultural production, albeit the product of a divided society, while expressing a certain moral cynicism about the reality and necessity of the secrecy. Simmel's emphasis upon secrecy in conflict situations of sociopolitical oppression (what he called "unfreedom") was the first positive treatment of the collective forms of secrecy known to comparative sociology and anthropology. Coming out of nineteenth-century pseudoevolutionary and rationalist concerns about the emergence of civilization and democracy, Simmel reflected the biases of the society of his times. He argued for the transitional emergence of the secret society as a lesser form of social evolution that would eventually give way to a higher form. He also found harmful functions in certain brands of secrecy as well and thus perpetuated the extant folk culture of romantic cynicism, which concerns all forms of hidden association. These were to be mistrusted, Simmel felt, and their secret form was regarded as selfish and generally as "anti-social." Power was part of the reason. Simmel was ingenious in connecting self-interest to secret formation. He argued:

The purpose of secrecy is, above all, protection. . . . Of all protective measures, the most radical is to make oneself invisible. In this respect, the secret society differs fundamentally from the individual who seeks protection of secrecy [because it is] not the individuals, but the groups they form, which is concealed. (1950: 345)

Here, Simmel wrestled with how to make a shared cultural reality out of the threads of individual secret acts.

Symbolically, Simmel's work viewed secrecy as "a second world alongside the manifest world" (1950: 330). This metaphorical relationship between part and whole comes close to a rethinking of the distinction between "culture" and "society," in which society contains a symbolic world—culture—parallel to a structure of social relations or a process of social practices. Yet Simmel's metaphoric term "world," and the subordi-nate term "manifest," suggest that he could not further explore this analy-sis of the multiple power structures associated with multiple cultural reali-ties within the same tradition. How can the members of the secret group and those excluded speak the same language and share in the same culture, but not belong to one "society"? Their leaders are the leaders of the con-taining society, yet they may attack or even assassinate those who are not members. The problematic extends into the secret formation as well, for this is no simple social solidarity (Allen 1967); secrets are status privileges that separate inside from outside, but within the secret formation, secrets create hierarchies of younger and older members of the hidden order. It may further antagonize segments of the population, such as the genders, creating secret and public spaces suggestive of secret and public persons and bodies.

When it came to non-Western societies, Simmel's assumptions of functional adaptation, harmony, and homogeneity further thwarted the understanding of divergent cultural realities. Simmel's work was thus instrumental in shifting but not fully analyzing the structural/historical assumption that a "society" contains but one cultural reality. We see this most clearly in what Simmel refers to as the "protective" functions of the secret groups, such as early Christian communities who were persecuted.

> The fact that secrets do not remain guarded forever is the weakness of the secret society. . . . The protection which secret societies offer is thus absolute, but only temporary. In fact, for contents of a pos-itive social value to be lodged in secret societies is only a transition which, after a certain period of growing strength, they no longer need. (1950: 346).

Hence, Simmel saw systems of collective secrecy as structurally unsta-ble, an element of theory with which I largely agree, notwithstanding the cynicism from which it derives. But what he fails to see is that consensual groupings can crosscut or dissect a society, shifting centers and peripheries of power. Even when Simmel refers again to the social amelioration that eventually transformed formerly persecuted Christian groups into the "dominant religion" within society, he imagines a complete change of the social economy and reality of the people, rather than a multicultural popu-lation or a divided social consciousness. The reified concept of "secret society" conflates time and space. All of these are problems stemming from the notion of the modern society as homogeneous and the assertion that secrecy must be a declining process of social evolution.

But there is the logical converse of Simmel's position: That secret rites are products of historical diffusion, derived from another place and time, but nevertheless preserved through secrecy and then reproduced in the contemporary group. Here is W. H. R. Rivers, the great riverboat doctor-ethnologist of New Guinea:

> There is reason to believe that the knowledge thus inaccessible to the people at large has come from elsewhere, having been derived from external culture of which even those who act as its custodians have no tradition. The knowledge thus guarded is closely analogous to the unconscious experience of the individual in that it belongs to a remote past that has become accessible. In the secret societies we seem to have guardians of unconscious experiences who only allow its content to reach the general public in some disguised form. It is worthy of note that such esoteric public knowledge is with especial frequency the motive of dramatic and symbolic representation. Of all the facts collected by me in Melanesia none show the dramatic quality and the use of symbolism more definitely than the ritual of the secret organization. (1917: 402)

Such notions are not far removed from those of Lewis Henry Morgan; they even employ some of the same imagery ("custodians" and "guardians"). We shall find that the same imagery hovers over the work of Barth (1987).

Rivers's ideas suggest how the sequence of time—the eternal unconscious that reveals regressions to infantile thinking in Freud's sense—becomes the storehouse of authority, and the core of symbolic meaning, in secret societies. Later, Rivers (1922) would review evidence on rebirth symbolism, discovering that death and rebirth were critical to the symbolism of secret societies in many areas of the world. Of course this text reflects the problems and opportunities of dealing with precolonial descriptions of secrecy. But what matters is his assertion that ritual secrecy derives its meaning not from present-day social functions or values but from the past, indeed, the archaic.

The fundamental imagery of this dualistic paradigm—society versus

why is western society totally obsessed w/ opposites as there are none...

secret society—is a distortion or, more accurately, a disruption of normative time and space relationships. An odd instance of "condensation," Simmel's model imagines that two social entities (secret society, secular society) can somehow "occupy" the same "space" and "time" simultaneously. This is a logical outcome of thinking of a "primitive" society as homogeneous, having "simplex" roles, in which each actor supposedly has only one role, or at least performs only one role at a time. Of course this fiction also imagines a linear progress from simple to complex societies that ultimately eliminates the need of secrecy (1950: 345–46). I shall disagree, as noted in the final section of this chapter on social economies.

Perhaps this model might work in mass societies, such as the United States, in which anonymity and secrecy are the means of the preservation of individual rights against the oppression of the State. For example, the secrecy of homosexuality is a complex means of hiding and passing, and dates back—in its classification as sodomy—to the early modern period (Van der Meer 1994). While the secrecy of homosexual relations began as an individual matter, it quickly grew into a semicollective concern in urban centers such as Amsterdam, Paris, and New York. Sexual secrecy is more a thing of the past, so it is said (Sedgwick 1990); but secrecy undermines political and social movements among lesbians and gay men, who were hitherto made invisible (and in some sense "protected") as well as victimized by secrecy and passing as heteronormal (Adam et al. 1999; Herdt 1997a; Herdt and Boxer 1993).

The extension of this idea of secrecy and neoliberal individual rights beyond the West into simple societies is very problematical, however, for its basis in contractual arrangements between individual concepts (e.g., sexual identity) is peculiar to the West (Teunis 1996). In the case of male secret societies in West Africa or Melanesia, by contrast, how might we construe male secret cults as protective of rights, especially in relations with their own women and children? After all, is not the power of public affairs lodged primarily in the male role, and in warriorhood, as the seat of the secrecy? Such questions were of course beyond the purview of Simmel and were unanswerable at the time because of the paucity of ethnography. Simmel's idea does not travel well primarily because the conceptualization of "society" on which it was based was too simple and nondynamic (see Murphy 1971).

This conflation of time and space—which is problematic throughout the scholarship on ritual secrecy, from Simmel to Hutton Webster and

Rivers—should be seen as an instance of a larger intellectual history. As the important work of Fabian (1983) has shown, such a concept of time probably derives from linear models of progression in the epistemology of nineteenth-century evolutionism with which anthropology has been saddled in its language of description and analysis. In this case, spatial relations between the "society and secret society," instantiated in notions of sequences, developmental transitions from secret to public groups, and progression from magic to science, all implicitly rely upon the crutch of evolutionary time frames (Fabian 1983: 17). Some of these preconceptions were carried over into the Melanesian literature through displacements that will become increasingly transparent.

One final point on Simmel. It is well known that Simmel posited two types of secret formations: one in which the group is itself hidden from the society, such as a subversive political faction; the other in which the existence of the secret formation was known to the larger society, but the identity of the individual members remained anonymous or secret. Without being entirely explicit about it, Simmel strongly implied that the latter form was more "primitive" than the other and was to be found in "nature" peoples. Conversely, the other, more "sophisticated" mode of secrecy was identified with the transition to modernity.

But there is a third ideal type of secret society, unknown in Simmel's time but common in New Guinea. The most important instances of secret societies known to Melanesia (Allen 1967) meet neither of Simmel's conditions, since, in many cases, the existence of the secret society is acknowledged, and its individual members are known and recognized as such by the public in these societies. In this light, Simmel's notion of "public" is far too simple for the multilayered cultural reality of ritual and public rhetoric discursive practices of precolonial and now postcolonial (Lattas 1999) Melanesian societies.

Contrary to Simmel, I want to stress that these distinct types of secret societies are not bound to a linear progression or evolutionary sequence, as we shall see; they occur across a range of societies, large and small, preliterate and complex, being reducible neither to a particular form of social structure nor to historical survivals from an earlier age. These formations of ritual secrecy are, however, created under the social conditions of unstable, chaotic, or breached social relations, whether as a result of some kind of political domination, intense warfare, mistrust, or gendered social conflict. For New Guinea, the chief outcome of these instabilities among males was to create ritual secret realities lodged in the men's house that signified a utopian male world.

From Secret to Private and Public

Whatever the status of these brooding questions for Morgan's generation and the cohort of Simmel to follow, few would disagree with the assertion that secrecy is nowadays felt to be a "bad" or antisocial thing for an "open" democracy such as the United States. Intellectually, I think, this view in social and cultural study still derives in part from the famous opinion of Simmel: "The secret is . . . the sociological expression of moral badness" (1950: 331). However, as we have seen, the roots of suspicion of secrecy are far older than Simmel. It is true that secrecy is more suspect than ever, as if the end of cold war has brought a deeper suspicion of the hidden and greater prize for transparency than before. A flood of books on the nefarious activities of the CIA (Prados 1996) and KGB (Andrew and Mitrokhin 2001) have exposed the paranoia, secret warfare, and attempts of these fallen boy scouts to disrupt the world powers' governments, including democracy within their own systems. Nearly a century after Simmel's influential writing, sociologists, political scientists, anthropologists, and other social scientists continue to argue, seemingly oblivious to this cultural history, that whereas privacy is "legal," secrecy is best seen as an "immoral" or "illegal" species of privacy (Tefft 1980: 13–14; 1992): "Privacy has a consensual basis in society, while secrecy does not" (Warren and Laslett 1980: 27). The clinicians often take an even more caustic view, as evidenced from a recent cross-country scholarly study of Alcoholics Anonymous that stated: "Originally, AA was more about disclosing the secret than about searching for the authentic self: 'We are only as sick as our secrets'" (Makela et al. 1996: 161).

Secrecy and the law again form a problematic relationship in the early twenty-first century—long after the Victorian lawyer Lewis Henry Morgan began to turn away from secret societies. A recent commentary on donor insemination by legal scholars in the United States, entitled *Lethal Secrets*, argues the anti-society position quite well:

> We firmly believe that the practices of secrecy and anonymity must end. . . . We are convinced that in all DI [donor insemination] families, the need to maintain secrecy and anonymity has had an

adverse effect upon all the members. . . . Whenever a family lives with a secret, the fear of revelation of that secret is a specter that haunts those holding the information, ultimately straining the relationship. (Baran and Pannor 1989: 152–53)

Here we see a convergence of clinical and legal opinions.

Secrecy was typically defined as the involuntary concealment of information, with privacy seen as a purely voluntary matter (Tefft 1980). The public/private divide in our society (Seligman 1998) comes into relief. What is at stake in this rhetoric is trust—shared social confidence, and perhaps even moral and legal degradation (Goffman 1963). Institutional secrecy, in this cynical view, poses a threat to the social contract, for it would create a culture that is "spurious" and inimical to the creativity of individuals, unlike a "genuine" culture, to recall Edward Sapir's view from the early twentieth century. The cynical view states that secrecy destroys the supposed seamless sociality that makes culture a "good thing."

Anthropologists working in New Guinea were not able to escape the powerful grip of this modernist epistemology, its preconceptions and prejudices, in their own ethnographies. The cynical attitude toward secrecy, inflected through Western ideas associated with antisocial tendencies and the individualistic public/private dichotomy, have been projected more or less directly into interpretations of ritual secrecy in non-Western societies. As noted before, these interpretations derided ritual secrecy and treated its permutations in Melanesia as way stations along the road to a "higher social evolution" that would eventually lead to rational "civilization." In the writings of Hutton Webster (1932), in particular, secrecy was interpreted as a device for manipulation or oppression. Even Simmel's highly creative work implied that social evolution would inevitably eliminate secrecy in favor of the confidentiality of personal contracts. Thus the ideals of sectarian Western civic disclosure suggested a change from group secrecy to individual privacy in culture and public affairs.

Later in the twentieth century, during the cold war with its schizophrenic ideologies, secular secrecy became virtually synonymous with communism and the accusation of homosexuality as a means to vilify and destroy marginal or nonconformist groups (Corber 1997). The efforts of secret quasi-military organizations, especially the FBI and the CIA, to "combat communism" and protect the "national security" interest were often thinly veiled manipulations of power-grubbing. All privacy, including sexuality, was open to surveillance, which became widely identified with international espionage networks or the misguided utopias of delusional individuals who founded personality cults based upon social hatred and predictions of apocalypse. Even today, nothing is more incendiary in Western debates on privacy and civic responsibility than to suggest that officials have improperly kept secrets from the public, even in times of war.

But what has this to do with initiation in New Guinea? A general principle, call it a rule of cross-cultural translatability, emerges (Herdt 1991a). As the apprehension of secrecy grows, and greater efforts to control the representation and performance of reality are exerted through secret means, the public order expands. The sphere of personal privacy contracts concomitantly. In precolonial New Guinea, typified by the enormous sweep of male secret societies, there remains little or no social space or cultural ontology accorded to late modern Western "individual privacy." Consequently romance and intimacy as embodiments of the self were scarce (Giddens 1990). As the historical secret societies expanded in importance and social salience, so says this view, the pressure on individuals reached its zenith: the "de-individuation" made famous by Simmel. What this meant for the production of masculinity was a greater sanctioning of men's roles and tighter monitoring of their adherence to secret rituals. The tension between domestic and secret (Tuzin 1982) increased; the opposition between rhetorical speech in public versus secret objectification, male subordination, mistrust, and fear of boy-recruits may have threatened to burst the seams of kinship and community consensus. Today, under the influence of postcolonial change and globalization (Foster 1995; Whitehouse 1995, 1998), the societies of Papua New Guinea are witnessing the emergence of new domains of individual commerce and mercantile individualism, bringing on totally new demands for privacy and the demise of ritual secrecy (chap. 5). This view has always precluded the idea of a counterhegemonic form of agency developed through ritual secrecy.

Historically, the modernist view of liberal democracies suggested that there could be but one legitimate form of social reality—transparent public affairs—which made secrecy a counterfeit form, whether in Morgan's secret societies or in East-West realpolitik. It further suggested that there could be but one form of valid subjectivity, indicative of one mode of subject/object relations, sanctioned by official or formal power, that is, the State. But consider this Foucauldian twist: the more secrecy was feared in the nineteenth century, the more it grew in popularity. And then again: the more secrecy was suspected of disrupting the twentieth-century State—as it was staked out in cold war politics, despised but also envied in spy novels and the Sunday papers, prompting an ethos of "national security" accusations against traitors who "sold secrets" to the Enemy (Communists, Jews, Homosexuals; you get the picture: Herman 1997)—the more did anthropologists in the mid-century portray ritual secrecy in so-called primitive cultures as "false consciousness": mistaken, fraudulent, or just plain silly.

This worldview, to sum up, was thoroughly modern in its prejudices; for its suspicion of secrecy radiated from a social order of neoliberal democracy and expressive individualism that derided the distance between self and society, and especially the harboring of a secret. I think such a cultural worldview was foreign to Lewis Henry Morgan. Indeed, the perspective that has hovered over the scholarly and popular literature on secrecy for at least a century interprets the secret as a "disease" of society and a pathology in the actor. This "romantic-cynical approach" to secrecy idealizes secular humanism and its romantic liberal democracy, much as it is cynical toward the hidden elements of private life. There is much good that has come from the liberal democracy tradition of the West; I complain only about its use as a foil against secrecy.

The fact is that such attitudes often confuse notions of privacy in matters of rationalism and individualism, the suppression of persons or the concealment of things from the public, as indications of subversion. But the collective secret should not be confused with the private, and the voluntary concealment of information must not be confounded with those forms of power that suppress knowledge or action against the will, however this is mediated. Our contemporary version of public affairs is generally suspicious of anything hidden, even those esoteric rites or religious practices whose ultimate concern is union with God, and that would regard as sacrilege the dissemination of religious experience in secular society. Perhaps this dour Western perspective on secrecy is itself antireligious: the transition away from a worldview that once prized religious faith more than reason, community more than individualism, embodied by living in complicated intimate attachments, toward the diffuse market relations and fragmentary contracts celebrated in anonymous urban life today.

An examination of this scientific cynicism reveals two primary postulates. First, social scientists generally do not accept secret practices as cultural conventions that are "real" or "true," except insofar as they indicate false consciousness or domination. Even in this regard, many social and cultural theorists ignore or disregard secrecy as unworthy of scientific scrutiny, and I believe that their reasons can be traced back to the epistemology expressed by Durkheim's "social facts," that is, society cannot rest upon a social lie, and therefore many scholars cannot take seriously the social and psychological meanings of ritual secrecy. The second postulate, however, is just as important and is more relevant to this study: the notion that without trust, communal or collective organization is impossible to fathom for social theory. The idea is explored brilliantly in a recent essay by Adam Seligman, who writes: "Without a shared universe of expectations, histories, memories or affective commitments, no basis of trust can exist." He goes on to warn that in the absence of trust, as in cases of "radically incommensurate life-worlds," "indeterminacy becomes intolerable" (1998: 36).

For the democratic theorist unable to imagine a society of "radically incommensurate life-worlds" that is stitched or held together by ritual secrecy, as occurs in New Guinea communities, the failure to trust is pivotal. Again, such a worldview misconstrues ritual secrecy as purely a fantasy or illusion in the mind, the result of wish fulfillment and unconscious forces, in the case of Freud and his followers, such as Bettelheim. It may disregard secret organizations as manifestations of power based upon lies or hoaxes, without credibility in "reality." Both images derive from the Western cultural imagination and have been exported to different times and places. But in both these imaginals, secrecy is scorned as perverse and remains underanalyzed in Western and non-Western societies.

This worldview is thus reinforced by the liberal democratic values of modernity, which counsel that, in all matters, the public arena is to be elevated over the private domain (Seligman 1998). Is it not striking that, amidst concerns over national security following the terrorist bombing in New York of September 11, secrecy has become more common and less attacked in the United States? In such times, "indeterminacy becomes intolerable," in Seligman's words; privacy and individual rights are sacrificed to State security. It is true that the same cultural tradition that produced the idea of civil society (especially in the writings of Hegel) and sacrosanct individualism values private life and the space of the person as beyond the legitimate intrusion of the Western State (Bellah et al. 1985). Secrecy is a constant threat to the perceived moral legitimacy of the State in such examples. Of course, some have suggested that the public ideal is created here as a means of generating resistance and transgression, especially in sexuality and gender relations (Manderson and Jolly 1997), where intimacy and secrecy hold sway. Perhaps it is the intimate romantic bond of late modern marriage and "partnership" wherein secret contracts achieve one of their highest forms.

Whatever the cultural reality in Western society of these postulates, they are of limited value for understanding the larger historical and cross-cultural phenomenon of secrecy. Certainly they do not address the socio-cultural interstices of secret practice, particularly in the paradigm of ritual secrecy. An obvious failing of the public/private duality is its difficulty in rendering individual differences and subjective meanings across societies—which is especially troublesome in matters of intimate discussions (Herdt and Stoller 1990). Conventional notions of the public/private distinction suggest that the public actor should not be subjected to surveillance and sanctioning with respect to her or his private rights; or if the private actor is considered in relation to social conduct, analysis typically hinges upon opposition to the rules of public life (Foucault 1973; Geertz 1966; Wikan 1990). Only recently have hidden or secret aspects of the system of meanings and action been deeply rendered in ethnographies (Lattas 1999; Ottenberg 1989; Schwimmer 1980; Stephen 1994; Whitehouse 1995, 2000).

Anthropology's Dilemma on Secrecy

The romantic and cynical attitudes about secrecy, trust, and social life reached their zenith when anthropologists working in other cultures regarded ritual secrecy as a rational or cognitive process that could be understood as linear and rational. This view led to the conclusion that since the secrets did not square with "reality," being outside of public affairs (i.e., "culture"), the secret content must be revealed as a hoax, lie, fiction, or fabrication, a series of dominations or modes of "false consciousness" premises that promoted domination or exploitation in preliterate societies.

However, such notions rest upon a false preconception: Because ritual secrecy is not a rational knowledge discourse, it rather depends upon the sensory, the embodied, the lived experience of being and knowing. Ritual secrecy is closer to living a life that is in accord with the imagery and sensations of beliefs, and the revelations of faith, as these are practiced, worshipped. The distinction thus drawn is similar to Whitehouse's (1995) division of religious phenomena into the "imagistic" and the "doctrinal," and his work lends support to our analysis. Clearly ritual secrecy belongs in the category of the imagistic, and I agree with Whitehouse's assessment: "Anthropologists have exaggerated . . . the extent to which Melanesian fertility cults possess certain transmissive features found in Christianity" (2000: 95). The evocative, revelatory, world-as-becoming quality of ritual knowledge through secret initiation is clearly less doctrinal, until it comes to the instilling of masculinity, which forms another stage for later doctrinal exegesis, and adult socialization (Herdt 1981). Ritual secrecy as a form of male discipline is about practices and duties, being devotional, pious, observant of worship, and so on. As we shall see played out in the ethnographies reviewed in this book, emotional imagery, subjectivity, and sexuality are foundations of ritual secrecy.

I want to suggest, then, that the received worldview of secrecy ought to be challenged on two levels: first with respect to the ethnographies of Melanesia, as we shall revisit them; and second with respect to the history of science, of anthropological science in particular, to explain why anthropologists in studying ritual secrecy often went against the grain of cultural relativism dominant in anthropology to proclaim secret practices a fraud. Why did some surrender to the Durkheimian tendencies to see culture and society as monolithic—as one reality, one worldview, one mode of consensual social action?

To return to the historical hiatus in the anthropology of secrecy laid out in chapter 1 on Lewis Henry Morgan: my guess is that the ethical problems of studying ritual secrecy have often proved too great and complicated for the lone field-worker. Secrecy, if it were based (as Durkheim might have said) on a "lie," or, as New Guinea ethnographers such as K. E. Read claimed, upon a "hoax," placed the phenomenon outside of the purview of anthropology. The notable ethnographers whose accounts we deal with later were burdened by the long suspicion of secrecy as antisocial in the West, particularly in the domination of women and children. The dilemma is that the cultural relativism of the day ought to have suggested that the anthropologist accept the ritual secrecy at face value. In a descriptive relativist approach, ritual secrecy would have been viewed as representing conflicting orders of cultural reality, of belief and unfaith, which were internal contradictions to these societies, not merely "lies" and "hoaxes." However, the liberal democracy values of these prefeminist period scholars, including their privileged position as white males, and their sympathy for women and the amelioration of women's lives, may have all played a part in their interpretation. That they effectively combined the historical view of secrecy as cynical with this sympathetic and therefore romantic skepticism of the men's customs was certainly understandable in its day. As I shall suggest in the Conclusion, the positionality of white heterosexual male anthropologists limited their ability to understand the conditional masculinity on which ritual secrecy, especially its homosociality, was based. It was after all so at odds with the colonial position of their own masculinity.

Ritual and Contractual Secrecy

We are studying ritual secrecy in the context of precolonial New Guinea societies, but as this chapter reveals, the interpretations of these forms have typically inflected the preconceptions of the dominant form of secrecy in the modern period of the West—contractual secrecy. To sum up the positive and creative ontological dimension of these forms: ritual secrecy creates a shared cultural reality through initiation as a means of negotiating personal and social ills that finds no other ready solution within certain historical conditions. Ritual secrecy thus shares with gift exchange (Godelier 1999) the qualities of indebtedness and relatedness attached to the original "owner" of the secret who teaches and transmits its power through hidden rituals. Masculinity of a certain historical formation was one of its products. The cultural problem of endemic warfare and unstable political and marital alliances in New Guinea certainly presented such a historical situation. The special genius of ritual secrecy, as we shall study its permutations, is to provide a means of living in two cultural realities simultaneously—a perfect or utopian one, that of ritual formulas and dietetics, with often hidden hierarchies, which elide all the messy difficulties that trouble an ideology of intimate, vulnerable bodies, situated in imperfect earthly existence, full of the human emotions of conflicted desires, demands, and impossible loyalties.

Contrarily, there are social and psychological dependencies incumbent upon secret contracts, particularly the intimate and relational modes (such as parent and child) that are removed from the public code of rational and liberal democratic values and that enable the exploitation of demands and power in small circles, to produce such secret contractual relations. As expressed between the lawyer and client, or between psychiatrist and patient, priest and confessor, secrets are poured into the contractual partner in exchange for money or another precious commodity or good. And here, too, there are characteristic social and psychological problems of a historical age, including possible abuses of power, that find their solution within these indefinite and conditional arrangements; and no other form of social practice can supply their rewards and punishments.

Although it is easier to identify contractual secrecy in mass societies, there are hidden forms of "naturalizing" body and supporting ontological practices that qualify for ritual secrecy in the modern period, as we have seen in Victorian male cults. In more recent times, however, British covens of witches around Cambridge provide a rich illustration of the embodiment of alternative concepts of time, space, and being, the accoutrements of special clothes, ritual utensils, magical spells, and so on (Luhrman 1989a). The British adepts, both women and men, come in search of mystical support for their desire to attain a divergent reality; they seem to reject the civic community as humdrum, unsatisfying, too messy and incoherent for an ideal pursuit of Spirit. And through a disciplined "interpretative drift," to use Luhrman's expression of it, these actors remake their precepts and concepts, reconstructing an existing consensual system of sensibilities and desires, which pave the way for the production of a new cultural reality. Seldom is this completely successful. But when it manages to invalidate the mundane and contest the fickle or polluted notions of a disliked way of life, it is clear that the contemporary witches of England have worked very hard to build an alternative secret reality that they prefer to the ordinary one. To study such a world as an anthropologist is no easy task. It reminds us of the difficulty of creating authority in the midst of studying the seemingly irrational or magical, not to mention the multiple problems of method and ethics that entail a radically different way of life. These are the issues that must be reconsidered in anthropology's encounter with secrecy.

Ritual secrecy is created out of conflict and fear, providing a means of trust and loyalty between people who are challenged to defend a way of life. Their worldview and shared realities express common desires for emotional and cognitive coherence and clarity of boundaries, and entities, inside and outside of the person/self as constituted in culture. The ultimate cause of this desire, however, rests in the political economy of social life and cannot be reduced to an internal process, even though the ontological characteristics of cognition and emotion are developmentally necessary to produce the outcome. Yet this is also true of language, and the one does not lead to the other, even though it is hard to imagine a system of ritual secrecy without language (cf. Forge 1966). Once the tradition of secret reality is laid down in ritual formulations, they may then be combined with collective drives for power. For the individual agent, ritual secrecy becomes a means of defending the person/self from all social criticism, as well as self-doubt. Critical feedback can unsettle the secret perfection of hidden social classifications. This is what the ideology and practice of ritual secrecy achieves, and the studies from New Guinea to follow are indicative of how often it succeeded.

ontology = branch of metaphysics concerned w/ the nature + relations of being

Secrecy among the Sambia, 1974–1976

✳

THE CENTRAL PROBLEM OF THE anthropological study of secrecy is to understand not only what a people believe in, but also what they fear and doubt; not what they celebrate in public ceremonies but how their mistrust is transferred into hidden acts and whispered stories behind the stage of society. It is hard to fathom how the secret masculinity vaunted in this book was conditional in a double sense: the men feared their inability to create and sustain it in themselves and they feared losing it once they had it. Moreover, concerning the reproduction of their own kind, they were frantic but also hesitant, and resisted passing on even the coveted secret masculinity to their sons. This paradoxical cultural reality is the ontological province of ritual secrecy, and it existed long before the historical Western concept of "utopia" was invented to cover the idea of "heaven on earth." Indeed the contrast of this archaic sociality of secret masculinity in New Guinea with what is hidden in Western life (e.g., the idea of a "family secret") is simplistic and terribly vulnerable to exoticization. But such an understanding was far ahead of me in my first fieldwork, as the following story tells.

August 1976

It is late in the dry season and I am near the end of a many weeks' long reconnaissance of the two dozen or so Sambia villages and their near neighbors, the feared Yagwoia. The patrol brings to a close a two-year period of field research with which I began the study of the Sambia. Traveling with me is a troop of ten Sambia men and youths, all from my village, Nilanga. They include the carriers of supplies and interpreters, as well as my key informant-colleague, Tali, a ritual expert well known to the locals from his younger years (Herdt 1981: app. A; see also Herdt and Stoller 1990: chap. 5), and my close associates Weiyu and Sakulambei. The weeks have been occupied with the collection of final census and genealogical information on the Sambia villages in adjacent river valleys. However, it is the collection of the Anga area epic myths and the incredible origin myth of parthenogenesis common to the region that has most riveted my imagination. My main job—to study how male identity develops through secret initiation—has come to an end. Many performances of ritual initiation, each of them elaborate, some taking weeks to complete, have been observed during these years, from the first-stage initiation to the final, sixth-stage initiation, which signals fatherhood and the achievement of full moral personhood for Sambia males.

And in the process I have been transformed, though not as radically as the Sambia youth who experienced embodied change. However, once my presence was accepted at the rites, I became sufficiently acquainted with rituals to be permitted to ask the elders a few questions about their meaning. My oh-so-tentative interrogations signified a status change, of course, away from being the know-nothing puny red-skinned youth who had begun without language or cultural knowledge nearly two years before. I worried that I might never be able to return to the Sambia and could not have dreamed that my fieldwork was merely the beginning of a long process of learning. Before returning to Australia, I felt a terrible need to finish tracking the myths of Sambia back to their fabled origin hole, Kokomo, a sacred place a few days' walk to the south near Menyamya. The trip, which had hitherto been attempted only once by the Australian government patrol officer, was long and somewhat dangerous, as it involved crossing the border of the territory of the neighboring tribe, the despised Yagwoia.

In precolonial times the Sambia rarely ventured there except to raid. Even today they are extremely reluctant to travel into Yagwoia country. Not only were these enemies hated for the raids they inflicted upon the borderland, but they were said to be cannibals as well, who enjoyed the taste of "long pig," which, indeed, the Yagwoia admit. Sambia successfully raided them enough times to have left behind rage and many scores to settle. After days of resistance to my pleas for help along the trail in Sambia-land, my companions consented to cross the mountain range that marks the tribal boundary.

Passing for long hours through uninhabited mountains, a no-man's-land of pine and palm that symbolizes the gulf between the groups, our troop arrives at dusk in the first Yagwoia-speaking village that straddles the mountaintop. It offers the benefit of a doorless government rest hut to sleep in. The weariness of weeks of travel has soaked into the Sambia, and yet Tali, an aspiring Great Man and my ritual consultant, has already gone ahead into the village, a place he knows from an adolescent journey long ago, to seek out his entry into a shadowy network of ritual contacts.

Tali has a distant age-mate who lives in the vicinity, and a runner is sent to fetch the man. It is Tali who negotiates the contract of hearing the sacred myths and more generally discussing secret things with the elders of their former enemies. Yagwoia men communicate two attitudes. First, the Sambia are the only group of warriors they feared sufficiently in precolonial times to undertake special alliances for raiding their territory. Second, Sambia are renowned throughout the area for continuing the "true" practice of initiations. Later I was to realize that the "truth" to which they alluded was boy-insemination, the secret masculinity the Yagwoia had long ago been required to forfeit to the native New Guinea evangelists who came to save their souls and establish a Christian order in their villages. As I learn of this I am stunned to discover the degree of radical culture change so close to Sambia-land—the accidental history of opportunistic colonialism. A bit later I am surprised to see the Yagwoia men show a keen interest in the young initiates of our troop. Off to the side are the Yagwoia women, and as some men in Western-style shorts approach us, they shoo the women away and begin to mutter hurriedly among themselves. The older Yagwoia half-jokingly mutter that we would have been killed and eaten not so long ago. The Sambia boys actually grimace and retreat at this joke. The whole situation so quickly becomes a tangle of strong emotions, as is typical of these parts, that second thoughts quickly creep into my mind, of guilty responsibility for having prodded my fellows here. Perhaps it was too much to expect Tali to access the local myths. Perhaps they are dead anyway.

What are Tali's motives in this strange place? Mainly they derive from his own ritual career, which is always uppermost in his mind. The dietetics of male initiation and secret masculinity are the manifestations: the quest for male health, potency, and bodily purity through the use of ritual knowledge and procedures; a quest for ritual lore as Tali's means to attain authority in the prestige system of the Sambia men's house that honors this power as equal to the warrior's. Tali came to the Yagwoia only once, a generation ago, in adolescence, along with a party of Sambia men, including his father and uncle—now long dead—who had distant Yagwoia in-laws. They wanted to trade bird-of-paradise feathers and vegetal salt to the Yagwoia in exchange for ritual secrets. These trading partners are passed on for generations from father to son among the Sambia; the feathers, salt bars, bark capes, and sundry elements of ritual that fold into an irregular stream of barter. But they also initiated Tali with their sons. Now, in addition to these manly purposes, there was also my entreaty as friend to learn the origins of the myths; and this favor, Tali knew, would mean a great deal to me—a gift of immense value, through which he might gain sway for years.

All the usual ways of scratching around politely for information are trotted out; the exchange gifts start to flow, calling into practice the etiquette of hospitality through smoking and chewing betel, or offering sugarcane and a bamboo of water, all typical of male hospitality in the area. It is a slow and pretentious process, taking hours, sometimes days, with formal appearances monitored carefully for any trace of treachery—or weakness. Since the Sambia believe it is impossible to see into another's mind, one can only assess intent by action. And so the other Sambia men watch and smoke and gab.

And I, dogged from the long trip, soon begin to doze. In fact, by nightfall, having eaten some taro while thinking of culinary pleasures far away, I grow tired and ready to climb in my sleeping bag. Then, out of the dark, comes Tali, smiling. He said he would locate the myth-tellers and was good to his word: "Come along," he says, "we will story now" with the Yagwoia elders. It is nearly eleven o'clock and pitch black, the perfect time for secrecy in a small village. I should not have been surprised, given the penchant for Sambia themselves to tell secret stories only in the deep forest or after nightfall.

But another happy circumstance, unknown to me till then, has made this possible: Kwip, a long-lost middle-aged Sambia speaker, Tali's old age-mate from his youth, half-Yagwoia by birth. He arrives mysteriously and without escort after dark from a distant village in response to the messenger sent earlier. Kwip's solitary passage in the dark is most impressive, and I can tell from the reactions of my Sambia friends that they are amazed at his courage. For to cross vast expanses of the lonely forests in the dark is dangerous to the stranger, and truly beyond the pale for the average Sambia, who fears the ghosts and forest spirits enough to bar travel outside the village at night, and certainly never alone. But this becomes a danger far greater in unknown lands, increased astronomically by the fear of attack by aging cannibals whose "true" appetite is never sated, so say my Sambia colleagues, by expensive imported Australian tinned beef.

The man is a savior, however; not only clever but also pleasant, and now a fellow ritual expert alongside of Tali. Initiated together a generation ago, Tali and the Yagwoia remain bonded in some curious way not at all apparent to me. As the saying goes among them, never forget the men who cried together from the ordeals of initiation, a poignant reminder of conditional masculinity.

At midnight, the dusty old government rest house has been converted into a new fortress of secret masculinity. It comes alive as a surge of Yagwoia men eager to participate in such a unique cultural event shuffle in and surround the fire. A large group of elders appear with Kwip, apparently ready to spin myths for a price. What is their price, I wonder? I make coffee and share it among this large congeries of strangers. My sleepiness evaporates, pipe in hand, as a once-in-a-lifetime opportunity awakens me. And here, under cover of darkness, removed from the now slumbering village nearby, we await this revitalization—a matter of local myth-telling and the necessary orchestration of determining who will sit and who will stand. What is most striking, however, is the generational split with the younger men who are so intensely interested to see who among their own elders will speak and what stories they will tell. The first sign of a terrible tragedy emerges when one of the younger men raises his voice unnaturally and is dismissed out of hand by an elder who shuns his face.

The old men and ritual leaders tell a long "rope" or sequence of interconnected narratives—origin tales, including the myth of parthenogenesis, and so on, which I have traced from place to place among the neighboring societies of the Anga (Herdt 1981). The tales tell not only how society emerged from the obscure past, but also how the sexes came to hold their proper biological and social roles in war, reproduction, and the economy or ritual. These myths are absolutely hidden from the uninitiated, but especially women, of course. They tell of the creation of life, of the hermaphroditic ancestors, and then of death and rebirth through the source of sexuality. This means that they are, by definition, strictly secret. And secrecy in this part of the world always means behavioral segregation—men from women, and men from boys—enforced by threat of death. This I know already; what I did not know about was the colonial hiatus suffered by the disruption of secret masculinity among the Yagawoia.

As I prepare myself for the role of scribe, armed with a primitive tape recorder and clipboard, a dreadful commotion breaks out among the Yagwoia hosts. I am immediately fearful for my Sambia friends. Never one to let events fall as they might—remember, I am twenty-five years old and every bit as ambitious and romantic as one might imagine—I turn to Tali for direction, fearful something has gone wrong. Tali whispers to his age-mate, Kwip, What in the world is going on? Meanwhile the younger Yagwoia men in their twenties and thirties have grown irritated and aggressive. Several Yagwoia men take charge; one of them, a huge, muscled man in his forties, barks out orders. I fear that the precious stories will be snatched from my grasp at the moment of their telling.

What could be wrong, I wonder? I fear that one of our men has gotten himself in trouble or offended our hosts. But no, Tali reassures me; it's on the Yagwoia side and has nothing to do with us. The young men "want to fight," he says, looking worried in the way he does when the swirl of things grows beyond the control of anyone. And soon I see for myself that we are irrelevant.

All of the Sambia and me are pushed off to the side as a nasty generational schism erupts between the older and younger men of the local village. Outside in the night air we can hear heated emotions and harsh words exchanged. A group of men set up a barricade and younger men outside are forbidden to enter.

Imagine, now, my profound consternation as the old men drive the younger men away from inside, forcing them to leave, the refugees of their own tribe! I cannot think what they mean and am unable to follow the heated argument that lies in store, because their tongue is not ours. A large group of Yagwoia adolescent and young adult men are once more literally blocked from entering the ramshackle hut. I see puzzlement turn into intense anger on their faces, as these chaps (quite a few of them older than me), citizens of the place, are driven away. I fear their hostility, as they might attack us, and it is dreadful to see. However, my heart sinks more when I see their desire to be in this place with the elders and hear the stories, hungering for knowledge long denied. But of course we cannot know that at the moment. Nothing is to be done. The murmurs and resentment die down as they wander off and the dust settles around the hut. After carefully shutting the door and posting a guard the elders turn back to us, ready to begin telling the myths.

You cannot imagine my extreme discomfort and self-conscious shame (being a recovering Catholic) at this wild turn of events. This should not be happening, I feel; it is so damn inexplicable. Sambia in their own land initiate boys at age eight into a secret warriorhood that guides their development for the next twenty years or so. During this time, the boys live exclusively in the men's house and avoid women and female things on pain of death. At first they are involved in years-long secret homoerotic relations with the bachelors of neighboring villages. This is followed by arranged marriages that are feared as much as they are desired by the boys. Finally in fatherhood they complete their agency and secret masculinity to ensure the continuation of their clan and souls. As they undergo successive initiations the men earn the right to hear all the great myths. It is their manly right and duty to learn of them, culminating in that most secret of all stories—the origin of parthenogenesis, telling how once upon a time the ancestors, Numbugimupi and Chenchi, both hermaphroditic, had homoerotic oral sex and then coitus, leading to birth and the founding of the society (Herdt 1981: chap. 8). It is incredible to see the youths' reaction to this revelation—like a kind of crazy dream, in that uncanny sense of something feared and wondered or sensed but never fully believed, and never dared to utter but also accepted as "truth." By right and duty this and all the other stories are theirs to know and pass on once they reach this point.

Ritual secrecy surrounds this entire system, entry and exit. Once the boys are initiated it provides entry into the prestige and knowledge systems too. With each passing initiation boys are socialized into ever more complex magical knowledge and ritual iconography. The result is impressive, the learning of a secret encyclopedia, echoing the Book of Leviticus in the Old Testament as a storehouse of ritual lore, rules, and esoterica. For example, initiates learn over two hundred ritually prescribed food taboos, including a huge number of leaves and plants, many of which have secret names. In addition, the secret edible plants have special meanings associated to them; to increase masculinity means to eat and use them, in rubbing the skin, like a system of dietetics the likes of which is foreign to a Western sensibility. Moreover, the boys are taught about many ritual icons, including a significant number of cultural interpretations of dreams that serve as augury for hunting and warfare. Furthermore, they learn of place-names and secret stories to explain them, such as ritual initiation sites revealed only to the fully initiated. Many of the secret dietetics have secrecy associated with warfare magic and potency procedures. As time passes their ritual guardians describe more ritually vital foods, especially forest plants, and myriad ritual dietetics for health, vitality, and moral welfare: a wonder-world of hidden knowledge, about humans, animals, plants, spirits, and heavenly bodies.

As the years pass and males mature they are also taught sexual taboos, techniques, and stories, more reasons for avoiding females or purifying themselves from heteroerotic contacts. And they acquire the most efficacious war magic and secret sorcery practices, which are especially hidden. Their increasingly sophisticated personhood is more complicated by the secrecy, of course; a secret self known to father, age-mates, and brothers; and comrades-in-arms, the latter of whom may be among the boy's inseminators until he takes their place; but always leading to adulthood and a public world of war and leadership, accompanied always by ritual practice from which women and children are forever excluded. Sambia boys continue to live in the men's house as prescribed by tradition, a practice the Yagwoia apparently abandoned long ago.

Why should Yagwoia men be excluded from the secret circle as if they were women? They carry the very blood of their elders. Why, I ask Tali, are the elders excluding their *own* men? Nothing could be more alien to the Sambia: to hide ritual knowledge or myth from one's own kin. I can tell by the puzzle on the faces of my Sambia friends, Tali included, that they are as deeply disconcerted as me. Apparently, in this strange land, a strange custom prevails.

Many years have passed now, and I think I can better understand the young men's anguish at their exclusion from the secrets, and rage at their fathers and grandfathers, not only because I am older, but also because I, too, am more remote in space and time from the ritual secrecy of the Sambia.

Ritual secrecy defended this tense, floating world, power-filled and gender-divisive, hovering timelessly between subjects and hidden objects of desire: certainly not inside society, but not outside of social relations either. Ritual secrecy was meant to purchase a foothold, a coherent reality, for political solidarity. Apparently it fell apart for the Yagwoia. The anthropologist may be skeptical or afraid of entering this system of hidden powers and desires, and for good reason. Many a well-intentioned scholar has smudged a career on topics less incendiary than secrecy. Such a caveat explains in part the worry I brought to the Sambia study many years ago, when fortune allowed me to enter their secret system, but in turn required me to use pseudonyms. But what of the Yagwoia?

Theirs is a more complicated colonial story, given secondhand to me. But I fear that the Yagwoia story will be lost on the reader unless I digress sufficiently to describe what I know best—how and why secrecy was a social fact among the Sambia during this time of my first fieldwork, in 1974 through 1976.

Placing Secrecy

I began to live among the Sambia in 1974, approximately fifteen years after their first direct encounter with Europeans and six years after the colonial government "derestricted" the area to outsiders following the forcible suppression of warfare. I was the first anthropologist to work among the Sambia, though the French anthropologist Maurice Godelier initiated fieldwork in 1967 among the neighboring Baruya people.

Until about 1956 the Sambia were isolated from direct contact with the Western world. About that time the first medical patrol passed through the area of the Sambia Valley. Soon, however, Australian government patrols followed, about 1961, so that local warfare was stopped. Occasional skirmishes continued until 1968. Until first contact, knowledge of the outside world had been limited to airplane sightings, interpreted as large birds. Rumors of trade with white-skinned men on the coast far to the south were constant. Sambia technology consisted of stone tools and bow and arrows. New imported material, such as steel machetes, and other trade items were slowly introduced. By the late 1960s, however, pacification was followed quickly by various forms of precipitous but often subtle social and technological changes, including the gradual introduction of a cash economy based upon coffee tree planting and, in 1979, a permanent airstrip, followed by bureaucratic installations: a local first-aid post, then a government school, in 1985.

At the time of my initial fieldwork in 1974 through 1976 the change was spotty and not very noticeable to an outsider. Only as I became submerged in village life did I gradually uncover how profoundly attitudes were changing beneath the surface of social life. Concomitantly, the elders were vigorously resisting this change in marriage and ritual practice. Sambia was still a tradition-bound society, without roads, airstrips, or any permanent government presence, though its existence in a colonial setup precluded autonomy. By the time of subsequent field trips in 1979, 1981, 1983, 1985, 1988, and 1989, secret masculinity was becoming as rare as the men's houses that were now abandoned; and by my final field trips in 1990 and 1993, Sambia society was altered forever (see Herdt 1987a, 1993). Ritual initiation in the sense described before is a historical reality only, a fact that is made evident in the British Broadcasting Company film *Guardians of the Flutes* (1993) on which I consulted. We should study the earlier period prior to the burst of change not simply to remember the past, but because this was a time in which the public and private spheres still held much of their traditional meaning; and the secret system was vibrant and responsible for the performance of numerous male and female initiation ceremonies.

Historically, the Sambia were migrants from the Papuan hinterlands some two centuries ago. They and their neighbors share in a core of common cultural traditions (ritual, myth, and social organization) derived no doubt from ancient non-Austronesian migrations perhaps ten thousand years ago (reviewed in Herdt 1984a; Knauft 1993). Warfare has always been central to Sambia social organization, and marriage, residence, and sexual and family relations were adapted to the threat of war. The economy was based upon hunting and subsistence agriculture, the staples being sweet potatoes and taro. Sambia was an acephalous society in which political power rested primarily in the hands of ritual elders, war leaders, and shamans, and where a few Great Men could achieve renown through force of personality, charisma, achievements, and sociopolitical networks of influence with multiple sources of power.

Men claim diffuse power and the authority to rule in virtually all public affairs and are rarely challenged by women in rhetorical situations. Still, a profound force of contestation exists in some private and intimate matters, sexual relations being one and political loyalty another, wherein women hold considerable influence and are mistrusted and suspect. Moreover, women exercise control over most aspects of their own secret ceremonies surrounding menarche, marriage, and birth in the menstrual hut. The exceptions involve those situations in which warfare disrupts events or the men suspect the women of disloyalty (see Godelier 1989). The men's house and the women's houses were the countervailing points of this power and rule. Where the women's houses were contexts of privacy and

intimate relations between men and women, the men's houses were protected by taboos of ritual secrecy, on the one hand, and the veiled rhetorical threats of male public discursive attacks against women, on the other
(Herdt 1981). Generally, domestic-private relations in village life were
complicated and unstable. Men continually worry over the women's
doings and fear the women will usurp them in one way or another. Women *domestic*
held considerable influence beyond the reach of men, for example, in garden production; while in fireside gossip, daily cooking, and early child care,
women exercised near total control of space and time and were seldom
challenged by men. However, in public affairs, women held little influence,
never orated, and were subordinated to men especially in times of warfare
and ritual (see the similar account for the Baruya in Godelier 1986).

In 1974 the Sambia were living in scattered communities over high
mountain valleys in a thinly populated rain forest. Hamlets are composed
of one or two great clans that have separate, constituent clans. Secrecy and
ritual knowledge characterized the internal organization of clan ritual.
Local descent groups inhabited two lines of hamlets generally in conflict
and straddling opposite mountain ridges of the Sambia River Valley
flowing down from the Lamari-Vaillala Divide.

Elders and war leaders were committed to the advance of their own village, and desire to best their competitors in a zero-sum game of constant
bluff and battle with their peers in other villages. The enmity often
embroiled them in armed conflict, more often than not the unanticipated
outcome of squabbles over women and pigs. Two kinds of hostilities thus
constrained what I have called the social economy throughout the region.
First, and most important for internal tribal life, was intratribal bow fighting. This was ideally limited to showy, blustering challenges of lofting
arrows between neighboring hamlets. Only unbarbed arrows (no stone
weapons or barbed spears) were allowed. The aim was not to kill but rather
redress some perceived wrong that involved no loss of human life, such as
arguments over pigs, women, or theft of ritual custom. Sometimes, however, wounding and death occurred, and this escalated the fighting to a new
level of intensity, no holds barred. Because Sambia value blood revenge,
every death required a quid pro quo, until the score was settled or—more
rarely—a truce arranged. Second, intertribal war raiding parties were peri-
odically launched against hostile others beyond the valley. All technology
was used, including barbed arrows and stone clubs, and all persons were
open targets; since enemies were not human, killing, raping, and looting

were not moral violations as they would have been in the group (Read 1955). Morality in war, as in everyday life, was situation specific, with moral rules being tied to the "security circle" of the village and its surrounds (Lawrence 1965).

Another organization, the ritual confederacy, linked nearby hamlets together as units involved in a men's secret society, generally isomorphic with the phratry as defined previously. These localized confederacies in places like the Sambia Valley did, however, sometimes cut across phratries, creating wider, tenuous political alliances. What united these neighboring villages as a confederacy, however, was their fear of attack by true enemies from other tribes. Every three or four years, the hamlets of a confederacy jointly staged ritual initiations for their boys. Grandfathers, fathers, and brothers were the key organizers, creating an intimate circle of kin and family relations for all these ritual affairs. The initiations thus socialized sons and grandsons into the hamlet's warriorhood, inevitably introducing a theme of intergenerational transition in all events.

All marriages were arranged between exogamous groups or clans, often resulting in the common Highlands pattern of women moving into the hostile hamlets of their husbands. Sambia do not say they "marry their enemies," as do certain Highland societies (Meggitt 1964), but they do feel mistrust of outside women and a generalized sexual antagonism toward these "enemy wives." Marriage is by infant betrothal or sister exchange with little or no individual choice of spouse. Hamlets also exchanged women as wives, with certain neighbor hamlets intermarrying frequently enough that warfare between them was rare, at least for certain periods. Sambia Valley hamlets thus intermarried, creating shifting, unstable alliances, provoking mistrust at all levels of social arrangements, and interjecting suspicion and often paranoia into the spouses' sexual relationship, living arrangements, care of their children, and daily interests.

Training for warriorhood involves socialization for independence, but only in the context of stringent social regulations that assure conformity to ritual hierarchy in the men's house. Extreme autonomy and independence are sometimes manifested even in small boys. Sambia parents point to this hardiness as a sign that anticipates how this child may become a strong man, a war leader (*aamooluku*), which in another way Godelier calls a "great man." Such males are close to the vaunted image of an ideal and glorified man. They are more courageous and daring than others, more intelligent and resourceful, having had numerous occurrences, in their early development, of the tantrums and sulking that the Sambia know only too well to announce the rise of a Great Man war leader (Herdt 1987a: chap. 4). They are expected to become great hunters and fierce warriors. Their unruly and antisocial behaviors are the cause of concern. "Never worry," grandfathers advise. "They will soon be initiated and feel the pain of a warrior." During this time they are producing the activities necessary for war-making and promoting homosociality among bachelors and initiates committed to the defense of their special, secret reality.

The village was always symbolically dissected by three gendered places, which curtailed the movement of men and constrained the agency of boys. Men, their wives, and their uninitiated children reside in women's houses, small igloo-like huts, whereas all unmarried initiated males live in a larger men's house, which is strictly taboo to all females. The clubhouse is the center of all secret ritual plans and discourse, especially war-making, and the sole residence for all initiated unmarried males. Yet married men, too, look to the clubhouse for social recognition and self esteem, and they often sleep there in times of ritual activity (as they did before, during war). The menstrual hut of women, placed somewhat outside the hamlet, is tabooed because birth and menarche are celebrated there, and the secrecy of fertility and procreation are protected by the "natural" flood of pollution surrounding the hut. Indeed, the entire hamlet is divided spatially into male and female spheres, with male footpaths and female ones, which are forbidden to the opposite sex.

Privacy, by contrast, is possible only in the garden or the forest (and on occasion the deserted men's or women's houses) for married couples or the pairs of boys and bachelors who hunt and conduct homoerotic relations away from the village. Privacy, in this sense, means a relational discretion, not a sense of being alone for the individual, for the Sambia do not recognize the need to be alone and generally frown upon such an idea, especially for children and young people.

Gender polarity was strictly enforced in the sexual division of labor, which viewed men as warriors and hunters, and women as gardeners. Men and women were generally forbidden from doing each other's tasks in hunting and gardening. Women are responsible for all food preparation and child care. Women are forbidden to climb trees or to chop down large ones. Women do not lead or fight in warfare. Men are ridiculed for caring for children. One of the problems of making the transition from being a boy to initiate is that the womanly tasks boys routinely took, including handling babies, were ridiculed by the men as weak or soft and polluted.

Sexual relations between men and women were conflicted and loaded with the secrecy and segregation that made difference into excitement. Early sexual relations between couples were also highly ritualized, first through fellatio (a woman sucking her husband), and later in genital inter- course, a woman expected to submit to the missionary position. Generally, marital histories reveal arguments, physical fights, jealousies, sorcery fears, wife beating, and, more rarely, suicide. But it is not as if women simply do whatever the men bid. Women may subvert and resist the men's demands, such as "forgetting to prepare his food, refusing to make love, shouting and commenting on her husband . . . using sorcery or semen sorcery, and pol- lution poison in the food," Godelier has written for the neighboring Baruya (1986: 150). Indeed, this is the fabric of contentiousness that makes men steal themselves into their secret realities in order to seek shelter and trust. The women's speech and behavior are not allowed beyond a certain point lest they infringe upon the men's secret masculinity.

As sex between couples is highly ritualized, it follows that intimacy is itself a product of very structured rules, sometimes broken by lust, which causes ill effects later. Men believe sexual intercourse should be spaced to avoid depletion and premature aging or death, and yet they typically react in frustration and sometimes anger when they do not have sex with their wives. Many a young man is jealous and vindictive toward any wrong move on the part of his consort when they are beginning their sexual life together. Couples normatively have sex every few days, or as infrequently as once every two or three weeks, depending on age, length of marriage, and so forth. However, the postpartum taboo forbids sexual intercourse for some two years following birth. No overt contact, such as touching, between the sexes is permitted in public. Ritual practices, beliefs about the fears of female pollution, prolonged postpartum avoidance, and these other taboos thus undermine trust and intimacy, while promoting the par- titions of secrecy in marital relations (Herdt and Stoller 1990). Couples who break the rules are swiftly visited by illness and death, and may suffer their children to be malnourished, ugly, weak, or diseased.

Precolonial Identity Politics

It is difficult for Westerners to appreciate the sexual politics and divergent realities of the genders in a world like this. A special trust and intimacy is created between people of the same gender, and for women, "evidence of women's driving motivations was structured through the device of secrecy"

(M. Strathern 1988: 114). Mistrust between adult genders is expected and all too real. Sambia strongly believe that such a special bond predisposes women to "grow" girls, and men to "grow" boys, after initiation begins (218). Homosocial trust attends being incorporated into the secret men's house and then being asked to protect these same bonds from all interlopers for the rest of one's life. The intimacy is itself generative of pleasure, and the pleasure has several manifestations. One of them is the pleasure of power and domination, enjoyed in the privileges of feeling superior to others. The other is the effort to create unity in the common threads of political and social interest vital in the maintenance of the clubhouse.

The Sambia division between what is "good for society" (i.e., the village) and what is "good for the clubhouse" is murky, tenuous, and often disputed—even in the internal discourse of the men's clubhouse. This difference in interest and privilege stimulates a kind of moral virtue and self-righteousness in support of the superior ways of male bonding and emotional attachments flowing from male secret sharing. For the men's (and probably the women's) secret circle is morally construed as being the right, necessary, and virtuous path: a dictate of faith and pure ritual orthodoxy to uphold the purity of essential categories, such as "growing" boys through insemination, and essential relationships, such as the ritual guardian/initiate bond that lasts for life.

What ultimately matters is the protection of secret masculinity, including the homosocial sensibilities and subjective pleasure that derive from being with the same gender. This experience is particular to the historical and cultural circumstances that generate it—the men's house, the women's house—and for the men this has to do with the pleasures of using and fashioning power. But who or what are the subjects and objects of this power? The men's house, with its own language, social relations, and secret concepts, enables the emergence of an alternative cultural reality, focused upon a system of "moral utopian" objects. Such masculine objectifications include the secret ritual flutes, the female hamlet spirits, the hierarchical relations between older and younger homoerotic partners, the absence of female pollution, and the presence of common concerns in the hosting of ritual practices. These moral utopian objects are largely constructed outside of the time and space world, and they are designed to meet the personal, social, political, and religious needs, interests, and life plans of men. Trust and the provision of internal confidence—a circle of shared strategic plans—are vital to this moral world. The creation of a security circle sufficiently tight to keep women and enemies out, and thus to preserve military secrets, social and homoerotic pleasures, and harmony, was ever-present in the men's plans. The male bonding that issues from this pleasure is very intense indeed, not sufficient to generate sexual excitement within itself, but certainly facultative of the ritual idolatry and fetishism of desiring and admiring idealized objects of desire in their purest "male" qualities (see Read 1965: 152ff.).

Does women's ritual secrecy involve the same processes and qualities? Not in the same way, at least among the Sambia. The reason has ultimately to do with war, and with how warfare constantly undermines and threatens to destabilize all relationships, especially those among males. For it is males who define public affairs, however tenuously, by creating boundaries: inside and outside the men's house, separating themselves from Woman and from their immediate social relations with married-in women, versus mothers and sisters, who are far more trusted, even if rhetorical positioning makes no such distinctions. As Godelier (1986) has suggested, women—the disempowered—have fewer means to create divergent secret realities, even in the menstrual hut, and have less to gain from enacting these counterhegemonic agencies. This view applies to the Sambia too, and for this reason, the attitude of women toward their soon-to-be-initiated sons was highly ambivalent. These ritual attempts are prerogatives of the ability to wage war or defend against attack, thereby manipulating relations through what is unseen and hidden in the men's house. Secret masculinity, as a form of diffuse power in public affairs, exists in the absence of strong social control, hegemony, and consensus in village life. There is, in short, no symbolic counterpart to secret masculinity in the form of a secret femininity, though the men are unsure of this. Their fears produce instability and paranoia, and contribute to the gender politics of male plans to ensure secrecy.

The initiation of boys—that is, the reproduction of secret masculinity—is iconic of these gender politics, which threaten but also reaffirm this instability. Boys sometime resisted being initiated, more often than one would have imagined (Herdt 1987a). Especially the younger boys, seven and eight years old, seemed too small, timid, and bereft of comfort to be resocialized and then indoctrinated into the harsh reality of the men's house ritual secrecy. I want to underscore the sense of counterhegemony in the resistance of these little boys who were the proxy of their mothers, both in resisting and in being dominated. The boys represented, in this conditional sense, Woman, and were objectified first as outsiders lumped with Woman. Only through the harsh means of ritual ordeals, including scraping the skin and bleeding the nose, among other efforts to "defeminize" the boy's body, was the maleness enhanced sufficiently that the men could reclaim or better yet, advance a new claim that they had "given birth" to the agentic boy.

I am less sure than was Roger Keesing (1982a) that precolonial New Guinea women devised their own counterculture and even countervailing mythological systems in response to the men's (Gillison 1993; Herdt 1997a: chap. 4). After all, men have the advantage and the disadvantage of going between the men's house and the women's house. Sambia women have their own sites of meaning and power inclusive of women in the menstrual hut. The diffuse power of women stems as much from how they learn to perceive what is hidden and to avoid the pockets of male aggression surrounding ritual secrecy—a coping strategy for incessant and sometimes incomprehensible demands from the men. But whether that is constitutive of a counter-mythological system remains doubtful. Nevertheless, the role of women to mediate and work between kin groups and networks, as argued long ago by M. Strathern (1972), is to some extent evident among the Sambia, particularly in domestic and extended family relations within the village, but only after they have become mothers and achieved higher social status.

Does the same argument apply to women's cultural ontology? What of the special, secret, or tabooed places for women, especially the menstrual hut? Might they also serve as cultural sites of the production of ontology and action? I think so. The evidence we have from a range of New Guinea village societies suggests that the locus of women's special ritual activities, fertility cycles, sacred songs and myths, birth-giving and parturition socialization, as well as the typical round of menstrual cycle practices, is focused on sites of ritual secrecy (Kyakas and Wiessner 1992). Moreover, a special status is attached to the menstrual hut in the cultural imagination of women (Brown and Buchbinder 1976). Indeed, it becomes an issue of some importance in testing the ontological theory to understand in what way women's secret spaces become alternate sites of cultural contestation and production (Gillison 1993; Lutkehaus and Roscoe 1995; M. Strathern 1987).

In contrast to prefeminist frames advanced to understand these dynamics, feminist anthropologists have analyzed issues of patriarchy, heterosexism, and male same-gender relations more than ever before (best elucidated by Marilyn Strathern [1988]). Challenging the idea that "men can grow boys" as nativist social ideologies, Strathern has suggested how this cultural reasoning has underanalyzed social relations. "It is relations that separate the genders, male from female and same-sex from cross-sex," M. Strathern (1988: 211) notes. In this way we begin to better understand gender segregation and the association of women's power with material structures or dwellings, especially the menstrual hut (Gillison 1993). As an archetypal theme in New Guinea, men greatly fear the menstrual hut—but how much of their anxiety is associated with women's diffuse power located in that hut? It is men who need a nerve center and secret space to plan and map, because of the pervasiveness of women in domestic spaces. The counterhegemonic force of women resides in their intimate network of same-gender relations, which persist without interruption by initiation for much longer in the female life cycle than do the men's. The leftover space—the menstrual hut—is not only truly feared and avoided by men because of "pollution," but is the object of the most intense gaze and warnings against the subversion of women.

The intensity of male/male secret attachments and Eros locked in male imagery of the Ideal or Great Man, as well as the intimacy and pleasure sought and largely attained in homosocial relations, virtually guarantee that women and children are demeaned as Other. By externalizing all the shared traits that attend to the excluded, and having a secret theory that precludes many of the precepts and concepts upon which the nature of this Other is understood to exist and act, it is virtually assured that women are attributed with influence and diffuse power beyond the men. Paradoxically, however, this process displaces qualities and traits from self to Other; for example, nurturance or verbal scolding, traits perceived as having their own value or virtue for the Other, may become manifestations not of desire but of envy, at least symbolically, in ritual action. The most dramatic and illuminating symbolic displacement of men's subjectivity is the ritual flutes, animated by their angry female spirits, and the strange manner in which the flutes create difference and fetishistic arousal (social and erotic) in men vis-à-vis boys (the proxy of women) (see Herdt 1982b).

Concomitantly such a process makes the ritual secrecy of protecting the body and secret personhood of men all the more passionate, imperative, and needy; for in such situations faith is too easily punctured by questioning, self-doubt, and criticism from the Other. The smugness of men in secret circumstances, looking down upon women, thus takes on a new meaning.

The men cannot abide irony in the experience of ritual secrecy, for that would undermine the very basis of faith, secrecy, and ritual absoluteness—purposively constructed reality confirmed to support the cozy homosociality of ritual secrecy. Here, the Sambia, unlike the Ilahita Arapesh (Tuzin 1980), do not narrate ritual secrecy as a construction of men; rather they see it as a dictate of nature and the sacred, thus without choice or conscious intervention. Irony, it seems, is the enemy of ritual secrecy. Trust in male comrades was both an affirmation of this absoluteness and a reaction to the conditionality of their masculinity. Their divergent reality could not withstand the self-attenuation of irony, contrasting reality with humor. Their utopia depends upon a grim and seasoned determination to shut out self-reflection. However, smugness—the ability to feel secure in one's superiority and sense of an absolute arrogance (meaning here to act without permission vis-à-vis the other)—is generative of their political legitimacy.

The creation of secret reality in the men's house thus smugly assures selfish satisfaction, too: secret desires and hidden objects, even the substitution of the hidden object of desire (the initiate) as a proxy for the public Other (women and wife). These formulations are vital to the internal coherence of the secret male reality making in the men's house.

Homosociality and Male Ritual Development

To enter the Sambia men's house is first to notice the lived-in and slightly sour smell of sugarcane peels, rubbish, and urine (from underneath the house) that ventilates the atmosphere. It is not so neat and tidy as it appears outside. A few young boys—first-stage initiates—huddle near the fire; some of them are clowning around, the older youths sitting silent, or morose, all of which may change in a rush of older men. Then the boys hush and the adolescents come to life, to show off for others with whom to rival. They are more "on stage" as the talk leans toward a hunt in the morning, in a ravine where cassowary have been spotted; and the best hunter of the village tells how he has already set his traps and will dream tonight of what may happen on the morrow. A fire is now roaring to ward off the late afternoon fog and chill. The men roast second-rate sweet potato, their only repast for the evening, since their wives have gone off to distant gardens. At its peak the clubhouse may seat thirty men, though typically only a dozen boys and bachelors sleep there. The younger initiates are pushed out the door and sent down to the creek to fetch water, or cut sugarcane, or do some other menial task, often at the command of the bachelors—just to prove that the boys will take orders. And the boys will go grumbling under their breath that they are not the bachelors' "women." This clears the decks for the older men's discussion of an impending marriage exchange which they were loath to discuss with the boys present. Such talk inevitably turns to the sisters of the younger boys and to sex with women, especially the relationship between coitus and menstruation. All such talk is completely forbidden to the boys; the secrecy of the men, their character as "in-betweens" who have sex with the boys and with the women too, is at stake, and must be defended, creating hierarchy—an internal barrier within the clubhouse. The rituals to rid pollution are touched upon; these are hidden from the younger males till later, that being privileged knowledge, and thus one form of power is kept out of their reach, for now. Of course warfare may come up; it is always just a matter of time until the challenges and heroics of warfare are spoken. But once the elders enter, the old war tales pop up, intermixed with ritual stories and—after the initiates are asleep—allusions to sexual relations with women.

This is what marks the fabric of the clubhouse: drab, untidy, and sour-smelling. The physical power of muscular male bodies is as omnipresent as male unity and intimacy; but also the competition of male peers, the routines of order via orders issued from the higher to the lower status. These accoutrements of male sociality actually merit study in their own right, for they massage the contexts of storytelling in matters of marriage exchange and sex with women, menstrual pollution, war stories, and ritual procedures for purity and preservation of masculinity, giving substance to masculine domesticity in the homosocial utopia imagined by the ritual secrecy of the men's house.

This physicality of the male body is what separates childhood from the subsequent development of secret masculinity. As the introduction to the men's secret cult and initiation into the mystery of the ritual flutes and bull-roarers, the revelations of the first-stage ceremony are so shocking and profound to the boy as to defy pat stereotypes or simple generalizations. But one thing is certain: the door to the men's house marks the separation of the boys from secular public life. Thus begins a long liminal period, roughly associated with the many years they engage in ritual boy-inseminating practices and sleep in the men's house. The absence of Woman in the men's house is so dramatic by comparison with childhood that it invites comparison to the screaming secret of the ritual flutes in village life (Herdt 1981).

Over the next fifteen years, boys undergo six secret initiations in all, which correspond to age-grades and ritual status. First-stage initiation (*moku*) males are *choowinuku;* second-stage initiates are *imbutu* (ages eleven to thirteen); and third-stage initiates are *ipmangwi,* or youth-bachelors, who have attained social puberty (fourteen to sixteen years of age). All three of these initiations are performed in sequence on large groups of boys who become an age-set cohort. These rites make boys and youths members of a warriorhood, the local unit of which is based in and responsible for defending its own hamlet and performing its rituals. The final three initiations are organized for particular youths, underlining their character as "life crisis" events in the lives of the young men and their brides. Fourth-stage initiation (*nuposha*) may occur anytime after the *ipmangwi.* It is a marriage ceremony, with secret rites and sexual teachings for individual youths who have a woman assigned for their marriage. Fifth-stage initiation (*taiketnyi*) takes place when a man's wife has her menarche. Sixth-stage initiation (*moondangu*) is held when a man's wife bears her first child. Having two children brings full adult masculine personhood (*aatmwunu*) and the end of exclusive residence in the clubhouse.

The formal marriage ceremony (*nuposha*) of the Sambia is often performed before menarche begins to alter the young bride's status. Ideally this introduced the newlyweds to oral sex, in which the younger woman fellated her somewhat older husband. The procedure was much like the homoerotic experience, but it was of course absolutely unknown to the younger bride, just as the pleasures of heteroerotic insemination were unknown to the boy-initiate. This point also highlights the non-subtle power difference between initiated men, on the one hand, and women and initiates on the other; and it amplifies the extreme prudishness regarding sex, in particular the remarkable measures of privacy taken to ensure that others do not observe the newlyweds having sexual relations. The mere mention of their sexual relations in public invites great shame and social distress. Only after the menarche (when coitus is permitted), and more particularly with motherhood, do women attain full personhood, which brings greater social influence and some measure of domestic power in the lives of women. Coitus never stops being secret; however, as the couple age and children come along, the imperative to hide sex or feel shame about it declines, as no doubt the absolute feeling of difference between the spouses is mediated across time. Ideally the young husband may continue secret insemination of boys in the men's house until he fathers a child by his wife.

In both cases, however, sexual relations remain hidden from others, secret with respect to the other partner, and totally silent.

In the secret ontology of men, first-stage initiates are viewed as symbolically equivalent to the menarcheal females in their late teens. We may see in this symbolic association the necessary symbolic transformation of the prepubertal boy-initiate into a sexual object of the postpubertal male youth. In addition it serves as the basis for the embodiment of the intense secret ideal that males "menstruate" through the nose to attain "pure" masculine vitality, physical growth, prowess, and, later after marriage, the continued well-being and preservation of health in spite of proximity to women, menstrual blood, and coitus (Herdt 1982c). Nose-bleeding rites must therefore commence the purifications of first initiation, preceding insemination; and then they must continue throughout the male life cycle, even in old age, ceasing only at senescence.

The secret imagery of the process in the cultural imagination of males signifies the perception of the boy's body as being ready for oral penetration as a necessary condition for the physical development and growth of his phallus at a later stage. While it is viewed as dangerous and also exciting for that reason, blood-letting is critical to the production of secret masculinity for the Sambia. Only after blood is let can the "birth" of the phallus occur, electing the boy to manhood, an irreducible intentional reality of secret masculinity. Both of these physical steps, elements critical to the dietetics of Sambia practice, help to essentialize the boy as a sexual object.

The sexual objectification of initiates, transformed from children to semen recipients, supports residence in the men's house. This years-long process of liminal seclusion has typically been ignored in New Guinea studies (Herdt 1984a; Knauft 1987); consequently we have only sketchy ideas of what actually occurs following initiation into the cult house, even when it is certain that initiation is typically the introduction to sexuality in all of its manifestations. Among the Sambia, initiates learn to ingest semen from older youths through oral sexual contacts in middle childhood. First- and second-stage initiates may serve only as fellators; they are forbidden situationally to reverse erotic roles with older males. No other form of sexual relations is permitted, including mutual masturbation. The sexual heat of a boy's mouth, while less than a woman's vagina, is thought to be stimulated by the expected gift of semen. The absence of any other sexual outlet assures older males of the control of boys. Sexual objectification is greatest when the boy's body is most like a prepubertal girl's and most

unlike an adult man's. Stated differently, the more like a man a boy looks
and acts, the greater his agency, and the less desirable he is as a homoerotic
object.

Generally, boy-inseminating rites among the Anga-speaking groups
require that semen is passed on from one body to the other, as if it were an
electrical charge or magical substance necessary to activate the other.
Semen moves so as to reciprocate the transmission of "blood," as a principle of marriage and kinship across generations (Herdt 1984a); thus, a man
who receives a woman in marriage exchange is expected to inseminate her
younger brother, the man's clan the recipient of a womb and child, the
woman's clan the recipient of semen to masculinize the younger boy.
Thus, secret masculinity hangs in the balance of marriage exchange.
Third-stage pubescent bachelors and older youths therefore serve only as
fellateds, inseminating prepubescent boys, who must wait their turn until
they achieve social puberty. All males pass through both social erotic
stages, being first fellators, then fellateds: there are no exceptions. After
marriage, a man is allowed both homoerotic and heteroerotic contact until
the birth of his first child, ultimately terminating all homoerotic activities,
at least ideally, just as he takes up more-or-less permanent residence in a
"woman's house" with his wife or wives.

A point of male vulnerability in this secret dietetics of initiation concerns "semen atrophy," men's belief in the rarity of semen, its absence as a
"natural" element in the body, and its depletion across time in order to
produce masculinity or reproduce in children (see Herdt 1999: chap. 5).
Since biological maleness is based on the accumulation of a semen pool
inside the body through years of repeated inseminations, the depletion of
semen threatens not only well-being and ritual stature, but also health and
life. This remarkable fear of male atrophy is introduced into the boy's subjectivity through ritual pedagogy. The male body—in this anxious, dreamy
narrative of men's stories—is conceptualized as an empty reservoir to be
filled up; however, it is easily emptied again, to its peril. Hence, once filled,
the "semen organ" of the boy sustains existence by supplying semen, but it
is diminished unless a source of replenishment is found. Such a great dread
may be the core of men's secret ontology, so closely guarded from the
women. Boy-inseminations (homoerotics) and relations with wives (het-
eroerotics) for reproduction require repeated ejaculations that stimulate
"growth" or "babies" in others by depleting one's only reserve.

Like a zero-sum game, semen atrophy imagines always that someone's loss is someone else's gain. The secret reality of depletion is difficult if not insufferable, and it has resulted in many compromises in defending one's personal fund of semen, especially regarding women. Regulation of heterosexual intercourse is a primary defense. But another is also vital: adult men practice secret, customary ingestions of white tree sap in the forest. Men say that this tree sap "replaces" ejaculated semen "lost" through heterosexual intercourse. So men regularly drink tree sap after coitus in order to replenish maleness. Interestingly enough, though, most bachelors—although they worry over semen depletion—do not replace semen lost through premarital boy-inseminating. Only with marriage are those personal anxieties reinforced through the institutionalized practice of tree sap ingestion (Herdt 1981: 248–51).

Tabooed as a cultural space, the men's house becomes their dormitory and barracks, shorn of any hint of women or femininity. The more spartan, the better to promote the boy's warrior characteristics, Sambia men feel. In precolonial times initiates were mostly being trained for war and were on call at all times, even when they were small. First-stage initiation embarks the boys on a developmental ritual career into adulthood that requires maximum sociobehavioral and symbolic "distance" from their mother, other women, and children, and maximal "closeness" to older males, elders as ritual leaders, fathers and brothers as seniors, older unrelated adolescent youths as sexual partners, and same-age peers as comrades and brothers (consanguineal or classificatory). Soon after initiation boys are expected to start showing their fiber and make a name for themselves as hunters. The second-stage initiate by age twelve or thirteen (the age at which Tali first visited Yagwoia) is expected to go eagerly to distant enemy lands and on long trade parties or up to the deep forest for months of rugged hunting, while girls at this age have never left their village and continue domestic routines, remaining structurally subordinated to their parents.

Secret Masculinity of the Kuwatni'u

First initiation for boys places them into the cultural category *kuwatni'u*, a general rubric and a term of address, shared with the class of second-stage initiates, signified by the acts of receiving semen and avoiding women. They are no longer referred to as boys or *kwulia'u*; indeed their boyhood name is stricken and may never be said by them again. It is insulting to a man's honor to refer to a man by his boy's name. At first-stage initiation he receives an informal *kuwatni'u* name (actually a nickname used informally by his age-mates) and a formal adult name (used by parents and adults). The name change symbolically marks the sociocultural status and personal identity change from childhood to initiation rank.

What does it mean to be an initiate or *kuwatni'u*? The category term signifies the lowest-ranking male in the men's house and secret system, suggesting the boys' deference and fear of their elders. The fearfulness is created through initiation ordeals and threats, and maintained through a variety of control measures that permeate life in the clubhouse. Some informants trace the etiology of the term to the general taboo that requires initiates always to hide themselves from women, especially their faces, when women approach them. So pervasive and strict is the rule that one gradually stops being startled and grows quite accustomed to the experience of having a whole group of initiates suddenly jump off the path from which one is walking and vanish into the brush at the sight of the most harmless old woman making her way piled high with garden produce back to the village. I once had such an experience. I was walking at the head of a line of initiates, talking with some and quite absorbed in what I was saying. They fled quite silently unknown to myself, while I continued talking rather loudly and greeted just such an old woman, who must have thought me quite strange talking to myself in the middle of nowhere. Moments later, as silently as they disappeared, the boys crept back like shades out of the bushes when she had passed on, shaking her head.

The deference, avoidance, and fear of the glances or looks of women implied by the term *kuwatni'u* leave a definite mark of shame on the boy's identity that he never wants to repeat in the years to come. However, it is precisely this ability of women to gaze upon them—first as boys, then as initiates, and later as adults—that contests the agency of males and lifts the power of women over men.

Kuwatni'u are completely under the surveillance and control of older bachelors and men in the clubhouse—and for good reason. Men fear that initiates will escape into the forest, or run back to their mothers' huts, not only during the first stage, but occasionally up to the time of the third-stage bachelorhood ceremony too (Herdt 1987a). Direct control of the initiates exposes them to constant hazing and the whims of the older youth, some of whom are actually the sexual partners or the comrades of their partners. In general, though, most of the older males are their kin and supporters, their elder classificatory clan brothers, cousins, or uncles. Their ritual guardians may or may not be present in this group, but their older blood brothers may help to protect them. In keeping with the spartan outlook of the clubhouse, again, protection means in the context of the warriorhood that the boys should be toughened and made obedient to the war leaders and elders, and not coddled or treated in ways that will continue their softness or unmanly demeanor. For example, boys are punished for laughing in public, which is considered undignified for adult men. At the slightest sign that a boy would be tempted to go back to his mother or younger siblings, which might jeopardize the men's ritual secrecy, the boy will be severely reprimanded and if necessary beaten, or worse. Many are the stories of boys threatened with death if they reveal the secrets. The threats are not idle. This is one area without compromise; for as Godelier (1989) has written, betrayal of ritual secrets is so terrible that the men will not countenance any threat and will eliminate a boy if necessary, without possibility of blood revenge or retribution by his kin, as stipulated by the men's secret covenant with each other at first initiation. But what happened to secrecy after the changes of colonial rule?

When colonial authorities suppressed Sambia warfare, an unexpected dilemma presented itself to the elders. The initiates gradually stopped being trained for warfare; the war raids ceased, and the vigilance that preserved the absolute sanctity of the men's clubhouse secrecy was undermined. The veils of secrecy began to be challenged, though not openly at first. Gradually, the secrecy of the men's house was jeopardized by the opening up of a formerly closed social system and by the increasing openness of physical movement. During the time of my first fieldwork I was continually struck by the fact that the older and younger initiates had so much free time on their hands. Although the ideology of preparedness remained, demands to train and prepare for war were gone. The budding initiates loved to roam in gangs, hunt and fish close to the village, occasionally play "king on the mountain" and warrior games, and of course chum around the men's house as if there were little else to do. Back in the clubhouse they would tire of hearing the war tales so common to their elders' gatherings round the hearth, with their ceaseless gab and gossip about the tales of old. With each passing year this secular trend increased. Moreover, the bachelors were going in greater numbers to work on coastal plantations or to live in the towns, which disrupted the tenuous structure of authority and hierarchy within the men's house, as I have written before (Herdt 1987b).

The Long Liminality of Secret Masculinity

A long-standing enigma in the creation of masculinity among the Sambia and kindred Melanesian societies concerns the huge length of time boys spend in ritual seclusion. Why does status change require ten years or more, among such peoples as the Sambia, the Baruya, the Gahuku-Gama, Baktaman, and others considered below? The key is the boys' agency—or lack of it—in the men's house. The political and ritual problem of the *kuwatni'u* as a structural category in precolonial times was that boys were lacking in agency and no longer classified as children, but neither could they achieve this without secret masculinity. Their adulthood depended upon their ritual careers: following the rules, making a name for themselves, contributing to the symbolic capital of the clubhouse.

The kind of conditional personhood created by this seclusion is reminiscent of the description of the Greek city-state as a permanently armed military camp (Dover 1978: 192, n. v). How else could the camp be prepared for attack or warfare at any time? As long as the cohort of unmarried initiates—age seven to their early twenties—are placed into a military clubhouse removed from women and are harnessed for fighting, the village could depend on a constant source of manpower for its military needs. Without it, the village might fail. Pairing off younger and older males into opportunistic couples was the consequence of such a political formation. Agency and military prowess go hand in hand in such a regime.

As amoral, liminal persons, betwixt and between the normative positions and regular outposts of social life, children (boys especially) are a fuzzy category in Sambia culture, being between sacred and profane, the men's and women's worlds (Turner 1967). It is a very strange threshold that extends into young adulthood. One might say that such a liminality is the psychocultural requirement of the creation of a sexual and social subjectivity based upon ritual secrecy. But from the social and political perspective of the solidarity of the men's house, this liminality is extremely useful, perhaps instrumental, in the production of warriors, through the social control of boys and their agentic activities. As the boys accepted being objectified in order to achieve manhood, they signified their acceptance of the ideological or utopian cultural reality of the men's house. This subjectivity included the creation of difference within them psychologically, a necessary step to their subsequent overcoming of the gaze of women, in preparation for eventual intimate sexual relations with their wives. All such measures of course ensured the regulation of women as a scarce symbolic resource by the men's house.

Thus, by creating very long-term secret ritual seclusion and female avoidance, the boys were removed from public affairs, where incoherence, compromise, and doubt are typical, because these qualities might have crept into their subjectivity. Neither could the boys be tempted to give away secret knowledge to women, being always under surveillance. As they matured, their reputation as warriors rose in the region, even as they remained largely powerless in village political life (indeed, married women, especially women elders, had a greater measure of agency compared to the initiates). The structural boundary inclined male initiates to identify with their mates in the men's house and compete with the others in villages outside.

A strategic masculine edge was being produced: for military preparedness; for growth and masculinity in boys' bodies; for strength and advancement in the entire male age-grade of the region; and ultimately for the individual youth's own marriage and the achievement of full male agency in adulthood. Obviously, it is in the self-interest of the initiate, then, to foster his own competence in handling ritual secrecy. To whatever extent he could do so, through the imposition of dietetics and self-discipline, such as inducing nose-bleeding in himself, then to that extent might he succeed over his fellows. Such a developing secret masculinity is omnipresent in daily activities, when boys monitor each other's behaviors and will occasionally report infractions of rules and violations of taboos of hiding to their seniors. The violators are invariably punished, typically by caning them or thrashing with sharp cassowary quill-bones. In such moments one sees the latent conflict and competitions between age-mates and generational cohorts become manifest. But in fact these competitions are given dramatic expression in certain ceremonies among men at each initiation. The net effect of the rivalries between age-mates and competition between generations within the men's house is to create horizontal lines that top off the vertical cleavages long discussed since the time of Read (1965: chap. 4) on up through Godelier (1999: chap. 2). Rivalries are encouraged up to a point within the ranks of the initiates as warriors-in-training, in learning to hunt and fight, and in mastering ritual practices and secrecy.

Nevertheless, in the clubhouse it was forbidden to discuss the disempowerment of initiates—that is, the boy's domination by older males and his lack of agency in certain areas, especially in his tabooed relationships with women and children. In the latter case we are dealing with what was truly a whispered secret, rare in the small hours of the morning or at the margins of the forest where boys were at some distance from their omniscient elders. The secret utopian ideology of the men created a different conscious emphasis that tended to displace and disrupt the boys' griping and insubordination—when and if they occurred. Elders were interested in but one thing: the production of a new kind of body, a warrior's masculinity and body, in each boy. This obviously promoted the older men's ideology and their individual self-interests. It also subverted the boys' fears and deflected the boys' desires away from the women's house, and kept them turning back upon the clubhouse. In the long years of living secluded in the men's house the ritual practices and common inseminations to which a boy was expected to submit, and eventually to become enthusiastic about, promised empowerment vis-à-vis women on the outside and eventually trust by seniors in the men's house.

Secret Masculine Desires

What subjectivity is created through secret masculinity? How are its desires inculcated and socialized through the men's house pedagogy? Initiation reveals to boys the "secret" (*ioolu*) meanings of practices never before known; this wonder-world opens the door to experiences only sensed or dreamed, such as actually witnessing the ritual flutes, dangerous and hidden from women and children. Of course, not all of the secrets are revealed to boys at first, only those appropriate to their age and ritual grade. In this sense, *ioolu* for Sambia has a strong connotation of things hidden from the public gaze, a notion apparently common to New Guinea systems (Schwimmer 1980). Like many other New Guinea peoples, Sambia also speak of the *kablu* (kernel, foundation, root) or "base" of something to signify its "inside" meaning. With each successive initiation more hidden knowledge and practices are added. By this notion the men explicitly demarcate a boundary between the inside (men's house) and secular affairs, which they think of as polluted, messy, dangerous, and uncongenial. Moreover, men implicitly differentiate between sacred knowledge known to elders and the lesser knowledge and practices of subordinates. Thus, they hierarchically structure knowledge and practices, linking knowledge to moral action and hence agency. For example, boys can know about the ritual flutes, but only after third-stage initiation do they have the right to use them—a metaphor for active, penetrative sex and social control.

Binding male subjectivity to a new, more adult form of agency is criti-

cal to the thinking involved in ritual initiation. Ritual secrecy is governed
by the general category *pweiyu*, or "ritual," ordinarily glossed as a noun to
refer to an extant practice, such as the nose-bleeding ritual, as well as by a
modification of *pweiyu* which can be used as a verb in the sense of tying or
binding "a thing together." Men will also refer to a "ritual binding" (also
pweiyu) in the same manner. For instance, a special vine from the forest is
used to bind ritual things; when it is cut the vine exudes white tree sap
(likened to mother's milk), and men mark this meaning *pweiyu* with a secret
name. Thus they can talk of how the vine is hidden in a men's net string
bag, making the container of secret paraphernalia twice-bound, first with
the vine inside and then with the bag around it. Such metaphors of ritual
secrecy are compared or analogically contrasted with "outside," the visible
and public that is impure or polluted, and of contrary nature, such as
women's net bags, used for garden produce, babies, and firewood, covered
in dirt and debris. The kinds of net bags have a radically divergent nature,
which reflects the divergent nature of male and female; they become
likened to enemies. In the broadest sense of *pweiyu* is the sensibility that to
initiate a boy is to bind his thought to the laws and customs of ritual
secrecy.

Ritual rebirth is the key to understanding these changes for Sambia
boys. We should think of masculine rebirth as an ontological process having subjective, body, and political ramifications. To create the necessary
shared secret reality of this rebirth as a subjectively "real" experience in the
objective circumstances of the men's house requires both a shared
mythopoetic image of the effect upon the body and an agreement about its
real-world effects for political organization. What is at stake is the effort of
initiated men as an organization to seize control of the cultural imagination and its influence over the women's world and the control of public
affairs. Subjectively, the mythopoetic imagery creates through many sen-
sual experiences a conception of maleness and manliness exclusive of all
womanliness.

For example, the bachelor as a category is referred to as *moongenyu*, a
term that means "new bamboo." It metaphorically refers to the prototypic
young bachelor as a type of muscular/virile body and as a form of partially
empowered agent following third-stage initiation. Politically, while the
bachelor has more freedom to move about in public life, he must still avoid
women in all contexts, but he is able to dominate boys and inseminate
them. Secretly, however, *moongenyu* also signifies a manly penis: the

imagery corresponds in men's secret lore to how the penis is believed to grow and enlarge, gradually enabling sexual intercourse. This is based upon the assumptive notion that successive inseminations result in the creation of a fertile adolescent youth, himself capable of reproducing the system of substance transfer. He is the very picture of what is regarded as sexy, lusty, and beautiful—an object of desire for both women and boys. This certainly is the case for the Kaluli people of the Great Papuan Plateau (Schieffelin 1976: 125), but without its being either totally mandatory or secret, and the Baruya (Godelier 1986), as noted before, who totalize boy-inseminating as an ontological principle of all masculinity.

Mythopoetics of Secret Masculinity

Thus the bachelor (or *moongenyu*) becomes an object of desire and social attraction that merges both the idealized mythic figure of the bachelor and the real-life person into a unified fetish-category. We might compare this imagery to that of Woman/Other as an idealized object that is substituted for the real-life woman to whom a boy is later married and with whom he will engage in sexual relations. But such a comparison, whether for the Baruya, the Kaluli, or the Sambia, imagines that the Man is fetishized because his body is or contains the essences or substances necessary for the chain of virility and reproduction. Indeed, the Sambia believe that the man creates virility/growth in the boy, in a manner analogous to how women create babies. Kaluli deny knowing where babies come from (Schieffelin 1976: 125), which their ethnographer seems skeptical about. However, such a denial is perfectly in keeping with the metaphorical intent of their beliefs, since they see men as the admired and desired sexual object, placing ideological and conscious emphasis upon the Ideal Man, not the Woman/Other. By comparison, the Sambia make it clear why they fetishized the *moongenyu*: they admire his phallus and they expect he will "grow" the phalli of the initiates whom he inseminates. Sambia men imagine that the glans penis grows in a last surge of ritual inseminations near the third-stage initiation, representing a final growth of manly phallus, signifying quintessential maleness and potency.

In fact, it is an image frozen in the developmental subjectivity of the male. The growth of the penis, in the men's ritual pedagogy and practice, suggests the notion that the inseminations result in an elongation of the phallus as a "pure product" of semen. The sense of this "growth" is forever constitutive of the man's sense of virility and body image as he approaches sexual relations with boys and then later contemplates the dangers of sex with women. This sense of timelessness pervades the formation of male subject/object desires and relationships in the lifelong practice of ritual secrecy. Adult men cannot do without the barrier of ritual secrecy that separates them and enables their negotiation of sometimes tense and challenging situations, requiring deceit and manipulation on a personal level (Herdt and Stoller 1990: chap. 5). In short, the subjectivity of secret maleness embodies what I have previously referred to as the ideology of an Ideal Man, but this is a split image, the public adult warrior's mature body and the secret subjective body that is still "growing" as if it were a boy, in the cultural reality of the men's clubhouse.

Eventually the bachelor must give up the receptor role and become the dominant player who bestows the gift of semen to younger initiates. But does the youth have enough semen, and is his phallus sufficiently close to the imagery of Ideal Man that he will not be silently mocked by the younger initiate who will drink his sperm? This question hangs in the transitional space from being the subject who desires penetration by the older male to becoming the Ideal Man object who desires to inseminate a younger boy. The older youth also begins to anticipate marriage arrangements. A key informant, the youth Moondi, for instance, once told me how he began to fantasize about inseminating a favored younger initiate soon after his third-stage ceremony (Herdt 1987a: chap. 3; Stoller and Herdt 1985). Until that time he had perceived himself primarily as an object, not as much as a subject, in the mythopoetics and secret practice of being male. Within the year, though, he began for the first time to consciously desire women, specifically a younger woman betrothed to him, whom he eventually married, largely completing the transformation from object to idealized subject.

Ritual rebirth is a key to understanding this transformation in sexual subjectivity, for it appeals symbolically to suckling and breast-feeding, recast into sexually intimate relations between an older and younger male. The concept of feeding or *monjapi'u*—the sense of "feeding to grow or nurture"—is critical here (see Herdt 1981, 1984a). The orality of the sucking links sex with feeding, and semen with breast milk, in countless ways, literal and figurative, all essential to the embodiment of the intentional reality of trust and utopian commitment that the men try to inspire in the boys.

As Sambia equate semen with mother's milk, and allow for the substitution of semen later in life by certain white tree saps and cassowary grease, they condition their masculinity on the secret ingestion of fluids and essences. The initiate who sucks the young man's penis is imagined to be like an infant suckling at the breast. That nursing is fully fetishized can be seen from the fact that an adult man is aroused by the sight of a woman's breasts or the act of her nursing a child (Herdt and Stoller 1990: chap. 7) and that gazing on this is forbidden to men, especially the young father.

Suckling as a trope thus opens up as a major symbolic arena of ritual/emotional/erotic relationships in the homosociality of the men's clubhouse. Its secret ontology conceptualizes penis "suckling" which men do to "grow and feed" boys as the vital dietetic process necessary to attain manhood. Men also inseminate their wives, first through fellatio, and then in genital sex, in order to "grow" her breasts and make her a strong mother. The bachelors thus believe (literally, not metaphorically) that they "grow" boys, with a power to create secret masculinity, just as the boys' mothers once "grew" them. To say that the bachelors have "faith" in this belief system is a necessary redundancy because the elders go to great lengths to shelter the initiates from the "polluted" world of public affairs. Of course, it will easily be seen that the public discussion of this idea would subject the men to skepticism and a variety of forms of accusation of exploitation and manipulation of women and the younger boys, as the men themselves acknowledge when they say that they are *bomwalyu* men—middle men—situated halfway between sex with the boys and sex with women, which they must hide from both sides. Ritual secrecy obviously protects them from interrogation all the way around. But we should not think for one moment that the men are skeptical that their inseminations make the boys into strong warriors, since they explain their own personal development in this same way (Herdt and Stoller 1990: chap. 4). Such cynicism is a luxury of the modern period that can ill be afforded by people at war.

We begin to see how the clubhouse tried to produce the utopian sense of a hermetic circle of self-sufficiency—especially during the troubled times of warfare. What the men are producing, I think, is something more inclusive than politics, and that is their shared commitment as a men's house to their own conception of reality in the world. Perhaps one might say that power precedes the practice of boy-inseminating by creating institutions over which men have control; thus, in these societies, political power is a necessary, but ritual secrecy is the sufficient, condition to satisfy social reproduction.

The imagery of the Sambia Ideal Man entails both sexuality and power in the role of the budding young warrior. Not only is it a demonstration of the warrior's sexual expectations, but the mythology of the role provides a context for individuals to reflect upon the changes in their bodies and erotics that are privileged to males and regarded as "the gift" of secret initiation. Men fear the loss of semen as a vital essence. They require replenishment of the fluid from a secret white tree sap, also compared to milk and semen, which is always consumed after sex with boys and with women, to stay healthy. But it is women who are feared more than boys, a point that probably contributes to the persistence of boy-inseminating. Because male status and social position depend upon this achievement, which is regarded as neither "natural" nor "inevitable" in secret masculinity, the desire for change in one's body and social advancement mirrors a whole new area of subjectivities that transfer the desires onto culturally approved and sanctioned objects.

The ritual flutes are a key to understanding this merging and transfer of ontologies. The sound of the flutes, the *namboolu-aambelu* ("female frog," or better yet, "cry of the woman frog"), signifies a complex system of desires that become a product of power, pleasure, ritual knowledge, and advancement, all rolled into the orthodox symbol of two bamboo tubes (smaller/larger), always played in pairs, that are said to be "married." By contrast, the bull-roarer (*duka'-yungalu*, or "bird's cry") is marked as a male signifier and is used less to attract than to repel spirits of the dead, as well as to announce the funeral of a boy, at which event the flutes will be played out of sight. The idea of the "marriage of the flutes" as a metaphor for the man/boy erotic relationship is evocative but hidden totally from the public meaning of the flutes, said to be a "female frog." In the men's secret reality, however, the idea fans out to encompass a whole network of relationships and practices, and together with the sounds of the bull-roarer comes close to representing the totality of men's secret collective consciousness (in Durkheim's, and then Read's [1952], senses). While the jural contract of the homoerotic relation is missing from public discourse and affairs, ritual secrecy provides the necessary envelope for embodiment of the daily practice. Hence, we can understand how, through the imagery of ritual percussion instruments and sacred music, the secret ontology of subject/object relations and idealized Objects is extended beyond the men's house into the secular world that came before the clubhouse. In another context, Gillian Gillison has made a similar point: "Gimi men design flutes—and, by analogy, their whole society—not to valorize female fertility but to cure the fatal consequences of men's own desires" (1993: 354).

The metaphors and sensations of boy-inseminating represent for the boy physical attachment to men—though not as much to an individual man as the collective pool of semen (*kwei-waku*). Indeed, this secret image provides the secret name for the bull-roarer, thus signifying the actor's connection to associates in his time, their body substance, and the pool of past transmissions of substance that created them in turn (Herdt 1984b). The ritual metaphor becomes an omnibus representation for thinking and talking about transforming a man's sexual partner into a cultural producer in all major areas of male advantage: warfare, ritual, and marriage for reproduction. According to this mythopoetics, males and females differ in most respects of their being, including the origins of their being in the cosmos. The ritual development of the male is designed to create and reproduce this distinctive ontology. Ritual "death" and "rebirth" are basic to it: out of the symbolic processes of initiation a new being, a new person/self with a body of different substance, is born, and thus the genders in society are reproduced.

The duration of sociosexual relations between older and younger males is roughly coterminous with their residence in the men's house, that is, their bachelorhood. But the transition from initiate to bachelor, from being more like a boy to more like an Ideal Man, is difficult, halting, and often filled with anxieties, particularly for the younger boys in an age-grade and for those without the social support of powerful clan-families. Since third-stage initiation signifies advancement to marriageable status, requiring the willingness of the father and elders to bestow upon the youth an appropriate, nubile young woman for marriage, the loss of a father or the lack of a sister to exchange suggests the tenuousness of the supplicant without suitable symbolic capital or access to a suitable bride to complete his male personhood through marriage and fatherhood. This tenuousness is forever threaded into the life-crisis subjectivities of the transition out of the men's house.

Secret Conditional Masculinity

There are three great ritual secrets of Sambia men: the practice of nose-bleeding, which forces initiates to nose-bleed in order to remove female pollution and toughen their masculinity; oral insemination by an older male that is supposed to produce strength and masculinity, as well as virtue and good health; and the final revelation of the origin myth, which tells that once upon a time men were hermaphroditic. This hidden knowledge and practice entirely belies the public male mythology of male dominance. The men themselves are profoundly concerned that the women might learn of this knowledge and practice, which would make the men feel deeply shamed and humiliated. This thought is such a source of distress and subjective vulnerability to all initiated Sambia males that it can only be whispered in the men's cult house (Herdt 1981).

Ritual secrecy of course protects against disclosure (more properly, against public discussion of these matters). On pain of death, women and children are forbidden entry into the circle of secrets, especially the practices of ritual blood-letting and ritual insemination of boys by older males to masculinize them. Here, clearly, we find the echoes of Simmel's conception of secrecy as an antisocial force in this notion of restriction and manipulation. Such quaint practices, heavily tinged with power, pose a double challenge to the anthropology of secrecy. On the one hand, they implicitly undermine the public ideology of the men that they are superior to women. The reason for this is that in both of these ritual practices, men are apparently in jeopardy of seeming to imitate, even to identify, with women: the nose-bleeding as menstruation, the insemination as birth-giving. What the men are creating is a new form of reality, which includes new subjects and objects that obviate the idea that men imitate women. But this is also a reconstitution of the desires and morality of the boys. It is this latter association of ritual secrecy with the production of cultural reality that interests me most.

A general relationship between social consciousness and subjectivity is implied in this change. To recall Simmel's (1950) brilliant insight: secrecy has the enigmatic effect of heightening the social awareness of actors, even as it reduces their self-consciousness as individual actors. In another sense, secrecy creates perpetual stage fright and chronic self-evaluation, which are tangible in the anxiety one sees in men who prepare to stage public ceremonies in front of the entire village. Of course the self-awareness is absolutely vital to managing impressions and hidden desires while living in close quarters. Boys have to be taught, via a secret ontology, how to render a public performance in a seamless and pleasing way. They excel and master the challenge, but they pay a price in social and psychic vigilance that requires vast social energy to keep things intact.

This aspect of ritual secrecy may seem paradoxical because, in the Western preconception, social and self-consciousness are conflated or equated. But being intimate with others is having to live perpetually on stage, and we must not confuse social awareness with social engagement here: the differentiation process of secrecy accentuates social awareness. The lesson of ritual secrecy is that to harbor a secret leads the self to withdraw trust and self-presence from social interaction, which may be seen as diminishing social engagement from the perspective of the folk psychology of the "true" or essential self in Western life. From the perspective of Sambia ritual secrecy, however, it actually produces the opposite effect. By intensifying the withdrawal of trust from the public to the men's house, there will be greater awareness of impressions and performances and the rules of the public role, whether being enacted as father or shaman, as the secret ontology is safe and contained in homosocial recesses of the men's house. The social role in public affairs signifies elements of what we claim on the front stage; while secret positionality signifies what we are not but what we ought to be. By comparison, the Western system of contractual secrecy privileges notions of individualized "fantasy" or "clandestine contracts" behind closed doors, following the divergent logic of Cartesian subject/object and Freudian reality/fantasy splitting of consciousness. These conflate "individual fantasy/cultural reality" and physical reality in the time and space world (Herdt 1987d) as experienced by the patient who confesses to his doctor, or the client who consults her lawyer.

We should not interpret this secret and emerging cultural reality as if it were the same as myth, or as the unconscious, for ritual secrecy does not observe the distinctions we have made in anthropology between myth and thought (Young 1983; Obeyesekere 1992). Rather, being always hidden from certain others, and being sometimes intensely intimate, this stitched-together reality forms the necessary developmental basis for wrenching the boy from domestic sociality and subjective imagery, providing the sources for the phenomenology of the boy following his initiation at age seven. This is what ordinary reality in the adult is made from. Secrecy in the rest of the boy's life has such a power to charm; he is made to reckon with its dramatic and sometimes brutal revelations; but soon enough he comes to feel a growing faith in this nature of things.

The ethnographer of secrecy is thus witness to an ontological production in a double sense: the ritual secret is the invention of a men's culture that has a vested interest in making situated ideological claims about reality and society seem totally natural; while the individual actor accommodates to this contested turf by producing desires and performing ritual acts that reflect back upon the body-self as if his secret subjectivity was as inexorable as life and death.

Thus is necessity transformed into pleasure. In everyday sociality, commonsense impressions and their ramifications in action no longer seem as fundamental as they once did. Secret obligation assumes the intimacy of a community of believers who yearn for support from each other and a mode of self-rationalization in all of the meanings of their public actions. Where the boys begin actively resisting separation from their mothers' bodies and yearn to return to their fold, years of living in the men's house and sharing in the teachings of women's pollution actively transform the boys' desires for renunciation into active fear of menstrual blood and its traces on the female body (though a good Freudian would say that this idea is itself a token or rationalization, and thus represents a mystification of some deeper meaning buried in the unconscious). Merely to think of menstrual blood or the public metaphor for it (*pulungatnyi*) is to produce a compulsive spitting by a man, since he has taken the thing (menstrual blood) in his mind and mouth and must eliminate it. From puberty, when it is first rather awkwardly performed, through adulthood, the experience of this spitting, if not in fact the desire for it, contains the pleasure of taking in and eliminating that which is so dangerous (Herdt and Stoller 1990).

It is through these small and diminutive acts of masculinity, loaded as they are with secret training and knowledge, that we come to understand the development of secret systems of desire. Where the spitting begins in trauma for boys, the result of a dislocation they despise, it ends many years later in the self-motivated and often solitary acts of an adult man who clears his mind and mouth continuously—the admired and ultimate graces of being a Sambia man. This progressive "naturalization" of secret gestures is as seductive and unconscious as the experience of what Americans experience as "spontaneous" erotic desires, which conspire to descend upon the self, much as the ancient Greeks believed ideas to come into their heads from the gods (Simon 1977) or as the Japanese novelist Mishima (1954: 92) similarly described the aesthetics of social masks emerging as if inspired by spontaneous forces in the heavens.

Totalizing Systems

The Sambia refer to their system of collective initiations as *iku mokeiyu*, a multivocal concept that signifies a complex sequence of rituals and a collective male reality. *Mokeiyu* refers to a kind of central sacred fetish, blood-red from the shaman's headband wrapped around the bundle, shaped like a phallus and filled with power. Its potency is fundamental to building ritual cult houses, bestowing a kind of "growth fertility" upon their structures and persons. The fetish is used in a thumping ritual to stimulate body growth in boys by pounding their chests. *Mokeiyu* refers as well to ritual authority, a specialist (often but not always a shaman) of high degree, who "sings out" for other men to assemble and begin the ritual initiation process (Tali is such a specialist, though not a shaman). Finally, there is the sense in which the *iku mokeiyu*, or "ritual cult," engages the notion of a group of man-trees, since *iku* is the common term for tree, but is also the common lexeme for "patriclan," which also stands as a general signifier for "man." The idea easily merges into the notion that the *iku mokeiyu* represents the larger cultural formation of a group of men's houses that typically initiate their sons together.

This latter sense of *mokeiyu* has excess metaphoric value in its reference to a variety of features that embody or link a whole group of men who are thought, again in a diffuse but definite way, to share in the same body substance. The utopia of a collective pool of men, their bodily substances, especially semen, is iconic of a system of villages and territories. The power of the medicine bundle also promotes an identification with a phallic red thing that brings good health and long life. It's a remarkable indication of collective consciousness that Durkheim would no doubt have liked.

In fact, the concept of *kwei-waku*, or metaphoric "semen pool," calls to mind some of the traits most admired in the Sambia sexual subjectivity of the Ideal Man. By linking the bull-roarer and secret flutes to the semen pool, as the men do at the time of the cult-house raising, they prevail upon a generalized power in the time and space world—albeit known only to them, and hidden from women—a literal, embodied polity. Secretly men believe that all the men who ever played the flutes or twirled the bull-roarer claim inheritance of this semen pool (Herdt 1984b). The practice of boy-inseminating, the men believe, links the boy not so much to individual men as to the collective pool of semen, timeless and indestructible. The strands of these concrete and metaphoric meanings, hidden in the secret folklore of idiomatic male discursive practices, take years for the boy to piece together in what I am calling the secret masculinity.

The constitution of the men's houses as a cluster to form a regional cult of ritual secrecy involves now a whole range of elements: (1) the creation of a collective *mokeiyu* system; (2) the initiation of all males without exception into this system, which instills many ritual practices; (3) the initiates' seclusion in the men's house, which goes on for years, until fatherhood; (4) the use of icons, flutes, and bull-roarers to promote the collective designs and practices of the men's house; (5) the use of ritual pedagogy to communicate secret texts, and to warn of the sanction of death if the secrets are revealed; (6) the embodiment of power through semen from the older generation; (7) the notion that all boys, temporarily residing in the clubhouse of another village, are given immunity from war and death, and safe passage back to their village; (8) the renewal of the pledge to keep the secrets from women and children; (9) the sharing in a pool of ritual secret words and concepts, as noted in the idea of *kwei-waku*; (10) the emergence of a system of imagery, which takes a focus in desires, for an idealized and desired male sexual object, hypermasculine, which I have called the Ideal Man; (11) the final emergence of a system of subject/object relations, hidden from the public, which requires secret language and objects, and the ability to master the social construction of appearances and impressions of reality in daily life. I would claim that this rather sketchy and crude formulation comes closest to what we might call the collective sense of a men's secret society among the Sambia.

In piecing together this image of the cultural reality of secrecy among the Sambia we are led back to question the fundamental problem posed by Kenneth Read in his critical work among the Gahuku long ago. Read asked what made the cult a functioning entity, for the promotion of the collective good or integration of the society. But he also quickly implied that the men were staging a hoax in their secrecy because he could not see how their goals could be the same as the women's. Once we take the reality of secrecy seriously we can return to an earlier question: Why do the men need ritual secrecy in order to create agency and sociality?

The Men's Resistance to the Boys

The answer—to return to my opening argument—rests with our faulty conception of society as a shared consensual reality. There are contests for the definition of reality being shaped time and again by war or the threat of war in New Guinea societies like that of the Sambia. The men in these secret formations are in dire need of solidarity and compelling ways to bend the realities of social relations toward the purpose of military and political alliance. This is never easy to do; betrayal, assassination, sorcery, countersorcery, pollution and poisoning by women, as well as sheer threats of domination by other men, especially bands of warriors from other villages, hang in the air, tugging at the seams of consensual agreements on morality and maturity in these intimate communities. All of this is made more difficult by the strong and compelling manner in which women and preinitiate boys share in one domestic household, with a different calculus of morality and maturity—a divergent cultural world (Herdt 1987a).

Here finally we must confront the basic mistrust of the boys by their fathers—the resistance of the men to having their sons initiated. Many accounts of initiation focus on the anxieties of the boys in their fear of being conscripted into the rites. The boys' fears and anxieties are real and must not be underestimated (Herdt 1982a). However, from the perspective of the reproduction of the men's ritual society and secrecy, it is the profound disquiet and anxiety about trusting the boys that is perhaps a far greater threat to the clubhouse. What do the men have to fear? Primarily that the boys, once let into the secrets, will go back to their mothers and tell all. This would be a great humiliation and a devastation. But since the men's clubhouse is the seat of military strategy and war-making, the mistrust of the boy means that he might alert his mother or other women and children to the plans of the men for battle, tipping off the enemy and creating a potential disaster in case of attack. Why would the boy-initiate do such a thing to his own father and brothers? After all, does he not admire and respect them, and want to be like them? Will their legacy not be his; their land his; and his wife bestowed by them? All of this is true, and the objections must be registered in this rational manner, as we shall see in Barth's account of the Baktaman (chapter 4). However, we are not dealing only with rationality, but also with social mistrust and paranoia, and the dread of being responsible for death and destruction, the ultimate conditions of masculinity.

The new initiate, before he has been socialized into the men's beliefs and practices, is feared because he may be an unwitting agent of destruction, just as he was as a boy. He may unwittingly transmit pollution from his mother into the men's house. Likewise he may unwittingly spill secrets and give away the military plans and secrets of his men's house, should he enter into intimate relations with his mother. The fear of all of this is inflected in later male development and all sexual subjectivity in adult men; no doubt this early trauma is reflected in the fear of men and fathers alike, when they ponder the question: Can we trust this child?

Here again, the boy-initiate's compliance with the demands of the men's society to be inseminated by older adolescent bachelors serves as a general proxy for how the men assess their ability to trust in a particular boy. One who agrees, who is compliant, who is thought to obey, but also to intentionally follow the necessary taboos and ritual rules—such a boy is to be trusted with authority in public affairs. The men gradually gain in their confidence of him, and his status rises. Perhaps he will become a Great Man, perhaps not. They no longer monitor his behavior, or force the bachelors into surveillance of his comings and goings, as typically happens in the immediate aftermath of first-stage ritual initiation. Thus the rise in male agency is a direct expression of the boys' agreement with the men to be entrusted by them with their reality.

A clue to the alternative mode of sociality and reality-building comes from the role of the erotic in these secret ritual traditions. Secret initiation is the introduction to sexual development and erotic life not only for the Sambia. From Aboriginal Australia to the Papuan Gulf to the Sepik River area of New Guinea, wherever secret formations flourished, the nature of all sexual interaction was generally withheld from boys and girls until initiation. Many such societies actually disapprove of childhood sexual play. Sambia boys are fervent in associating the awakening of the erotic in them to their debut with adolescent bachelor partners. Surely the structuring of cultural reality is at issue, the stamp of the divine on the homoerotic a particular sign of a divergent ontology in these societies. Equally contested is the site of social reproduction—men's house or menstrual hut?—and how one gender or the other is ideologically shut out of the process. Perhaps it is the case that where local ontologies, placed in the service of gender differentiation and hierarchy, lead to the formation of secret societies, these will almost always be exclusively in support of male privilege, even domination. Among the Sambia, the excitement of homosociality and boy-insemination draws upon both its secrecy and the devotion to such privilege. Thus, among the Sambia, exclusion of women creates an idealized and fetishized Woman/Other, whose nature precludes understanding the ontology of the homoerotic in the development of the male. Surely we might think of this as a permanent misogyny that stems from too much liminality and too much of a division of community into permanent armed camps, all signs of a world of war.

Secrecy emerges from the tribal world as a form of differentiation that both solidifies and divides the genders, age groups, and thereby the known world. Contained within the ritual secret is a theory of being: of being male and female, young and old, higher and lower, social practices that create boundaries and formations. The effect is to reproduce these in the social order, as objects apart from the actor, a point that is difficult to grasp in the secrecy systems of Gahuku-Gama or Baktaman or Baruya. The insight is best grasped when these societies undergo rapid change, and we are, for a few moments, witnesses to the cultural realities of secrecy, before these die. *such*

Secrecy Disrupted

And this leads me back to the opening story. I had come with the Sambia, that quarter century ago, to hear and learn the secret myths. The Yagwoia elders were eager to tell them and were prepared to do whatever was necessary to bring this about, including scuffing up and removing their own grandsons. But why, I did not know; I know only that I felt bewildered and highly self-conscious; a White man, younger than some of the men's sons and grandsons, who had been shown the door. Of course politics and colonial power were in the air, but had I known they would re-create this conflict, I would have stayed in my village rather than witness the exclusion of a whole generation from the reproduction of the hidden reality.

Of course there was an accidental history to this "barn dance," one of those unexpected quirks of social change common to colonization: The younger men had never been initiated! Not one of them. Here they were, strapping youths, twenty-year-olds, and even men who looked thirty or more, who never knew the glories and grinds of initiation ordeals. They could not possibly have fathomed the embodied meanings of insemination the Sambia boys among our group had known.

Among the Yagwoia, the missionaries had done their job well; had arrived a generation before their beachhead among the Sambia. They were too numerous and remained too long among the Yagwoia, and the traditional secret practices were among their first targets. Their first step was to get rid of the ritual flutes. They did their best to oppose initiation and largely succeeded, at least in the elimination of all new recruits into the men's house. However, the adult men still had their secret reality, tucked away, in the form of the wonder-world of secret lore and all the stories and ritual teachings. They wanted to teach this; the urge to pedagogy was strong. No wonder the older Yagwoia men had shown such fascination with the Sambia lads in our company: the boys still practiced the tradition of boy-insemination, and it provoked the uncanny desire of those visited from the past by the shades of who they once were and never could be again.

A new taboo was issued: the ritual traditions would be kept secret from all subsequent generations; the sacred stories would survive in silence among the older generation. In that strange disconnected reality of secrecy, the elders could abide this only by teaching each other all they knew—a kind of reciprocal process of idealizing and making of each other Ideal Men. They had no choice when it came to the missionaries' oppression. But still, of course, they were dissatisfied; who was to receive and pass on the sacred stories and myths?

How could we know the problem that the Sambia and I presented to the cultural production of these old men? Their own grandsons were not initiated but we were. And not only were we not their offspring; we used to be enemies. But their sons—seemingly in defiance of the timeless quality of the secret world I have painted, and at least as far as their ritual system was concerned—were symbolically dead and gone forever to them. And even though we came from far away and I was White and the hour was late, I reckon that we, and I, offered the best chance to preserve their cultural treasures. Indeed, the plaintive note of this writing leads to my end point: the older cultural reality—the one produced in secret, and then hidden from the missionaries and ultimately from their own offspring—that world of hidden subjects and objects, and all it represented in the glory of their manhood—is now dying, if not in fact dead.

This is a romantic view, of course, and it is meant to counter the feckless cynicism that would see the secrets as empty vessels hidden from the missionaries who suspected them of being filled with subversion. Of much greater importance is the reality of the Yagwoia stories, for that is based upon a dialectic of what is secret and the corresponding system of desires and objects in the public domain. And all of that is of course gone and impossible to salvage except in the most crude and formulaic way. The sons and grandson-insiders were excluded and the enemy-outsiders included, a corruption of the creation of ritual secrecy as I have outlined it here. Obviously my status as a White man, a token of the colonial outside, as well as my privileged status as confidant and initiate of Sambia, allowed me to sit in and tape-record. I am not proud of the power contained in that fact; I am only grateful that the stories, however fragmentary, can be preserved for some future generation of Yagwoia. It was my social responsibility, living among the Sambia in those times, to share in the cultural ontology of the boys and men in these matters. They made me privy to their greatest secret, the myth of parthenogenesis (Herdt 1981). I am forever grateful to them for it.

What the Sambia see at that final most secret part—the revelation of the myth of parthenogenesis, at the end of the ritual cycle—is not empty, but a cosmic myth that explains not only the origins of human society, but the creation of the genders out of the original hermaphroditic state of humankind. Thus, the men see in this final stage vindication of their secret masculinity—that is, the lived experience created through ritual and now reflected back upon their long lives.

"Myths treat of origins but derive from transitions," Victor Turner (1968b: 576) once wrote, a bit of wisdom that links the Sambia with the Yagwoia in reckoning the nature of being in the world of war and ritual secrecy. For their sacred myth tells that once upon a time the world was originated by two beings of hermaphroditic nature, a blend of male and female anatomy, whose sexual interactions impregnated one and masculinized the other, thus founding society, but also initiating the secrecy on which male power and warfare were based. Sambia reckon their sons are too green to hear this story until they have already achieved fatherhood, and I think they are right. The hidden reality of the culture heroes and what they did and desired is too much for the youth to take when they are still growing up.

But for all of these indigenous and colonial bits and pieces of a drama of power and cultural loss among the Yagwoia, what really mattered in my hearing the stories, the Sambia have said to me, is that *they* had already staked a claim on my soul. This is a normative claim, by the way, typical of the religious sentiments and oaths that mingle between the generations. Sambia seemed to worry not only about the loss of names and souls being stolen by the Yagwoia—the sense of the power in those myths was still very great, in spite of the commotion—but about the peril to my own soul, in hearing, taking in—embodying—those myths. The evidence of their claim, as I have often been told, is that people have seen me—to be more precise, my "totems" or "spirit familiars," the iconography of my soul according to Sambia dream theory—in their own night dreams (Herdt 1987c; Herdt and Stoller 1990).

My "nature" was not the same as theirs because I had not grown up with the Sambia; my "growth" and "strength" as a male knew none of their embodiments. But it is equally true that I had come to share in the ritual world of Sambia men by witnessing so many of their initiations. Whatever differences existed between these two tribes, and indeed, the differences between the Yagwoia and their former enemies the Sambia were considerable, this much they knew that they secretly shared in common: an ancient practice of boy-inseminating rituals that created manhood. The Yagwoia elders seemed to know this in their first meeting with our troop, and the recognition of what was lost, and what might have been, was a powerful indicator of their decision to tell the myths. Their reality-sharing posited absolute faith in the hidden initiations as a time-honored means of the elders and ancestral spirits and the essences of semen to make a man out of what was once just a boy-thing. Perhaps in this peculiar way, too, my person (apart from the skin color) and ritual knowledge were closer to the Yagwoia elders than their own sons were, since the latter could never be initiated, or even see an initiation performed. My participation in Sambia rites, and my interest in them now, suggested a rather complete identification with the local theory of both being and doing secret male practices—totally at odds with the teachings of the missionaries. Before the time of European contact and missionary efforts, ritual practices had been a screaming secret in Yagwoia society, too, separating male from female, and elder from younger. Today, however, the rites are dead, truly a whispered secret unknown to the most recent generations, suggesting the kind of historical hiatus that brings down empires and raises new ones. Perhaps the one thing worse than having lost the power to regenerate reality, the legacy to pass on to sons, is the absolute dread that the secrets, if passed on, might be misused, laughed at, and spoiled, the kind of betrayal that might end in the self-blinding sacrilege of an Oedipus.

We must not think that the story of the loss of secrecy among the Yagwoia is by any means unique. Maurice Godelier has observed for the Baruya:

The initiation ceremonies—which had never been discontinued among the Baruya during the colonial period but had merely been held far from the gaze of the missionaries and the soldiers—

increased in scale albeit still without the rituals associated with war, which was now forbidden, and with homosexual relations between the initiates, which were on the decline. (1995: 73)

The decline hastens, and wherever secrecy is at stake, the pressure is increased.

These younger Yagwoia men, shamefully excluded from the secret stories by their elders, were excluded because their *elders* felt shame that their offspring were not initiated. The youths were not proper, virtuous, moral masculine persons in the eyes of their fathers and grandfathers: they were the Other. While this allusion in their remarks seemed to indicate the missionaries, it will be clear that the exclusion from the clubhouse (which used to be primarily directed against the Woman/Other) somehow also discolors their relations with their own uninitiated sons. Today their sons have souls claimed by others: namely, the Christian missionaries. How could the young men understand their elders' form of secrecy at all, the latter wondered out loud? Not only does this Christian civilization not know their sons' real Yagwoia names—the childhood names that should have given way at the time of initiation to grander, warrior names of old—but their sons carried Christian names that were utterly foreign and meaningless to them. In the great song-ropes of the civilization of Anga-speaking societies, including the Sambia (Herdt 1989b), a man can only be known by his inherited ancestral name, which is celebrated in a name-song, linked to many other names, past and present, of his lineage and their territory, a wonderful rope of identity-songs. All of that is lost to the Yagwoia. Truly, their fathers felt, they no longer shared in the same substance, the same being, as themselves. Their nature cannot be the same as that of their fathers. And my willingness, indeed, my eager desire to hear those sacred stories and take them into my being, made of myself a means to reproduce their cultural reality temporarily.

A generation ago, Roy Wagner wrote of another New Guinea people in a completely different context: "Life, then, is for the Daribi a matter of retaining one's soul in its association with one's body, of keeping one's free will and mobility, and of holding at bay the world of influences and entities which would 'bind' the soul and tear it free of its matrix" (1967: 61). The idea rings true also of the Sambia and the Yagwoia, except that there is a secret ritual embodiment that they provide and demand, which they believe vital to create and nurture the soul, through long years of gender-segregated seclusion. This ritual embodiment is their manhood. A man's soul is the embodiment of all that tradition and secret ontology, which, when torn asunder, renders all of sacred life meaningless.

Here is what the Yagwoia elders found so intolerable: the terrible old threat of betrayal of the secrets by their own sons. They felt that the influence of the missionaries could never be trusted. As Godelier has suggested for the Baruya, betrayals of all kinds occur in social life, including terrorism, rapes, and so on, and these are usually "forgivable"—with one exception:

> Such are the betrayals by initiates, men or women, who pass on to members of the other sex the secrets and powers of their own sex. These betrayals jeopardize the very foundations and mechanisms of domination and exploitation of one part of society by other. They run directly counter to the major contradiction in these classless societies, which is the subordination of one sex to the other, of women to men. They impinge upon people's conceptions of the order of society and the universe. They flout the ideological teachings and the whole edifice of legitimization built around this order. (1989: 179)

We begin to understand the intolerable plight of the Yagwoia elders, who felt not only that they had been "robbed" of their own sons by the missionaries. The chaos visited upon them and the treachery of their sons' and grandsons' rejection of the secret initiations were unpardonable. For surely to feel rejected by one's own son because of what one is, the very nature of one's flesh and being, a product of secret ritual, is a kind of castration on a cosmic level. The elders cared nothing for Christian heaven. They felt only the betrayal of their sons' necessary support since the elders' souls depended upon their sons' ritual observances and memorization to ensure their own immortality. Pity them for what they have lost in the virtues of society as much as for how they fear an indefinite future and loss of immortality. Here we see at last that the stakes in ritual secrecy are the material world as it is, and the utopian world as it is intended to be, forever.

My fate will be complete when, on another day, those Yagwoia myths, published and then recycled back to their real origin hole, fall into the hands of the by-then literate grandsons and great-grandsons of the men in this story, who receive them as completely strange, not familiar at all—the token of some weird lost tradition; or worse, they are greeted with hostility and thrown back in my face as the inventions of a strange old White man who obviously never knew the culture because, after all, there never was secrecy.

It is through such stories that anthropology remains forever humbled by the small role it has played in such dramas of change; not in causing it, for we have but little power; rather in witnessing the creeping rationalism of Western expansion that normalizes reality by rejecting the lessons of all other cultures. The practice of ritual secrecy is a way of dealing imperfectly with messy and incoherent threads of social relations, especially the anguish of being unable to live up to one's rights and duties in such a warring society; this creates a torment of being male and having a masculine nature that is incomplete, not strong and big enough, to match the image of the Ideal Man. The deployment of secrecy for domination is a common result. For some, the demise of secrecy is liberating; many women experience it this way. For others it represents the loss of the treasure of aboriginal rituals and the role they played in creating the reality of people of all kinds. The elders experience it this way. What stands in their place is denuded and secondhand; the former certainty of their place in the world—created by ritual secrecy out of the cultural imagination—now gives way to another mode of social life based on principles of opposition to secrecy. But these are no more open or certain than before, though they are much more drab.

CHAPTER 4

Paradox of the Men's House

�֎

Handwritten margin note: Herdt does seem to write like Derrida in that there is often no simple point to a q but a chain of ideas

THE DAILY LIFE OF RITUAL SECRECY in the precolonial societies of New Guinea depended upon the shifting political economy of local peoples—especially their sense of how the world was forged in war, and what trust and loyalty meant for survival in a volatile world. The institution of the men's house was vital to communal security in many of these communities. Its secrecy enabled political alliances in the never-ending play of local politics that underlay the arranged marriages vital for offspring if not in fact military advantage. However, all of these advantages were purchased through conditional masculinity—the warrior's contingent agency of limited duration, dependent upon the context and ritual secrecy of homosociality in the men's house.

A paradoxical theme emerges from the ethnography of conditional masculinity in New Guinea: in public affairs the men professed their superiority to enemies and women, while in secret they confessed their inferiority and dread of woman as Other (Herdt 1982a). Ritual secrecy, however, was the means of creating and itself became the divergent reality of the men's house, ultimately expressing an idealizing, if not utopian desire of the men for trust in their comrades—a call to a purer, cleaner, orthodox, and resplendent masculinity, removed from the pollution and instabilities of the world.

The creation of ritual secrecy requires an institutional nexus for its symbolic location and the political uses of privileged space for the provisioned reality. Generally in Melanesia this need was met in the men's clubhouse of precolonial communities. Centrally located in each village, but unapproachable due to ritual and gender-segregated taboos, the clubhouse was the nerve center and massing place for male action in secret, private, and public affairs. Likewise, "ritual power" was stored there, in the implements and body decorations of initiation, which ensured not only the preservation of ritual authority, but also a continuous and inalienable link to distant dream and myth time ancestors (Herdt 1987c; A. B. Weiner 1992). The men's house served political strategizing, suggesting a crude grass-roots intelligence organization, the internal discourse of which was suspicious of everything beyond its immediate surveillance. Its grip was not uncontested, however, as can be inferred from its taboos marking all others as *the* Other. This difference, between the spatial centrality of the clubhouse and the taboos that roped it off, forms the enigma of screaming secrets in New Guinea villages.

The men's house was by definition a culturally constituted homosocial and male-privileged space, as seen from the fine ethnographies of Kenneth Read, Fredrik Barth, and Maurice Godelier (reviewed later). Access through initiation was thus age-graded and hierarchical: first by gender; second by age; third by the commitment to emulate and aspire to be a Great Man; and finally, toward the end of life, by that die-hard sense of clinging to power and hence to utopian immortality. But how is it possible for a house of conditional masculinity to "produce" immortality?

Quite simply: through rituals of rebirth and regeneration in which it is claimed that men have the ritual power and means in secret to "grow" boys into men. As boys matured they may have developed a social desire to be included in this inner circle, even before they had the faintest idea of what it meant. Nevertheless, the same small boys were highly ambivalent, many even resistant, to joining the secret club. Life histories of Sambia males typically remark on the dread of the men's house; the fear was heightened by an intense curiosity about what was going on inside this forbidden place only a few steps from where mothers nursed their children (Herdt 1987b). Already, desire for the hidden was taking shape in the form of the child's hide-and-seek, the forerunner to secrecy. A cultural ideal was stamped into the clubhouse: in that space lives another, more powerful reality.

Initiation into the men's clubhouse in Melanesia is a species of what we in the West would call "religion" as broadly defined by the concern with ultimate matters and the appeal to spirits and spiritual dimensions of human life. Ritual secrecy is especially necessary to the development of the moral and social career of the person. It enables the initiate to deal with the conflicting demands and competing realities of everyday life. As Peter Berger once remarked of a parallel matter, "It would be erroneous to think of these situations as being rare." He continued, "The reality of everyday life, therefore, is continuously surrounded by a penumbra of vastly different realities." After debating the merits of these competing points of reference, he concluded: "Where religion continues to be meaningful as an interpretation of existence, its definitions of reality must somehow be able to account for the fact that there are different spheres of reality in the ongoing experience of everyone" (1969: 42). However much this holds true for the West, it captures precisely the struggle to predict reality in precolonial New Guinea (Knauft 1995).

Ritual, in Melanesia, is, among other things, a form of property—spiritual property—which requires secrecy to ensure "copyright protection" for its powerful and most precious form of production: existence, being, and reality. The sense of this was heightened by kinship and clanship, of course, as the proprietary agents claimed common descent or blood or geographic provenance (A. J. Strathern 1974). The protective secrecy, a privilege of the men's house, warded off assassins, shamanic opponents who might rob one's "soul," and women who would pollute or deplete a man through sexual intercourse and thus damage the fighting force of the local clubhouse. In such a cosmological conception, individual actors are dependent upon others for their well-being, which is, of course, the elementary structure of the age-grade and age-mate principle in such societies. To have the soul removed, to be polluted in one's being and body by menstruating women, to lose the secrets of ritual purification and regeneration—these are the great fears of male secret societies located in men's houses, and protected against by secrecy (Lawrence and Meggitt 1965; Read 1965). But I hasten to add that all these are significations of impermanent reality beyond control of the self (Harrison 1993).

However, as we have seen, religious initiation in these Melanesian cultures was often an introduction to sexual life—an extraordinary idea to contemporary Western thinking. We can add that the intimacy of men's house, and the desire for the male as the idealized object, placed sexuality in the context of conditional masculinity. Earlier reviews of the evidence on boy-inseminating rites (Herdt 1984a, 1993) barely touch upon the element of ritual secrecy. In general, however, Melanesian homoerotic practices were ritual secrets, typically guarded by men, though there are exceptions to this, as among the Marind-anim (Van Baal 1984), for whom the secrecy was semipublic. But what of those New Guinea societies that lacked homoerotic traditions? We can infer clues from the tropes of ritual secrecy and sound instruments (Herdt 1982a). The ritual flutes among Gahuku-Gama, for example, were said to be "age-mates" (Read 1965: 144), a very close bond. Their music was said to vitalize, even eroticize, relations between males, though homoerotic relations among them were absent (Herdt 1982a; Read 1984). The liminality created by the protections of ritual secrecy thus provoked intense, intimate, and sometimes erotic feelings and desires, as among the Gebusi (Knauft 1986). Thus, homosocial coresidency allowed but did not enjoin homoerotic relations, and the men's houses created closely hovering desires indicative of these cultures, though rarely marked as such by the ethnographies in question (Herdt 1991b; also see Knauft 1987, 1995).

Little was taken for granted in the close quarters of these feudal villages. And yet, in a peculiar way, ritual secrecy was accepted as being so close to reality that it moved into the background. As we have seen in the Sambia (chap. 3), people did not fully realize that they "practiced secrecy" or avoided thinking about someone else's secrecy. This was mighty strange in view of the fact that many of these situations involved people living within a tiny hamlet or village that defined itself as an extended family or clan, sharing in common ties of blood and marriage (Bateson 1958). However, at the time of initiation, this ordinariness was dismissed, and ritual secrecy with all of its risks and excitement moved into the foreground. Let us at least recall the difference between these two shifting atmospheres within the same small social field as the contrast between screaming and whispering secrets (Herdt 1981).

In New Guinea cultures ritual secrecy frequently involved a kind of gendered knowing and unknowing—a domination of imagery and language, requiring duplicity or complicity on the part of both sexes, who played their respective roles in the social drama of contested village life. The knowing of secrets inevitably led to divergent gendered lifeways (Herdt 1997a). People's narratives of these lifeways often mention threats of death and the fear of discovery or the "temptation of disclosure," as noted by Herdt and Stoller (1990, esp. chaps. 5, 6). Fear of "accidental" disclosure inculcated more dread than is typically registered in the regional ethnographies (e.g., Lewis 1980; cf. Gillison 1993). Understanding these anxieties is vital to the political psychology of precolonial New Guinea, particularly in times of war.

The use of ritual secrecy to constitute politics and individual developmental experience is of course not unique to New Guinea. As Ottenberg brilliantly summarized in his seminal study on West Africa, "I believe that at Afikpo it is through secrecy associated largely with the boys' and men's secret societies, and with sexual matters, that the child is often provoked to thought and action" (1989: 56). He goes on to suggest that their ritual secrecy is thus formative of culture and individual life course in tandem. Ritual secrecy is a device for "masking" or "screening" or "veiling" the self—that is, fueling personal intentions in the time and space world amid the contradictory intimacies of domestic routines, particularly sexual relations. This point is especially germane to the relationship between ritual secrecy and warfare. If it is true that secrecy shields the intentionality of individual actors, then we begin to understand how difficult it must be to secure trust between villagers, even male comrades (Poole 1982).

Ritual secrecy was traditionally vital to the maintenance of all social control, including warfare, in and between social groups. For all genders, it provided concepts and mechanisms for essentializing or naturalizing (Keesing 1982a) the production of social rank, deference, and social interaction across age-cohorts and genders. It regulated the social distance of age groups, thus maintaining the necessary opprobrium between peers in tense situations of conflict. It is in such situations that we should speak less of "secrecy" and more of social relations that contain hidden dimensions that made masculinity contingent (M. Strathern 1988: esp. 207ff.). The hidden reality for males orders a parallel system of social rank and status, directly or indirectly expressed in public (Bercovitch 1989b). Secret initiation thus stratified males and pitted them against public classifications of all other person/actors, women and children being essentialized as Other, which forever foreclosed the possibility of harmony and did much to precipitate trouble in village sociality.

However, as Harrison has brilliantly observed in his study of the Sepik River area Avatip people:

> War is therefore not an absence or failure of social order but their attempt to *make real one of the alternative conceptions of social order*. It is action aimed at imposing an objective, sociocentric order upon what, in ritual context, they conceive as a subjective, interpersonal moral order of relations of kinship and marriage. In the tradition of thought which Hobbes and Sahlins belong to, it is war that is taken for granted as the natural state that has to be transcended through the imposition of political order so as to create peace. But to Avatip

men it is rather sociality that is taken for granted. This sociality is
the background state that men must overcome [to] establish . . .
political relations between enemies, between men and women, and
between senior and junior men. (1993: 145, emphasis added)

I am fundamentally in agreement with this view. But I am emphasizing
conditional masculinity and how war can produce or "make real" a "conception" of the world. Cultural reality in turn anchors gender and intergenerational differences, and these are refracted back through ritual
secrecy—an idealized, alternative reality at the core of the men's house (see
also Lindenbaum 1984; Whitehouse 1995). Thus, the term *social order* in
this model is codependent upon *cultural reality*, in particular, the shared
male reality created through initiation that maintains power in the men's
house. That may be why Harrison stresses the distinctively New Guinea
preconception that war is a social, not a natural, state.

The social construction of masculinity was contingent upon this state
of affairs. Hence social reproduction required the production of a special
form of conditional masculinity via ritual secrecy. But this suggestion
impels us to think further about the relationship between ritual
classification, male agency, and social regulation.

Ritual Classifications: Persons and Agency

Major sources of ritual and ceremonial activity in New Guinea and
Melanesia begin with reviews of Codrington (1891), Haddon (1920),
Lawrence and Meggitt (1965), Mead (1933, 1949), Read (1954), Watson
(1965), Wedgwood (1930), and then are followed by the sophisticated
comparative studies by Allen (1967), Barth (1975, 1987), Godelier and
Strathern (1991), Harrison (1993), Herdt (1981, 1982a, 1982b, 1984a),
Keesing (1982a), Lutkehaus and Roscoe (1995), Poole (1981), Schwimmer
(1980), A. J. Strathern (1968), M. Strathern (1988), Tuzin (1982), Van Baal
(1963, 1966), and Whitehead (1985, 1986). Many unpublished disserta-
tions from the period contain critical information as well (e.g., Bercovitch
1989b; Jones 1980). Generally, with the exceptions of Allen (1967, 1984,
1998), Gillison (1993), and Tuzin (1980, 1982, 1997), these studies have
not specifically addressed the phenomenon of ritual secrecy. For example,
Whitehead was critical of past work on male cults and suggested two
"dominant emphases" for understanding variation in New Guinea: "Forg-

ing a common ritual manhood between men of disparate, kin-defined units," the so-called manhood cults, versus "those cults the dominant emphasis of which is upon reinforcing solidarities within kin-defined units" (1986: 82). Ideas of clan substance and inheritance or transmission of the corporeal or incorporeal properties of clans from generation to generation link putative male ancestor to grandfather, and father to son (Feil 1987), regenerating kin groups.

Michael Allen's structural-functional classification remains useful in understanding two pervasive cultural patterns of ritual secrecy in New Guinea. Allen's (1967) project was to compare, classify, and argue the merits of solidarity and male social grouping in the ethnographic record of Melanesia (see Feil 1987: 133f.; Hays 1992; M. Strathern 1987: 288–89, 1988; J. F. Weiner 1988, for recent critiques). Later surveys were amplified by A. J. Strathern (1979) and Paula Brown (1978) for Highland peoples, Roger Keesing (1982a) for Coastal and Highland groupings, and Herdt (1984a) and Lindenbaum (1984) for fringe societies that practice boy-insemination (see also Feil 1987; Knauft 1993; M. Strathern 1988). Allen's distinction between puberty rites ("change in individual status rather than change of group membership") and initiation rites, which in turn are organized by men's societies (Allen 1967: 5; 1984), remains a pivotal refinement of Van Gennep's (1960) model of the rites of passage. Allen (1967) drew the following contrasts and definitions between the two sets of rites.

Ceremonial coming-of-age and puberty rites were often organized for boys, but also well recognized for girls; and in a few rare places, such as the Orokolo on the Papuan Gulf, jointly organized for both sexes. In the Lowlands these matters are often viewed as causative of "fertility" (a much misused term: Hauser-Schaublin 1989), or necessary for residence transfer (Williams 1940). In the Highlands they are usually constructed around bachelorhood cults, associated with purification, purging, and sweating, which typically embody sexuality as a theme of maturation, though not always (Brown 1978; Meggitt 1964). Secrecy may be played down and even disappear toward that end of the spectrum of societies in which relations between the genders were more harmonious and institutionalized sexual antagonism was largely absent (Herdt and Poole 1982).

Initiation rites are typically organized through secret associations or cults, almost always gender-segregated, generally male-dominated even if female-sponsored, and symbolically preoccupied with growth and fertility of the body, especially the male body (Allen 1967; Barth 1975; Gillison

1980, 1993; Keesing 1982a; Hays and Hays 1982; Herdt 1982b, 1984b; Langness 1974; Poole 1982, 1986; Read 1965; M. Strathern 1988; Tuzin 1980). These rites are typically divided into two forms: those that utilize boy-inseminating practices for the purpose of "growing" the body or fertilizing it (Herdt 1993) and those that utilize analogic practices and body fluids, sweat, blood, milk, and so on, as the means of stimulating and promoting growth, health, and social maturity (Allen 1998; Barth 1975; Knauft 1993; M. Strathern 1988; Whitehouse 1998). Allen's work was foundational and heuristic in its attention to ritual secrecy.

> I suggest that the criterion of secrecy be included in the definition of initiation ritual. Those rites that are in no way secret, yet in all other respects are similar to initiation rites, could be termed induction rites. Like initiation rites, but unlike puberty rites, induction rites result in the novice becoming a member of a discrete social group or category. An example of such rites would be those performed when one or more individuals assume a new title in the public graded societies of the Banks Islands and the northern New Hebrides. (1967: 7)

Allen's insight is important for suggesting that secret initiations into relatively exclusive male groups, typically organized around beliefs in spirit beings, hidden power, and knowledge, are residentially organized in men's clubhouses. The aim of initiation into these secret collectives is to refashion or radically resocialize (Herdt 1981) the boy-initiate, often by ordeals that deconstruct basic elements of reality itself—gender, sexuality, power, and their subjectivities in desires, drives, concepts of emotion and ideation, beliefs, and attitudes that condition the agency of the male person. Such an analysis must take account of the classical model of the rites of passages and "life crisis" changes that are distinctive of anthropological study in New Guinea as elsewhere (Turner 1967; Van Gennep 1960).

However, this model never explained the remarkably long duration of liminality, that is, the removal of male initiates from secular social life in New Guinea communities. As hinted before and discussed later, years of liminal seclusion were necessary, I believe, for the suppression of anxiety and ambivalence and for the production of trust between older and younger males. Secret masculinity, dependent upon ritual secrecy, ensured authority and rule in the men's house.

What recruitment criteria govern entry into ritual secret formations? Is entry voluntary or involuntary? (Wedgwood 1930 emphasizes this definitional criterion.) When ritual secrecy underlies the development of the whole person and the competent performance of vital areas of social life, initiation is generally obligatory for all individuals who belong to a larger group or to the stipulating criteria (e.g., male or female) in the developing person. First, by making ritual secrecy the force behind agency in the group, actors understand that the whole person will be "motivated" by ritual knowledge, practice, and the desire for advancement into greater authority in the internal hierarchy. Second, to permit exceptions is of course to call into question the totalism of these fundamentalist ideologies. Thus, in the vast majority of New Guinea Highland cultures, wherein developmental criteria stipulate ritual initiation to attain competent adulthood, initiation is obligatory for all members of a gender category (i.e., males), and typically for the other gender as well. No exceptions are permitted (see Herdt 1987a, where it is reported that even the blind, deaf, and mentally disabled are initiated). Why? Because masculinity is conditional, even the possibility of exceptions would threaten to undermine the absolute imperative that all males join the ranks and fill up the men's house. Third, in interethnic relations, the perception that ritual secrecy lies behind roles and social order serves to mediate regional and intertribal relations (Barth 1971; Van Baal 1966; Whitehouse 1998).

Ritual secret status advancement, either hereditary (Deacon 1934) or achieved (Godelier 1986), at least in part (Schieffelin 1982) depends upon a variety of factors, well outlined by Poole (1982). Among these are age, which is primary (both age of onset and subsequent initiations); age-grade and cohort peer advancement; pace of individual growth and maturation; ability to marry; perceived moral responsibility; economic and political achievements; and support by wider kindred, clan, or men's clubhouse group. Generally, "competence" and "rectitude" in demonstrating and handling secret knowledge are acclaimed, as M. Stephen's (1994) brilliant and beautiful ethnography of secrecy in a Papuan sorcerer reveals. We might contrast prescriptive initiation, typical of male initiation systems and bachelor cults in Highlands and Lowlands New Guinea (Brown 1978; Feil 1987), and "optional" or elective membership based upon provisional interests or concerns of female actors and male/female groupings (Allen 1967; Wedgwood 1930). However, the distinction is not absolute; Schieffelin (1982) speaks of Kalului growth and insemination ceremonies as a kind of bachelor cult that serves as an "alternative" or "optative" paradigm to initiation. Intense social change complicates this account, as initiation was linked with marriage arrangements, and Schieffelin suggested that the contracts were uncertain in the life course of the boy. How far aggressive mission pressure to end traditional ritual practices was a factor in this is unclear but it must be relevant (Schieffelin 1978; Schieffelin and Crittenden 1991).

Four theories of ritual secrecy merit outline for the following ethnographic comparisons. The first of these, historical diffusionism, follows the ideas of Codrington (1891), Haddon (1917, 1920, 1924), and Rivers (1917) that rituals were diffused from one place to another, that they had an "unconscious" aspect, and that they revealed something of "primitive character," in keeping with the last breath of nineteenth-century evolutionary anthropology. These writers—and Rivers was especially influential—suggested that ritual secrecy had been "invented" in prehistory and then exported from place to place, along putative coastal or trade routes, ultimately finding its way symbolically into the cultural traditions of others. The second theory—dominant throughout the twentieth century—is the structural-functional model, which posits that ritual secrecy is for the generation of male group solidarity and cohesion in agnatic societies (noted in the review of Allen 1967). Durkheim's problem of the existence of collective representations over individual experience is relevant here: these theorists argue that ritual secrecy counters the tendencies of individuals to dissemble or dissolve their commitments and loyalties to the ritual group (Keen 1994). Generally, this approach suggests that secret fraternities maintain "the society" as a whole, avoiding the major contradictions such organizations posed for internal cohesion, as noted in chapter 2 (Read 1952; and see below).

The third theory veers away from structures and functions and instead emphasizes the symbolic, especially discursive meanings of ritual practices themselves. As modes of meaningful or semiotic expression, this line of theory can be traced to Malinowski's (1922, 1935) practice-oriented accounts of gardening spells or *kula* magic, in his ethnographies of the Trobriand Islands. In this great corpus we have, I think, the first sophisticated and compelling study of "primitive" secrecy, albeit one that is closer to the form of what I earlier referred to as contractual secrecy. However, in making an overly sharp distinction between magic and science in later writings, associated with an overly blurry definition of science, Malinowski fell into the trap of nineteenth-century comparisons between primitive and modern that confused and undermined his contributions to the study of secrecy (see also Tambiah 1990: 67–68, 140ff.).

In more recent work on initiation rites some elements of this discursive theory of ritual meaning have implied the subjectivity and agency of the individual in cultural production. Critics of the structural-functional approach have pointed the way, suggesting the limitations of consensual theories of meaning for secrecy studies (J. F. Weiner 1988). My own work belongs here, but is critical of reductive aspects of the literature (Herdt 1981). Precursors to this approach can be found in the ethnographies of Bateson (1932), Wirz (1933), certainly in Mead (1938, 1949), Lawrence (1964), and Schwartz (1973), as well as Van Baal (1963). A later generation gave credence to what Schwimmer calls the "semiotic function" of secrecy, most noticeably in the comparative ethnography of Forge (1966), Gillison (1993), Knauft (1993), Lewis (1980), Schieffelin (1976), A. J. Strathern and M. Strathern (1971), and Tuzin (1980), among others.

Power and Ritual Secrecy

To understand power as the central paradox of conditional masculinity in these societies we must continue to rethink the role of the men's house as a means of the production of culture and the creation of reality. Deconstructing the multidimensional functions and meanings of the local men's clubhouse in ideology and practices of secrecy is vital to interpret the strategic uses of ritual secrecy for agency and social relations in public, private, and secret. Rather than treating power as a given, or as rule by men as given by power, we should instead critically interrogate how power is generated through the men's house. As Langness (1974) once argued, the power to dominate is oblique, especially with regard to the internal discourse and ritual practice of males who form stable identity systems (Herdt 1982b). Here, Langness apparently equated rule with power and assumed the inherent "natural" tendencies of male power to be exploitative of women and children. This not only misunderstands the character of precolonial power in these societies and the authority that rested upon a tenuous intergenerational trust in the men's house, but it also underrates the incredible uncertainty, vulnerability, and contingent qualities of male agency beyond the men's house in public life.

Again, why secrecy? The fundamental issue is to consider why these systems of male power vested in the men's house are unable to achieve their goals through physical means. Why do men need the aid of ritual secrecy (Herdt 1990)?

Generally, ethnographies of male initiation in the structural-functional approach have not problematized power sufficiently to answer these questions. Power was typically regarded as having the generally positive function in the Durkheimian sense of producing social solidarity (explicitly by and for the men: see Read 1954 and the critique in Herdt 1982b). For this reason there is a special historical interest in tracing the intersection between ritual secrecy and power in the work of K. E. Read. By the next generation of the late 1960s and 1970s, however, "ritual power" was equated with "male power," and it was interpreted more cynically, even in a destructive light. Ian Hogbin's (1970) Wogeo narrative is the more benign side of a romantic cynicism that makes fun of the men's power, and indeed the book is paradigmatic of what was wrong with this approach in the 1970s and 1980s prior to feminist writing. Langness's (1974) study exemplifies a more negative cynicism, suggesting how men's ritual secrecy exploited "power" in the most general sense, the domination of women and boys by physical force. By contrast, Godelier's (1982, 1986) work on the Baruya, coming out of French neostructural theory and neo-Marxist philosophy, critically explores male domination as a contradiction in political economy, trust, and loyalty, and their symbolism.

In the following reinterpretations of the literature, we shall try to locate these shifting sands of theory, with an eye to understanding the unfolding intellectual history of ritual secrecy in New Guinea studies. Many of the studies previously addressed and those to follow labored under the burden of the highly negative attitudes within our own society that suggest how secrecy is antisocial. Moreover, the conflation of "ritual secrecy" with "contractual secrecy" has also confused individualized versus collective interpretations of issues that require separate social, political, and ultimately historical explanations.

Agents of Change: Unprecedented Women

The story of Lewis Henry Morgan with which this study began is about the transformation of personal experience and objectification of the culture as the means to becoming a cryptographer of secret realities. Just as the change in Morgan's historical period ushered in a contest between the followers of Handsome Lake and Native American revivalism and those of traditional medicine societies among the Iroquois, so too have anthropologists working in the Pacific more broadly and New Guinea in particular found themselves in situations of irreversible change. As agents of colonial rule in the indirect sense, the observer on the scene, as instanced by the remarkable observations of K. E. Read (1986) at first contact in the Highlands, is placed in the precarious position not only of witnessing but of actually participating in the demise of traditional secrecy.

While cargo cults are no longer prominent in New Guinea, extensive and sweeping forms of fundamentalist Christianity are everywhere present in Melanesia. Airplanes in New Guinea stepped up the search for the "brown gold" of fundamentalist Christianity: locals to be washed and refined for eternity. Missionaries are shaking the doors of the men's house, and shaking up the received theories of realities that ritual secrecy once defended. Indeed, in many a place the traditional men's cults manage a tenuous coexistence with these messianic Christian movements. The missionaries are critical to these processes of change, though anthropology has until recently been too skeptical of their intents and purposes to study them as social phenomena in their own right or to discern regional patterns of messianic work (Barker 1990). Fortunately, a spate of new studies has made these versions of fundamentalism an object of serious study in Melanesia (Carrier and Carrier 1989; Lattas 1999).

Most of the scholars who initiated fieldwork after the 1960s have had to grapple with myriad traces of the decline of ritualism in Papua New Guinea and the off-lying island societies of Melanesia. They have generally not studied ritual secrecy in depth or have relegated it to the margins of comparison. In part this is due to the overall decline of ritualism and ritual secrecy. Yet it may stem from the longer and more pervasive intellectual and social history already alluded to: an intellectual trend away from the study of traditional religion and cosmologies and their forms of enactment because they seem to be "exotic" social practices.

We might call this the "missing discourse" on secrecy in the experience of anthropologists. Just as secret ritual practices protect against the outside, so do they present the most formidable barriers to ethnographic study. These barriers, as we have noted from the study of the Sambia, protect against the corruption of outside and unfettered knowledge. In such systems there is no conceptual contrast between secret and private as we know it. However, what is prevalent are "spiritual" or holy places that are restricted to those who are initiated, who belong in their circles of power, who believe in the hidden on the basis of faith, even when it cannot be seen. Among the interlopers and uninitiated Innocents, we must count a new and unprecedented species of woman—the anthropologist on scene—as a prime suspect.

Of course, Margaret Mead surely ranks as the first unprecedented woman of this kind during the time of her famous fieldwork among the Mountain Arapesh in the Middle Sepik. She must have been remarkable to the locals, a woman who was White, a woman unafraid of the men or their ritual secrets, as a story from her field notes will illustrate. Mead explains that the Arapesh revered the cassowary as what she called an "initiatory monster" (1970: 425). By comparison, among the neighboring Abelam tribe closer to the river, it was the crocodile that took on the terrifying role of swallowing the ritual initiates whole, regurgitating and thus rebirthing them as adult initiated men. "The secrets of manhood are enormously extended," Mead suggested:

> Besides learning to blow the flutes, the boys are shown all the marvels that the large group can muster, especially the carved pig bones, called the *loh*, which lie in the wooden bowl of the old men's blood, the masks and carved figures which adorn the Tambaran house and other noise-making devices. (1970: 425)

The Arapesh men had many secrets, of course, forbidden to Arapesh women, but not to Mead. They would show her their bone awls used for incising and scarifying the backs and brows of the boys and discuss these bloodletting procedures with her, conveniently and opportunistically ignoring the fact of her femaleness. Perhaps they treated her as an "honorary man," as Gewertz (1982) reports of her own experience among the neighboring Chambri. They were willing to discuss these material items with the young American. Because of their openness, she then assumed that she would be permitted into the deeper recesses of the men's clubhouse. However, there came a limit to their hospitality: the cassowary costume used for the initiator, the incisor, which has a "thoroughly terrifying appearance." When at last Mead dug out her camera, the men drew a line and said, "No." "One of my informants so far forgot the dictates of caution as to show me how these were worn, but he refused to let me take a photograph" (Mead 1970: 425). Their secret reality would permit them to go no further. But why? Since they went that far, why not go all the way? Mead insinuates the answer in the next paragraph, apparently unsuspecting of the significance. "These sacred masks are called *abuting*—the same name as the long yam which is so closely associated with masculinity; their makers were subject to rigorous taboo and the form was religiously reserved" (1970: 425). In short, these were icons of the phallus, and direct signifiers of conditional masculinity in its various guises (Forge 1966; Tuzin 1976). It is one thing to show a phallus to an honorary European "man" who looks awfully like a woman (Mead's "show me" may seem a bit ambiguous, but we must infer that he, and not she, wore the phallus). It is another matter to be photographed and have "its" image—that is, in the ritual ontology, an identification with secret masculinity—removed to an unknown and impure place.

More than half a century later, anthropologist Jane Fajans (1997) found herself tangled in a situation of comparable ritual delicacy. Consider the following report regarding how the men excluded her from secret male ritual performance among the Baining people of New Britain:

> It did not occur to me that this was intentional. I saw it as an accident and consequently I betook myself to the bush site. The men there were quite surprised at my arrival, having been under the impression that I had been forbidden to come. I had no inkling that this injunction had been issued, the implicit suggestion having obviously gone over my head.
>
> Although there was a definite air of mystery around this particular project, it seemed more like a mood than a specific secret. For example, when I asked the name of the piece that they were working on, Kariangi immediately told me *"avuganam."* Ukusak, who was working alongside, told him to be quiet. While one might interpret this as an expression of a desire to keep the name a secret, somehow it appeared to me more like a more diffuse caution against irreverence. (1997: 193–94)

Of course, there is no necessary difference between "irreverence" and ritual secrecy: they are neighboring chairs in the same theater. However, she added: "People reiterated that these things were taboo and dangerous to women, but they confessed they had no idea what would happen if women saw them" (Fajans 1997: 195). The inability to control a powerful white woman is not only a sign of what has changed in such local places, but a sign that the change already transpired threatens to erase what came before.

The scenes change but the theme remains: As these ethnographies suggest, ritual secrecy is a never-ending headache for the field-worker because of the risk of violating the divergent and contested realities they contain. In turn, the ethnographer is a never-ending headache for the ritual leaders. Ritual secrecy, we see, is a symbolic form without a top or bottom; its sides can become its middles; what was public can become secret with the change of a syllable; its genius is to leave Margaret Mead always one step behind. And the ethnographer does not, except vicariously, share in this being and apparently must not photograph it. To repeat: ritual secrecy creates reality as means of ethno-differentiating the being and agency of secret-sharers versus the Other; that is, those excluded and by nature divergent from themselves, including the anthropologist.

The Gahuku-Gama

A generation later, the anthropology of the Highlands would be opened up by the late Australian Kenneth E. Read, a younger contemporary and friend of Margaret Mead. There exists no finer articulation of the structural-functional model of ritual secrecy and the contradictions it posed for the role of power in postwar Highland New Guinea studies than Read's work (1952, 1954, 1955, 1965, 1984, 1986) on the Gahuku-Gama of the Eastern Highlands, Papua New Guinea. Read, as is well known, was the first anthropologist to conduct long-term fieldwork in a Highland society (Hays 1992). In addition, however, Read would return a generation later in the early 1980s to conduct fieldwork under the influence of massive social change, producing a new ethnography that is virtually unique in the history and ethnography of the area (see also Brown 1995).

Read's initial encounter with New Guinea was as a member of the Australian army, as he lived for two years in the Markham Valley. His second, as an anthropologist (1950–52), came during the time in which the colonial government had recently curtailed warfare in the area of Goroka, where he conducted research at Susaroka village, focused upon the men's secret *nama* cult religion and society among the Gahuku-Gama. In a significant review of Highlands studies by Hays (1992) it becomes evident how impactful were the early publications of Read's ethnography in laying the foundation for subsequent interpretations of the entire culture area, particularly with respect to the hegemonic role played by the men's clubhouse in village society. Read's fieldwork, like the man himself, was romantic and reflected first the sentimental and later, the cynical sides of this epistemology (see chap. 2).

To a significant degree, K. E. Read was in a position not only to understand the workings of the Australian colonial administration, but also to profit from its recent pacification of the Asaro Valley. Read's career involved being Senior Lecturer in Anthropology at the Australian School of Pacific Administration in Sydney (1953–56), where he was instrumental in teaching culture and language to aspiring young patrol officers destined to administer the Territory of New Guinea. He made contact with some of the most influential names in the history of colonial New Guinea. In *Return to the High Valley* (1986), he details his extraordinary first patrol around Mt. Michael, chaperoned by Dudley-White, *Kiap*. However, contrary to what one might have expected for a man of his social class, Read shunned other colonials and turned to the Gahuku for solace. This was consistent with his confession that he was "permanently elated" being with the Gahuku-Gama the first time around (1965: 7). Moreover, while he tolerated the *kiaps*, he disliked the missionaries intensely, as revealed by his thinly disguised invective against their efforts to destroy Gahuku ritual traditions (1951). However, the functions of secrecy in the men's house generally stumped Read, who saw them as the "contradictions" that the *nama* cult created for "society."

The Gahuku-Gama were a colonial amalgam of patrilineally organized tribes in the great expanse of the Asaro Valley near the emerging frontier town of Goroka, the provincial capital of the Eastern Highlands Province. Traditionally, warfare and ceremonial exchange systems, interspersed with frequent male initiations, preoccupied social relations in this area. Tuber and pig production were highly developed. Male and female relations were generally segregated and polarized, with men living in men's houses and women and children in women's houses. A male belief system concerning menstrual blood, fertility, and pollution infused all aspects of the exchange of women between distant and hostile groups. While in many respects the Gahuku thus resembled the Sambia and their Anga-speaking neighbors, they did *not* practice boy-inseminating rites, as Read (1984) has described. Among the results of this system was the consequent social problem of removing boys from their mothers' houses and placing them in the age-graded warriorhood of the men's club. The men's house created the necessary social and political fabric for village cohesion, especially male solidarity, but it introduced terrible pathos in the relationship between the generations and genders.

Through a series of now classic papers and books, Read demonstrated that the social and political uses of ritual secrecy empowered men and complicated all gender relations among the Gahuku. His work effectively introduced into Highland studies the notion of ritual embodiment as we think of it today (A. B. Weiner 1992). But when it came to explaining the ritual secrecy and its tentacles of diffuse power, Read was at a loss. He showed that the men's house was the site of male cultural production of all kinds, especially the fabric of supernaturalism and orthodoxy represented by the men's secret flutes, called *nama*. According to male ideology these flutes created the economy, the conduct of gender roles, the men's ritual initiations, and a variety of practical tasks and technologies in the social economy. The clubhouses of each village were linked to the "*nama* cult," named after a species of giant and monstrous birds, signified also by the music of the men's flutes (Read 1952). As if this were not already sufficiently diffuse, the *nama* cult designated as well the affiliations and age-graded associations of the local group to a broader political network of similarly appointed men's houses throughout the entire culture area, competing with enemies who were not Gahuku-Gama. In this model, the village, the men's house, and the local *nama* ritual cult were the building blocks of social structure and religion, constituting a vast but vague cabinet of Durkheimian collective representations (Read 1954). Though represented as units of a larger whole, these groups sometimes warred, their loyalties shifting amid tensions and even oppositions.

We must look to the enigmatic symbol of the men's secret and sacred flutes, the *nama*, as the Rosetta stone to unlock the men's secrecy. According to Read's (1952) classic paper on the *nama* cult, it worked for the "regulation, maintenance and transmission of sentiments upon which" their society depends (1952: 1). The "*nama* cult" was of course a social and political construction, no less than communities or congregations everywhere. Yet its claim by men to being a supernatural agency invoked awe and *mana* in the most general animistic sense of a life force or cosmic power. It made of the cult flutes, according to Read, a "symbol of unity: representing the 'solidarity' of males" (1952: 7; 1965: 113–14). Indeed, "there is no real challenge to the belief in ancestral power, the generalized concept [of] which lies at the heart of the indigenous religion" (1952: 236). The flute sounds were heard in public but the knowledge of them was secret, entirely in the hands of initiated men. They were thus given to "exploitation" or manipulation, and there was a strong sense, Read believed, that women saw through this secrecy as a "charade." However, women suppressed their doubts out of fear of the men and respect for the *nama*. It was certainly problematic to conceptualize the Gahuku-Gama as a monolithic "society" in public affairs, men and women agreeing to singular purposes and the blessings of these spiritual and orthodox powers, for women were hemmed in and oppressed by them. Herein lay the romantic and cynical contradictions of ritual secrecy for power.

Kenneth Read never explained why the senior men of the *nama* cult that regulated "the society" should also wish to subvert it; this was taken for granted, and I think I can guess why. Like most of his generation, Read simply assumed that men were more powerful and were superior to women, at home in Australia, no less than in Papua New Guinea. (I believe that the same assumption holds true for Margaret Mead, in her famous 1935 study of sex and temperament in New Guinea, also insinuated in Gewertz 1981.) Read did not question whether men would assert their power over society; male power was assumed to exist. He suggested that as an "index of male dominance and [as] an institution serving to maintain the status quo of male hegemony," its advantages to men were obvious (1952: 15). However, as we shall see, Read did critically question the source of masculinity and understood secret beliefs to be constitutive of how men can "grow" boys.

As to the men's belief, it was clearly the men who had faith in the *nama* and saw themselves as its protectors "in charge" of the flutes. Yet males were equally dependent upon its spiritual powers for growth, fertility, and military survival. Read argued that political "deceit" and "conscious deception" through the manipulation of the flutes were the common experience of women and children (1952: 9; 1965: 116). Women were "deceived," not because they "believed" in the spirits (as the men did), but because the men could "control" and "manipulate" the flutes, whereas the women could not. Were the men also "deceived" by their beliefs? Read is never clear. He hints of an appropriate Durkheimian skepticism that the spirits were inventions of society, and as an atheist, Read was comfortable with this existential position. At the center of social and cultural reality, this model suggested, ritual secrecy was illusory, like the famed symbols of the *churinga* of Australian Aborigines that Durkheim (1915) thought to be nothing more than a "reflection" of society. The men manipulated these symbols, not to the detriment of women and children, but for the good of society—images of Rousseau's social contract and Durkheim's God-as-false-consciousness in nineteenth-century discourse.

His early articles in the 1950s paint a picture of a unified people sharing in a common language, moral customs, and social order, but which was of more advantage to men than women. In a classic piece that still has much to recommend it, Read summarized the issues.

> Male dominance, and the preeminence of male values, is affirmed by the differential importance attached to male activities, particularly to warfare; but it is also given a symbolic, supernatural expression in the cult of the sacred *nama* flutes. The flutes belong to men exclusively; women are not permitted to see them; they are compelled to hide whenever the flutes are played, and the penalty for disobeying is death. They are led to believe that mythical birds produce the sound of the flutes, a deception that is also practiced on boys before they become members of the club house. On initiation, however, the secret of the flutes is the most important revelation given to the novices, and thereafter, in daily life as well as ceremonial context, the *nama* are the supreme symbols of male hegemony. (1954: 25)

Notice that in this passage Read has carefully underlined the physical sanction of death threats, which explain why women and children offered no resistance to such a "hegemony." But since they could threaten in this way, why did the men need secrecy for hegemonic control? As I have argued before, Read concluded that the men's secret cult "was therefore a one-sided species of Durkheim's religion: society worshipped only males" (Herdt 1982b: 47). Today, however, that view is incomplete, for it does not address the question of the sources of male agency and power: Why is it necessary to create such a male-worshipping religion in the first place?

Read offers the following addendum that is a partial answer: "Legend held that the most sacred and most secret symbols had been discovered by women and thereafter taken away and appropriated for male use only, to be viewed by the women on pain of death" (1965: 112). That the flutes were produced by women but "stolen" by men is a common story in the Highlands (Gillison 1993; Herdt 1981; Keesing 1982a). To be entirely cynical about this mythopoetic origin is to interpret it as a contrivance for justification of male power, as did unreconstructed feminist accounts (Faithorn 1975; cf. Gillison 1993).

K. E. Read's great and unspoiled insight into the Gahuku-Gama was to suggest that while men "believed" in the spirits, they nonetheless "manipulated" the flutes as a political weapon. The men were acting upon the basis of a hidden reality, a subjective agreement that revealed a deeper ontology that does not fit neoliberal Western categories of "true" and "false." There was only one way into this reality—initiation—and there was never an exit from it during one's lifetime (Herdt 1987b). That is the compact with ritual secrecy: All or nothing: For life or death. It should have as its oath: Till death do us part. Read understood this. The trouble is that Read would lead into this but then back away from its premises, which were disturbing to the prevailing structural-functional, relativistic, and neoliberal premises of his day.

What is missing from his insight is an explicit analysis of internal male relationships and hierarchy to illuminate the relations between the *nama* cult and the wider social field. It would take another generation to translate this account into gender relations (M. Strathern 1988: 53ff.), and even then, the conditionality of masculinity, which Read understood but could not connect to theory, remained misunderstood. Read's account (esp. 1952) subscribes to the Durkheimian conception of a singular tribal "society," in which masculinity was but a part of the way in which social processes introduced inequalities, manipulations, and deceptions. By use of double-edged tropes ("men playing with reality," conscious "deceit," "charade," and so on), Read set up the means to analyze conditional masculinity and actual relations between men and women, and between older and younger males. He also anticipated the collapse of the *nama* cult later, when he returned after twenty-five years absence (see Read 1986). But his account fell short of being able to provide an insight into ritual secrecy.

The original tropes must be reinterpreted, their indications reconsidered, because the meaning of the flutes is so general and all-encompassing. In later writings Read suggested a culture in which all morality was situational, so that Gahuku regarded themselves as humans, and all others as enemies or nonhuman (including their imported wives from neighboring groups). While Read himself emphasized not the universal but the contextual morality of their rituals (1955), he tended to back away from the "bad" aspects of male domination, in favor of a rosier picture of the Gahuku-Gama (1965). His student Langness (1974) was critical of this. Only years later did Read question his more relativistic tendencies when it came to the area of gender domination and male ideologies of "growth" (1984). In fact, though, he did not reject his views from before, and even appealed to Hogbin's Wogeo (1970) for a much more static account of how male ritual secrecy was used to "grow" boys into manhood.

What Read's romantic and later cynical interpretations did was to intrude one reality (the ethnographer-outsider's) into another social reality (the ritual actors'), without a complete understanding (Lewis 1980) of why the ontology of Gahuku-Gama men required ritual secrecy to "make the world work." The men's house needed a mantle of trust, and secret rituals bestowed this upon their untidy and somewhat dangerous marital alliances with surrounding tribes (Read 1965). Gender segregation was more thorough and complete than among the Sambia, and yet masculinity was forever conditioned on the practice of secret rites. Read suggests that the nature of Gahuku-Gama cosmology is animistic and thus requires calendrical fertility rites and initiations to renew it. "Renewal" or "rebirth" are tied to the local ontology, however; that men had to feign female reproductive work, such as menstruation, in their secret rites was already a sign of a disparity in social status and power not predicted by and generally suppressed by the men's ideology of "superiority."

Here is where I think that Langness (1967) was right in understanding the political need of men to play down their dependence upon women and exaggerate the role of sex antagonism and political competition. But it seems that within these structural-functional accounts there is no attention to the relations *within and between males*. In fact, both Read's work and that of Langness (1974) later are alike in assuming that all males are equal, at least in principle (see also Meggitt 1964; M. Strathern 1988: 62–63). There is also the assumption that intergenerational relations are smooth, and the transmission of rule and authority to youngsters from elders is unproblematic, which is perplexing because of Read's detailed ethnography that reveals exceptions to these notions. Read's own sensitive life-histories in *The High Valley* were highly revealing of the tremendous social pressures and anxieties experienced by boy-initiates for conformity to senior males. Moreover, rivalries between men aspiring to become Great Men were swept under the rug (Forge 1972; Godelier 1986; Watson 1971). Perhaps Read believed that these aspects were the result of social change.

A generation later, a revolution had occurred. When Read returned to study the Gahuku-Gama, he found that their ideology of male political unity had collapsed in the face of massive social change, unrest, and individualistic self-interest. Social conflict and violence were all around; the men's houses were gone. They apparently did not require the secret trust and agency of the men's house reality; instead there was a new social fabric of money and the ability to purchase the security of a new technology of armaments. Secrecy was gone.

"What holds Gahuku-Gama society together?" Read's answer was much like Landtman's (1917: 236–37), writing on the Kiwai of Papua at the mouth of the Fly River: the ritual process of masculinity was not confined to any single ceremony. Rather, Kiwai youth were introduced through a range of "great ceremonies" to sexuality—forming a diffuse power system for "admission to secrets." This idea invites an understanding of how ritual secrecy fuses or merges male homosociality with male sexuality, "maintaining the whole society." Like his structural-functional contemporaries, Read did not sort out how ritual secrecy created divergent realities in men and women, and how these lifeways precipitated unequal intergenerational relations between males within the *nama* cult. There was a contradiction: How could the *nama*, based upon the "hoax" of ritual secrecy, be the means of unifying the "whole society"? Of course it could not, for that was not its aim, but the imposition of the term "hoax" and other cynical attacks on it merely obscured a closer analysis of the reasons why not.

I do not want to dismiss Kenneth Read's ethnography merely because of its allusions to "deceit" and "fabrication." But I disagree with the insinuation that these traces of ritual secrecy should be described in a moral language of individual or personal tomfoolery—a kind of moral failing or personal flaw in the male self. Not only Read's (1952), but also Hogbin's (1970) and Langness's (1974) accounts all suggest such a cynical interpretation. Read's own evidence reveals that whatever shenanigans or posturing were involved, Gahuku-Gama men were deeply immersed in what we in the West would declare to be authentic "religious experiences" (Gellner 1992). I do not deny that Read's account also portrays the physical and social domination and intimidation of women and children, or that the flutes were mystifying and frightening to them. Certainly they were to the Sambia (Herdt 1982b). I would however be skeptical of the idea that the men were engaged in a bogus practice, a guilty secret, which signified their defensive or protest masculinity, as implied by Read and others to follow (Faithorn 1975; Hays and Hays 1982; Herdt 1981; Hogbin 1970; Mead 1949; Schieffelin 1976; Tuzin 1982).

Read never fully comprehended how tenuous and incomplete was Gahuku-Gama men's control over all public affairs, including warfare. Village-based political formations, including the men's house, were as disparate and given to internal squabbles and feuds as elsewhere in New Guinea (Harrison 1993). The women's positions as intermediaries and plural citizens were more effective and necessary under the old regime and through the colonial period than either the Gahuku men or K. E. Read could grant (see M. Strathern 1972). In this sense, the masculinity of men had to be more conditioned than the femininity of women. The men needed the women to make themselves complete, to finish the symbolic processes of making parts whole (M. Strathern 1988). The Gahuku men's secret cult posed an analytic problem for the structural-functional theory of society that Read espoused, namely, because the *nama* cult allowed a much diminished role for public culture. It also depended inordinately upon a Western public/private dichotomy that pitted the deceitful individual male agent against "society" as a whole, which was a misreading, for it omitted the role of women, who controlled and belonged to another symbolic seat of power: the women's and menstrual house. Far too often we have underestimated the great force of homosociality—of living and sleeping together in the same house—for shaping gender-divergent realities (Herdt 1989b). I believe that Read well understood the influence of this homosociality, but he downplayed its implications for gendered notions of public and secret realities, an ethnographic hiatus that still remains in spite of the remarkable efforts of Marilyn Strathern.

I suspect that there were always intergenerational problems of social control and having the will of the elders played out. It is more parsimonious to conceptualize ritual secrecy as a powerful set of devices—material, discursive, and symbolic—that produce and articulate differences between social and ontological categories of Gahuku, while maintaining ideologies of cohesive sociopolitical relations for internal discourse and rhetorical relations with groups in adjacent territories. Long ago it was debated whether there was an "African model" of influence in this social theory (Barnes 1962). Today we would see the matter in a broader light. Was "Gahuku-Gama" an actual "society" in the first place? Surely this rhetoric implies an abstraction, built out of a variety of observations about interrelated, neighboring, and sometimes hostile groups, who united for certain purposes, and fought for others: a sense of a polity that is socially constructed, not natural (M. Strathern 1988; Wagner 1975). The whole idea of "Gahuku-Gama" was of course an ethnographic construction of Read's textualism, like all the other constructions of this kind emanating from the colonial period (Geertz 1988). The Gahuku-Gama were consolidated in some sense as a confederacy by the colonial administration itself, but the implications of this were not clear until a generation later, when Read completed his sequel to his first book and found that the unity once observed had disintegrated; the village had split and was unable, in the absence of a leading Big Man, to find a center within itself. The Gahuku-Gama as a tribal entity was no longer.

In fact, Read hints of this when he deals with social change on a later occasion. His early works, like those of his peers, largely ignored the social change and colonialism, significant for understanding the domination by men of women. Gahuku-Gama culture was already undergoing great change by the time of his arrival in the late 1940s and early 1950s. The Lutheran mission was making strong inroads, including the destruction of the *nama* flutes in public and the resistance to other iconic elements of the *nama* cult (Read 1951). This social change introduced a kind of "fearful" attitude about the fate of the men's secret reality, at the time, as Read (1984: 220) later wrote, much as Margaret Mead (1956) had done before in her more general re-study of Manus.

At the time, Read only hinted that Gahuku men feared the collapse of their conditional masculinity. Ritual secrecy kept the sexes living in different houses, leading different lives—a separate habitus. When the genders were put together in intimate quarters and could observe each other, wonder, and interrogate, the fabric of precolonial social difference began to disintegrate. In the process, the subjective and counterhegemonic forms posed by the younger boys, ambivalent or even angry about their initiation ordeals, and by the women, who were left out of decision making, erupted in a cataclysm, as revealed in that great work, *The High Valley*. When Read later found Gahuku society full of tawdry "Western culture" and devoid of ritual—and thus absent ritual secrecy—he did not care for it very much; all the romance was gone, leaving only cynicism (cf. Lévi-Strauss 1974).

The rise of modernity imagines a romantic civic society based upon trust and openness, a single "truth" and consensual reality, the expression of its own ideologies of nature and culture. Many have followed Read's stance of moral relativism here (see Lawrence and Meggitt 1965; and see the critique in Herdt and Stephen 1989). Such an appeal to a different, utopian world, in which social reality would be of one piece, and not so divided, is alien to Read's description of Gahuku-Gama social existence in the 1950s. But this is a morality play; to recall Milton, it looks upon fraud as a greater crime than theft. I do think that Read understood this dilemma at the end of his poignant and sad conclusion to *Return to The High Valley*. The *nama* cult was "dead," and so was the consensus of society.

It is not surprising that Langness (1974: 209), Read's student and the primary ethnographer of the BenaBena people (neighbors of the Gahuku-Gama), would have concluded from his studies that secrecy is a fundamental manifestation of "male power." Long after colonization had impacted upon the area, Langness conducted fieldwork in the 1960s. The initiations were gone. What Langness reports is based primarily upon memory and idealized accounts of ritual events in the context of accelerating social change, as the BenaBena were brought into cattle and coffee production near the Highlands Highway. Langness hypothesized a male desire or "need to dominate or aggress" against women, primarily as the result of a compensation or masculine protest against the men's intrinsic bonding with their wives. Only ritual secrecy, through a combination of power and threats, would effectively undercut this "drive" and ensure male solidarity in the face of enemies (1967). Thus, men used secrecy to support their physical and symbolic domination—"power in its most fundamental sense" (1974). Such a model is predicated upon a historical displacement of time and place (Fabian 1991), much as in earlier studies of secrecy reviewed in chapter 2. The effect textually elides the vulnerable and highly conditional masculinity and the alternate reality it creates through ritual secrecy.

Whatever its value as a claim on innateness or universal (phylogenetic) "nature," Langness's model of human development adds little to the meaning of local male agency or ritual secrecy. He fails to explain the meaning or function of *close-bonded homosociality*. Why is it necessary? What "work" does homosociality produce for the men's house? The answers lie in how we conceptualize cultural reality. In terms of gender and sexual development, I think that both male and female bonding are "cultural" and "natural," but there is a difference that Langness elided for New Guinea: local folk psychology in most of these communities, the Gahuku-Gama and BenaBena included, desire homosociality as the norm. In fact, the evidence of the cross-cultural record makes us skeptical of the bourgeois norm of *yes, coming from a homosexual*

heteronormativity as being typical of the human condition (Herdt 1997a).

Why should power be connected to secrecy (to de-essentialize the construct of "power") or be expressed at all in the context of ritual secret ceremonies unless this form is vital to the creation of cultural reality in a people? Secrecy is necessary to define the foundation and defense of incorporeal and corporeal property—territory, goods (including women and valuables), ritual rights and duties vested in persons in many Highlands societies. However, it seems that in addition to this necessary condition, it also provides a sufficient means among the BenaBena and Gahuku-Gama to structure social relations between the genders. This is because the social economy is built upon highly political, contested, or tenuous theories of being about what it takes to be a full person (or "man" or "woman"). These ontological categories have social and political charters as well; like warfare (Harrison 1993), they objectify the necessary achievements and signs of male personhood, such as "fighting" and "virility" and "renown." It probably was not possible, as Margaret Mead (1935) once suggested for the Sepik River Mountain Arapesh and others, to build the kind of rugged masculinity sufficient and necessary to get all these jobs done *without secret initiation.* That is a social, not a biological, outcome, if such a spurious distinction can be made at all.

The Baktaman

Fredrik Barth's original (1975) study of Baktaman, a small tribe of Mountain Ok speakers in the area of Telefomin, Northwest New Guinea, goes further than prior structural-functional studies in demonstrating both the analytical power and limitations of idealist or Platonic notions of ritual secrecy as noted in my initial remarks on Lewis Henry Morgan (chap. 1). The work of Norwegian anthropologist Barth is notable in spanning a variety of cultures and in advancing critical theory in anthropology. His 1975 *Ritual and Knowledge among the Baktaman of New Guinea* and a later 1987 account, *Cosmologies in the Making,* both provide fascinating and highly readable ethnographies. Though based upon short-term field study, these valuable contributions stress the cultural and ecological constraints on information flow that create sociality and secrecy. Barth's study of the rational-intellectual (Evans-Pritchard 1964) and nonverbal dimensions of ritual initiation is elaborate in many domains, including ritual meanings, taboo, secrecy, knowledge, spirits, and initiation rites. His was the first study to reveal the widespread import of male cults and secrecy for sociality building among the Telefomin area Mountain Ok speakers.

The Baktaman, a "nation of 183 persons," was broadly concerned with the premises of Baktaman knowledge in terms of the explanation of self, man, and environment which they transmit to each other through discourse and ritual, much of it organized in an instituted system of male initiations (Barth 1975: 1). The sympathetic account continues the romantic tradition of cynical-romanticism initiated by scholars such as Margaret Mead and, as we have seen, K. E. Read. It also provides an extraordinary example of the vitality of the Durkheimian conception of religion, with its emphasis of ritual over belief, albeit lacking some of the premises of structural-functionalism to be found in Hogbin's or Read's accounts. Parting company with the universalism of Lévi-Strauss, Barth was later to remark that his work is a "struggle to *get our ontological assumptions right:* to ascribe to our object of study only those properties and capabilities that we have reasonable ground to believe it to possess" (1987: 8, emphasis in original).

Baktaman inhabit a high mountain terrain once marked by chronic warfare, the fear of cannibalism, and a heightened social anxiety over sorcery. These endemic social conflicts were sufficiently great that they intruded into all levels of social grouping and sociality, even into the intimacies of filial bonds. Economically dependent upon taro gardening and hunting, the Baktaman were living in dispersed homesteads, with men's houses. Their diffuse political and social organization contributed to a pervasive sense of anomie and social disorganization.

Male/female relations were distant, often strained, and generally expressed an intense dualism of essential bodies and natures. These interests were apparently acute for the Baktaman and their neighbors (Poole 1981, 1982). The gender segregation of the village, based upon men living in clubhouses with initiated boys, and women living in separate houses with uninitiated children, was as complete and totalizing homosociality as any New Guinea culture known (Herdt and Poole 1982). A regional ritual complex of extraordinary power and symbolic richness long known but little documented throughout the wider area of Telefomin has since been documented (Barth 1971, 1975, 1987; Bercovitch 1989b; Jorgenson 1996; Poole 1982). Barth's ecological approach to culture, society, and interethnic relations treats the complex ritual initiation system of Baktaman males as a system of "actually received messages" (1975: 47) that reproduce their overall tradition (cf. Whitehouse 1998).

Barth saw the Baktaman as a singular cultural tradition, a unified "society" with a shared "religion" that required mandatory initiation of all males. Its purpose was to stimulate abundance and fertility in domestic production, especially of the taro. Their sequence of seven consecutive initiations conducted over many years "also constitute the major cult events of Baktaman religion" (1975: 47). Elaborate "codes" for ritual performances distributed across categories of persons suggested a metaphoric tendency to elaborate partial realities. The development of knowledge in the construction of the person is based nearly as much upon concealment as upon revelation, including numerous occasions of spoofing, deception, taboos, lying, hiding, silence, and distortion—a veritable wizard's bag of tricks deployed to terrorize and thus shake boys of their sense of absolute, rooted knowledge and reality. Poole's (1982) work has dramatically illustrated this aspect of initiation. However, the boy-initiates' experience is typically described almost entirely as victims, as an exploited class, while the elders themselves are described in largely cynical terms.

In keeping with a tendency of nineteenth-century writers, including Morgan, Barth agrees with scholars who think of New Guinea male secret formations as "mystery" and "fertility" cults (Whitehead 1986). Symbolically, it is suggested that "Baktaman experience arises less from their logical articulation than from their cryptic, vital character as the secrets of a mystery cult" (Barth 1975: 264). Barth means the term "mystery cult" in a literal sense: even the elders of the men's cult are unaware of the deeper source of the meanings of the ritual secrecy. This point about the "unawareness" of elders is a critical claim (see Tuzin 1980). It is difficult to know how much of this claim was the result of the brevity of Barth's fieldwork and the understandable problems of working in the vernacular. Nevertheless, Barth's view is close to the theoretical model, the "cryptological view," that holds ritual symbolism to be "empty" or "meaningless" (Sperber 1976). As we have seen, New Guinea precolonial systems apparently varied greatly in the extent to which exegesis characterized their symbolic meaning systems (Forge 1966; Gell 1975; Herdt 1981; Lewis 1980).

Barth provides the beautiful metaphor of nesting Chinese boxes to describe his understanding of the unfolding process of Baktaman secrecy and revelation. I quote the key passage:

I have previously used the image of Chinese boxes to characterize the structure of Baktaman knowledge: it is constructed with multiple levels, and each level is organized so as to obscure the next level. There is every indication that this depicts the distribution of actual knowledge, and not just pretenses about secrecy; and the information made available at one level bears witness, in terms of knowledge at deeper levels, of having been purposefully distorted and garbed on certain points (61) to preclude independent deduction from one level to the next. (1975: 218)

The effect of this ontological process upon sociality is very destructive in the long run, Barth suggests: "Fathers must systematically deceive sons, men deceive women and vice versa, all public life is permeated with the protective tactfulness of sorcery fear" (1975: 219–20). Moreover, when added to endemic warfare and sorcery, intertribal relations were virtually impossible.

As we shall see, however, this negative and destructive view of the effects of ritual secrecy is entertained simultaneously with a communalistic and rosy picture of male responsibility for "fertility." We might hasten to think of this as a paradoxical view of conditional masculinity for reasons quite similar to those noted before, except that among the Baktaman, the paradox of ritual secrecy is not that of male superiority expressed in public, versus male inferiority voiced in secret, as it was for the Gahuku-Gama. Instead, the paradox of male initiation concerns the communal responsibility voiced in public versus deception felt in secret. This difference will focus the interpretations that follow.

The Baktaman men's house does not differ substantially from the account of the Gahuku-Gama, or neighboring BenaBena, for initiation was mandatory and conscription provided warriors with their resources and introduction to adulthood. All males except one (a feeble-minded deaf-mute) were initiated, Barth says. Notice why:

> The justification for this, somewhat incongruously in his case, that he might tell the secret to the women—a conventional phrase, emphasizing the trust and responsibility imposed on initiates and their differentiation from the irresponsible and dependent women. (1975: 47)

In this passage, the appeal to conventionality suggests the sign of the romantic-cynical approach to ritual secrecy—placed in the service of the local ideology of communalism and political innocence. Clearly, the Baktaman men fear this disastrous possibility, at least in their minds. Whether fantasy or cultural reality—and what is the difference?—it would seem that their fear is perfectly congruous with the voices of men who say that they mistrust the "irresponsible" women as interlopers. But why is this rhetoric more of a "conventional" idiom than any other, if not to imply that men act out of conformity rather than conviction?

The ideal and rosy side of the paradox of Baktaman male ritual secrecy, much like K. E. Read's model, would surely have warmed the heart of Emile Durkheim (1915):

> The view thus seems to be primarily that men are saddled with a responsibility, on behalf of the community as a whole, to assure prosperity by achieving ritual purity and performing the cult; it is not a male cult but a communal cult performed by men. (47)

Typically, it would not be possible to check the counterpoint of the paradox against an ethnographic text, but fortunately, Barth's own interrogation provides the dialogical account necessary for this.

> However, since the conventional blessings enumerated as springing from good cult practice include growth and strength of sons, and there is some public concern about the low reproductive ratio for the Baktaman population, I did once suggest the possibility of a parallel female cult to assure the growth and strength of women. This elicited a warning that such a cult would make women *too* strong, if they had initiations in addition to their natural fertility they would want to be on top when copulating; and this led further to the telling of myth no. 3. . . . Despite this sexual dichotomization and rivalry, recognizable as a persistent secondary theme, the main focus is none the less on the rites as a cult for the Baktaman nation, or its component clans. (Barth 1975: 47–48, emphasis in original)

This, by the way, is one of the few mentions of sexuality in Barth's book.

The romantic argument that Baktaman have a "communal" rather than a "male" cult is much like Read's prior model. However, it is unconvincing with respect to the Baktaman, since the ethnographer's account contradicts the claim of communalism on two points: Barth's opposition to the idea that the Baktaman have a men's secret cult, operated through the men's clubhouse, and his general view that Baktaman men are not engaged in the domination of women.

What about the existence of a parallel tradition of secret practices among women? This issue has long perplexed Melanesianist scholars. Among the Sambia, there are no early initiation events for females, nothing like that of the males, until they are older, when the marriage ceremony is performed (Herdt 1981). They are then secretly instructed in sexual and reproductive knowledge and tasks, and female folklore and ceremonies. I have never witnessed these events, because I was a male and this was not permitted, but female informants have described a strong emphasis upon the intricacies of the marital relationship. The menarche ceremony is the main ritual event of Sambia women, since "marriage" occurs prior to menarche. The secrecy surrounding menarche is profound. Perhaps this remains a central mystery of the human condition to the Sambia, much as Barth suggests for the Baktaman. Certainly many New Guinea peoples compare menarche to fundamental processes of creation, of life-making, fertility, and power. Sambia go a step further and compare the menarche of girls to the first-stage initiation of boys, which provides a major clue to this mystery. Women's own sexual and ritual development suggests an emphasis upon menarche and the flow of blood as processes of vitality and distress, forever linked to female sexuality.

The Baktaman ethnography searches for a community of equal faith, and upon failing to locate this, it turns into an apology for the failure of Baktaman culture to create standards of communalism, truth, and enlightenment—a dramatic example of anthropology's rebellion to the Enlightenment (Shweder 1984). Barth thus provides a rebellion to the Baktaman's own ethnotheories; I am not entirely unsympathetic to it. Barth argues that ritual secrecy is not so much a misguided or failed attempt to control and dominate women as a desire for harmony and tribal unity that he feels the Baktaman ought to seek. There is no need to discount either of these accounts; they are not mutually exclusive, but rather pertain to two fundamentally different narratives of reality: the one for public consumption, the other for secret discourse. In his later work, Barth parts company with neo-Durkheimian and Lévi-Straussian neostructuralist views, because he felt these were unconvincing in the analysis of ritual symbolism (1987: 6–8). "I feel intuitively committed to an ideal of naturalism in the analytical operations I perform: that they should model or mirror significant, identifiable processes that can be shown to take place among the phenomena they seek to depict" (8). Alas, there is no simple "naturalism" in charting the territory of ritual secrecy, as will now be evident to the reader.

The Baktaman study depends upon a "lumping" conception of society that describes a relatively homogeneous and egalitarian society occupying a space surrounded by its secret society. The spatial imagery of this nineteenth-century model is now familiar. The use of the concept of "communal" is complicated; it appeals to a utopian sense of mutualism and shared commitments that seem qualified for the Baktaman, but may reflect the aspirations of elders to embrace the entire community. Since they have highly seasonal patterns of social organization and demographically small hamlets, the diffuse nature of their ecology, including dispersed residential settlement, seasonal migrations, and exclusive men's house residence in the village, gives the picture of a people who are often scattered, out of communication, and even anticommunal. The sociological sense of the term implies less division and more communalism than actually exists. But if Baktaman sociality is unenthusiastically communal, it qualifies even less as a unified polity and social economy. More glaring is the rhetorical claim for nationhood, however. Notice that in rejecting his informants' ideas that men and women have different origins, interests, and natures, Barth ignores the cultural reality they have painted for him—one that they apparently fear enough to warn against. To invoke the modernist concept of state-formation implicit in "nation" suggests an epistemic tidying-up at a higher level than the Baktaman would recognize in their messy and fragmentary social relations on the ground.

The evidence offered in support of these constructs—community, society, and nation—derives of course from the claims of Baktaman men themselves. Seldom in Barth's book are we able to see the extent to which women might agree or disagree with the men's belief system. The Melanesian literature is replete with notions that the men's house and secret formation are vital to the fertility and the "blessings" of spirits. According to their view of things, Baktaman men must practice "good" ritual cult practices in order to attain purity and prosperity for the "whole community." Barth agrees with the men's self-justifying language of being "saddled with responsibility" for the "whole community" without critically examining how this male rhetoric is instrumental for the recruitment of initiates and the promotion of trust and alliance in the men's house.

Indeed, there is a naive realism in this element of the ethnography that is hard to understand. Surely if one is going to invoke the men's rationalization that they are morally bound to carry the "burden" of leadership and control for the entire "community" one might expect the account to establish what is gained or lost by doing so. Perhaps this romantic approach may be seen in the light of prior cynical accounts that caricatured male secrecy as "fraud." If this is so, then the balance in the account is easier to understand, a tilt in the other direction. Surely these are opposing views, the reader must wonder? Hardly; it is better to think of these as dialectical positions, one entirely romantic and the other cynical, thesis and antithesis, but part of a piece: the denial of secret masculinity. They form mirror images, a Janus that seeks either to completely dismiss the content of ritual secrecy as a deception or to stake it out as an altruistic communion without deception.

Need we understand why the men claim female powers of symbolic reproduction—just as they exclude real women from their secret rituals? Baktaman insistence on exclusion is prima facie evidence that gender segregation is the precondition for maintaining male feelings of superiority over the women. The men perceive the women as fundamentally different in being and nature from themselves, like the Sambia do; they even refer to the women as a separate species. Using the metaphors and analogies of nature as the primary source of their ideology of difference and hierarchy, Baktaman men build a view of necessary exclusion based upon their fear of menstrual blood, meticulously documented by Barth's original study iterating "maleness" and "femaleness" as distinct entities or properties of things. Baktaman men say that menstrual blood is dangerous and inimical to men. But contrarily for the women, blood is an elixir; it enables them to bear and suckle children. That the men are deeply fretful toward this gendered difference in nature and nurture is patently obvious from Barth's informants' warning against Baktaman women having their own secret cult. Rhetorically, men assert that ritual would make women "too strong," suggesting that they are already strong enough in opposition to men. Are Baktaman men not implying that female rituals would create a secrecy and alternate reality, overwhelming the men's tenuous hold on things? This anxiety, in turn, propels the ontology that male and female are different beings, and initiated boys must move from female to male quarters and be instructed into the "mystery" of male life.

As soon as this dire possibility that women could create reality raised its head, the men's ontology was suddenly and starkly visible. The warning that women would be too strong is but the tip of the iceberg: The men fear that if women "had initiations in addition to their *natural fertility* they would want to be on top when copulating." Ritual secrecy, in short, mediates sexuality and intimate sexual exchanges, another aspect of conditional masculinity. Somehow, like the Sambia, Baktaman require secret masculinity to practice sexuality with their wives. The reasons may differ, but the outcomes are the same: secret ritual prepares and fortifies men for sexual intimacy with women.

These Baktaman metaphors of ritual secrecy are essentializing, taking the body and the fluids and materials of the body as the focus of all contact with the world, and thus in need of urgent protection. Among such peoples this secret ritual protection involves constant attention to the boundaries of the body and the intense and painful procedures of purification that are suffered by the male agent (Bercovitch 1989a). The variety of blood-letting rites in New Guinea (Herdt 1982b) are widely thought by locals to constitute and generate the whole person—body, soul, and thought, inside and outside. The creation of secret blood-letting, for example, differentiates principles of "female" blood versus "male" blood, urgently requiring the male to let "female" blood in secret to "grow" or "be strong" or "procreate" and so on. Baktaman ritual expresses and enacts deeply rooted notions of such being and reality, connecting the secret dietetics of the male person to the hardships of living in highly compromised, potentially polluting proximity to women. Yet these anxieties and the dread of the menstrual blood are part of their reality and connected to cultural processes that have been systematically discredited by certain Freudians and other cynics (Bettelheim 1955). From the ethnography of ritual secrecy a generation ago, in which Wogeo men were said to equate penis bleeding to women's menstruation (Hogbin 1970), it now seems as if Hogbin misunderstood this ontology, as reinterpreted by the meticulous Gilbert Lewis (1980: 111–12).

Thus, to follow M. Strathern's (1988) critique, these practices readily convey the sense in which initiation separates the genders by the relationships that follow from them or lead to certain forms of relational exchange. This "essentialized" ontology in New Guinea is typically based upon the belief that the whole person derives existence (not to mention meaning) from properties, conditions, and essences originating in secret rites. These essences may be metered and exhaustible, but can be replenished—though again only through the proper secret attitudes and techniques (Gell 1975).

Such a gendered life-plan is part of a system of secret desires for survival against invisible threats, in order to endure into old age, always necessitating adherence to the canons of secret ontology and the exclusion of women along the way. All this requires faith in the cultural ideas that male virtue and health are moral contingencies stemming from ritual secrecy. Masculinity, in sum, is conditional, never absolute: and never as absolute as femininity.

Hence we begin to understand why men fear women's fertility and sexual positions. It is remarkable that Barth never returns to the mythic warning of the men, whose apocryphal warning about the harmful effects of female authority over men typifies the structural tendency of pseudomatriarchy and Amazon myths in the New Guinea Highlands to charter tenuous claims of power by men asserted in these unstable social formations (Gillison 1993; Herdt 1981). Consulting Barth's appendix III, we find that the myth in question is filled with imagery of the original theft of the cult house stolen by a brother from his sister. These were the first ancestors, indeed, those of the famous Afek myth in this corner of New Guinea (Bercovitch 1989a). "The sister would not let her brother into the cult house, but sent him off to hunt and garden" (Barth 1975: 278). When he refused, she killed him and used his bones for their magical and fertile properties, especially to grow taro. Another one of her brothers eventually tricked her, however, and she moved out, "and so the men took over the cult houses" (279).

In the narrative following the myth, Barth dismisses the warning again, in spite of how mistrust, theft, displacement, and reproduction hover around the story (1975: 279). He tells us that only a few senior men know the myth, and that it is typical of the kinds of "cult practice" and gendered relations one finds throughout New Guinea. That may be so (Roscoe 1995). However, it does not justify his next statement, that "among the Baktaman it seems to provide a justification for a *premise never questioned*, and thus does not constitute an important explanation in the Baktaman system of thought. Its telling was the result of my active prodding" (Barth 1975: 279, emphasis added). The premise in question is that of sexual polarity, more specifically, the latent idea that women might oppose the power of men within intimate exchanges or in public affairs. Once again, this interpretation stresses the conviction that gendered dichotomies or "sexual rivalries" are nothing more than a "persistent secondary theme." The "main focus," he asserts, is the cult sponsored for "the whole congregation of the Baktaman nation" (48).

Notice that at this critical juncture, contrary to what male informants have indicated, Barth resists their attribution of the causes or effects of ritual secrecy to male/female differences, apparently due to the other side of the paradox, communalism (of course, Whitehouse [1992] has criticized this; different demands upon memory may exact different meanings or rhetorics in these texts). After suggesting that gendered differentiation is of no import in the "Baktaman" system of thought (not "male" or "female," but "Baktaman" system), he states that we had best ignore it. In fact, Barth expresses puzzlement at why "women conceptually epitomize the excluded category" in Baktaman male secrecy (1975: 205). His perspective is curious in the face of the insider's view—even more so because of his later book, in which Barth (1987: 43) espouses a naive essentialism of sex/gender differences as causative—the "raw materials" that motivate the creation of ritual imagery![1] The conclusion: "There is nothing puzzling" about the emphasis upon sexual imagery in Baktaman ritual in spite of the absence of a "systematic picture" of male and female, since "we are merely seeing how familiar models are brought in as aids to the understanding of problematic topics" (1975: 211). In short, gender and intergenerational age differences are dismissed for understanding ritual secrecy and its hold upon reality-making.

Since Baktaman practice gender relations that are profoundly disjointed, there is reason to be skeptical about this formulation (M. Strathern 1988: 212), given the intense gendered imagery and attention to male/female differences rampant throughout the Mountain Ok area (Poole 1982; Bercovitch 1989b). The dramatic imagery of the Bimin-Kuskusmin is emblematic here, with all signs of the feminine literally "burned out" of the flesh of boy initiates in one way or another, and as repeated in the complex ordeals of the multistage initiations. Nevertheless, Baktaman and Bimin also differ in important ways, one being the role of exegesis among the Bimin-Kuskusmin, the other being their emphasis upon discontinuity and continuity with the past (Poole 1986). After a reading of Bercovitch's study of Nalumin, it is difficult not to wonder how much Barth (1987) systematically underrated the meaning and significance of gender in the men's house tradition. But "gender" is not a thing, but a set of properties and relationships to compose and decompose, and these are unstable formations (Knauft 1999).

To make what is politically necessary for men into a seamless utopia, the Baktaman created specifications of social advancement into the men's house a necessary religious purpose as well. One started a ritual career in childhood and expected, having undergone domination by older males, to attain status and authority over other men (Read 1959), in the local ideology. This also formed the basis of embodiment among these groups and was the basis of "immortality" in the ontology of the Baktaman. The development of ritual secrecy in cultures such as the Baktaman elucidates conceptions of difference and inequality in the time and space world. These folk theories underline the implicit status hierarchies that initiation creates in what have generally been considered "egalitarian" societies. Indeed this idea is vital to the early contributions of such great ethnographies as *Papuans of the Trans-Fly* (Williams 1936), *Sex and Temperament in Three Primitive Societies* (Mead 1935), and *The High Valley* (Read 1965), among others. The studies of New Guinea religions and cargo cults that followed (Lawrence 1964; Lawrence and Meggitt 1965) strongly suggest that under colonialism, ritual secrecy promoted social change (see chap. 5). Why then exclude ideas of social difference and political stratification from the account?

Barth suggests that ritual secrecy worked upon generative or structural principles that were internal to the imagery and signifiers of nature and culture, rather than signifying gender and other forms of difference or "power" that claimed its own reality. But no simple inside/outside dichotomy explains Baktaman male ideology: Baktaman sociality apparently does not work that way; and one of the primary reasons why, not fully reckoned in Barth's account, is the profound remove of the genders in segregated houses as these exist in the hamlet. An organizational key is the seasonal round of hunting and gardening that transcended ordinary sleeping and residential arrangements, as the family left the hamlet and ate and slept together in the bush. In the bush, then, the normal barriers and taboos were elided, and the fear as well as the freedom that this presented for Baktaman men and women must have been considerable.

Here is a problem of margin to center. How remarkable that the Baktaman initiated male can negotiate these large changes in sociality, and the intimacies of enclosure with wife and children, never allowed in the village, while having to maintain the ritual secrets and social distance for which they are renowned. The bush house created a kind of "private" space off- or backstage of village life. The men's house is productive of the cultural creation of male/male trust, a distinctive reality that differentiates men from women and enemies, much as their myths and lore warn. But a man was vulnerable offstage. Through the provision of secret masculinity, a system of subject/object relations removed from public scrutiny, the men's ritual desires conspired to reign forever in a timeless world—whether in the hamlet or out in the bush in proximity to wife and children. The Baktaman male hierarchy of men over women, and elders over boys, endures in all these habitations.

Having rejected gendered realities as the cause or effect of ritual secrecy, Barth appeals to the tropes of "deception" and "mystery" in understanding the "communal cult." But here he encounters considerable trouble in trying to reconcile this romantic ideology of collectivism with the "pervasiveness of secrecy and indirect deception" (1975: 219) repeatedly encountered. Ritual secrecy creates fear and mistrust, even between fathers and sons within the secret collective:

> The novice develops a fearful awareness of vital, unknowable, and forbidden power behind the secret and cryptic symbols. He realizes the existence of veil behind veil, and how modest and largely incorrect his own understanding has been. He comes to recognize the futility—and danger—of speculation and curiosity about ritual knowledge. (219)

Instead, the metaphor of Chinese puzzle boxes begins to yield emptiness: in the core, the outside observer sees nothing but deception and untruth. What a very different view from the richly textured ritual reality that the Baktaman have revealed, though it is not a tidy, or rosy, reality. Such a metaphor of mystery in explaining "primitive society" certainly reflects late Victorian tropes favored by Sir E. B. Tylor and Sir James Frazer (see also Carrier 1992: 16). Ironically, Barth suggests that because the elders are not a concrete class or group, "a straightforward Marxist explanation of the structure of knowledge as a direct reflection of social differentiation and privilege is unsatisfactory" (1975: 219).

Hence, the reader discovers that Barth's general theory of society rests upon a pronounced romantic-idealist interpretation that depicts the necessary badness of ritual secrecy. The elimination of secrecy—if it could be done without destroying the "welfare-preserving cult," as Barth (1975: 220) argues—is the solution to the problems of the social economy of the Baktaman. Because secrecy is destructive and infects everything, its "deceptive" qualities distort "truth" and goodness in all relationships. "Fathers must systematically deceive sons, men deceive women and vice versa, all public life is permeated with the protective tactfulness of sorcery fear" (220). Here, again, we see the imputation of individualistic moral flaws and the failure of contractual society conflated with the cultural reality of ritual secrecy, a confusion of the civil public and secret formations. While other ethnographies in the region generally confirm a picture of the spiraling effects of ritual secrecy (reviewed in Bercovitch 1989b), they do not reach the same conclusions.

Here, the European ethnographer Barth favors, as did Morgan before him, philosophical comparisons with classical Western traditions, especially the ancient Greeks, "where conviction through dialogue represents the supreme confirmation process." Lewis Henry Morgan in the nineteenth century could have authored the next interpretation: if Baktaman only had an "all-knowing god" or "Socratic traditions," as Barth pleads, they could—as a "society"—cherish a single "truthful ideal" (1975: 220). Stripped of their "veils of disguise" and "mystery," they could find more instrumental or practical "epistemologies" and "theories" of the world directly. Because no one can ever be sure of what is real or illusion, the Baktaman system of entangled secrecy creates "the ambivalence of fear of ignorance/fear of knowledge" (221–22). All social relations are thus constantly in turmoil. It is striking that all references to the desire for male intimacy as a source of solidarity or comfort are lacking in this final interpretive image. It is obvious from this omission that Barth conflates the public rhetoric of "secret mysteries" directed toward women and children with the secret male homosocial reality that distances and ropes off the men's house. These are separate realities that create and sustain gendered relationships.

The purpose of the Baktaman cult is to make sacred the "mystery of fertility" itself. "Secrecy is an essential precondition of this mystery," Barth concludes (1975: 221), which emerges through the deceptions of Chinese boxes, one box nestled in a larger box, leading on and on, finally to an empty box: the realization of the initiated adult man that the core of the men's mystery cult is "empty." Though Barth rejects the Marxist view as "unsatisfactory" and is skeptical of Durkheimian formulations, it seems to me that his interpretation enjoys the romantic-cynical confidence and even some of the conceptual thinking of both of these late Victorian positions. We would do well to recall the seasoned advice of that old colonialist Frances Edgar Williams in this context, when commenting on the supposedly "mysterious" and esoteric meanings of the bull-roarer cult among the Orokolo in the Papuan Gulf.

One thing is certain, that while the bull-roarers in their magico-religious character are felt to exercise some influence over the prosperity of the community at large, it is not with the express idea of promoting that prosperity that the particular ceremony is undertaken. (1976: 88; see also 1936)

Baktaman life was a bundle of competing men's house formations, competing male realities. They were engaged in chronic war and sorcery to an extent that creates demographically precarious splinters, rather than a monolithic "society." Baktaman faced formidable historical problems of adaptation: how to marry and rear children, how to negotiate war raids and chronic fears of sorcery, how to find a way to create dignity and confidence in a world saturated with gender polarity and secrecy. It seems to me that the men's collective secrecy is a means of addressing these complicated and contested "truths"—that there never was agreement or consensus about the meaning of death, reproduction, survival, morality, and virtue. I would rather argue that the men's secret collective is a gendered formation, built up from the self-interests and struggles of its exclusionary male cult. Nor should we assume that women were all of one voice. Mystery may be an essential ingredient to the cultural reality of Baktaman men, as it is in many peoples' attempts to understand and define the nature of the unknown in social reality or the cosmos. However, I fail to see why mystery should be so privileged, for the Baktaman account suggests that mystery is critical in the public discourse and beginning initiations of boys, as in the sense that mystery separates the inside from the outside of the men's house.

Is mystery *not* the sole desire or outcome of ritual secrecy for the elders? Barth's account of "fertility" is missing a lot; were we privy to the description of the stories of these rites—both the screaming secrets told to the boys, and the whispering secrets hidden from them by the elders—a different picture might emerge. It might in fact jeopardize the "fixed nature" of masculinity and male/female relations; it might supply the missing whispers of the old men and women that seem lacking. I wonder, Would these narratives sustain Barth's idea that the Baktaman are searching for Platonic Truth? Instead we might discover the more humble truths of Baktaman male reality, which are preserved, like a treasure, in the stories of myth, ritual, and folklore. They would not, I daresay, disappoint us.

The metaphor chosen by Barth, of the Chinese box as ultimately an "empty" box, and the complaint regarding the sad failure of Socratic truth are revealing of the slant toward Western idealism, which neglects the controversies of local ontology. Barth's communication theory conveys the context as one in which boys learn something, or learn to do something (i.e., practice secrecy), or acquire a way of handling it, or—even more vulgar—they internalize the received secret content in a passive way that changes neither the boys nor the secrets. No role is assigned to sources of the code or meanings for social relations, especially sexuality. The youth are not a blank slate; secrecy is inscribed upon a prior cultural awareness. Immense effort is needed to dispel that prior cultural world—the discontinuities Barth describes in his vivid depiction of initiation and the men's trickery and debunking of the boys' sensibilities are real enough. Yet we are never told why these energies are directed at the prior awareness, if, indeed, the Baktaman cult is simply concerned with mystery. Clearly, the preritual experience or sociality of the boys is being urgently contested. The men tell with certainty that they must create new gendered ontologies in the boys—perhaps in response to the desires and longings and objects left over from childhood that no longer have appropriate signifiers in the context of the men's house (Herdt 1987d).

What Baktaman ritual reveals cannot be verbalized or taught easily, if at all, and here I agree with Barth's view—but for different reasons. Ontology cannot even be learned in a linear mode, and here I also agree with Barth's (1987) later "analogical" emphasis. Ritual secrecy can only be entered into, participated in, and acted upon in intimate and social relations. However, contrary to Barth, we should not conclude that there is no underlying theory of being. Belief and faith can be enhanced; once the boys are securely ensconced in this system, they can be verbally coached and folded into existing hierarchies of quiet conformity to the Ideal Man ideology that becomes their commitment against the incoherent world of public or womanly and domestic affairs.

Here we might recall the role of the monstrous. Poole (1982) has emphasized the exposure to the grotesque among the neighboring Bimin-Kuskusmin. Much of Bimin ritual impinges upon the cultural reality of maleness and femaleness in the bodies, minds, and souls of the lads. Indeed, the grotesques and monstrosity of the liminal sacra in the Bimin ceremonies seems aimed at making neophytes sharply and pointedly aware of what to fear—and desire. As Whitehouse once noted, memory here is the result of "the unique and intense quality of ritual experience" (1992: 787). Initiates learn new meanings to access new awareness of their desires for objects. That is, the boys are acquiring the secret ontology of their gender, which displaces and substitutes for ("female") subjectivities that came before, with the insistent fears of ritual secrecy directing this in a seemingly mysterious way. That conditional masculinity is tenuous. "Monsters startle neophytes into thinking about objects, persons, relationships, and features of their environment they have hitherto taken for granted," in the words of Victor Turner (1967: 105). Turner's oft-cited conception is helpful in debunking the public and semisecret rhetoric of the Baktaman men, since they inhabit hamlets and social fields that are sufficiently fragmentary that no inclusive ideology will serve to make coherent the discontinuities of their lives. Such an intense subjectification of the secrets of ritual is of course the very texture from which ritual ontologies of Otherness are created.

As ritual initiates come to handle secrets, they participate in newly gained power and agency—the heightened order of cultural reality so different from before. Each successive stage of initiation leads to new meanings and revelations: to an increasingly coherent scheme of things, as instantiated in the general agreement the men had with respect to their myth of the origins of the men's cult and women's fertility. These steps require years of field study to observe (Ottenberg 1989).

Ultimately, Barth canonizes "mystery" as the key mechanism for the maintenance and stability of an uneasy partnership between Baktaman social life writ large and the men's ritual secret formation (cf. Durkheim's [1915] "conscience collective"). Such a Durkheimian idealism is surprising in view of his criticism of the emphases of other anthropologists (Barth 1987). However, it is precisely this kind of conceptual loophole that characterizes the powerful legacy of the romantic-cynical approach to secrecy. Perhaps, like Kenneth Read in an earlier generation, Barth was instilled with the values of the social democracy that saluted open communication in society and despised secrecy. The paradox of "the conventional blessings enumerated as springing from good cult practice" and the dire image of mystery-secrecy that defies truth-seeking and spoils all social relations is ineluctable. However, such is the Achilles' heel of conditional masculinity. Baktaman men have infused such worry over diffuse power into their ontology, but without either fully recognizing it or denying it.

We have not examined how local notions of desire and sexual need, as well as sexual harm, are placed in the service of building social economies. No analysis of the deployment of local concepts of power and the Idealized Man in these societies can afford to ignore what is being done with Eros and the energies of intimacy. Now we will study notions of male desire, male beauty, and boys' and men's sexuality in the context of the production of masculinity and femininity—the focus of the next ethnographic case.

The Baruya

With the work of French anthropologist Maurice Godelier on the Baruya, we arrive at one of the most recent, detailed, and important accounts of ritual secrecy to grace contemporary New Guinea studies. Indeed, I must confess that I have found myself marveling at this inspired treatment of the topic of secrecy in the Baruya ethnography, which may seem very odd, in view of the fact that Godelier began his career as a Marxist and I as a Freudian. Of course there is a danger that my reading of Godelier is prompted by my own familiarity with the Baruya, and their similarity to the Sambia, their neighbors. I am critical, however, of some of the tenets of male domination that Godelier asserts, especially as these contrast with the wider literature, as well as my own work among the Sambia. Yet there is much to learn from Godelier's study; of special importance for understanding the role of the men's house is Godelier's appreciation of an ontological theory of ritual secrecy.

The Baruya live on the fringes of the Eastern Highlands and number around two thousand. Beginning in 1967, Godelier began a long-term field study of the Baruya in what was at that time restricted territory due to local warfare. An Anga-speaking people of similar geographic and cultural origin to that of the Sambia (Herdt 1984a), the Baruya are an acephalous and patrilineally organized people with a ritual complex and rich initiation system not unlike the Sambia. War was very common, and its mythology and practice colored all aspects of social life. Most marriage is arranged. Direct exchange of women is common and plays a role in the creation of alliances between groups. Women can have a say in the arrangements, particularly through the ministrations of their brothers. The Pax Australiana not only effected pacification and led the way for missionaries, it hastened the transformation of a ritual system already changing. Godelier has coined the important concept of "great men" as a major prototype of symbolic action and power in Melanesia as a whole (Godelier and Strathern 1991). Whereas Godelier's project commenced with the study of land tenure and political economy, it later fanned out to understand leadership and gender domination, ending with a major analysis of these areas in the book *The Making of Great Men: Male Domination and Power among the New Guinea Baruya*, which will be the primary focus of the following interpretation. He focuses on "the machinery of male domination, the production of great men, and the ideological justification of this social order" (1986: xii).

This picture of Baruya ritual secrecy emphasizes homosociality in the men's house and trust among initiated males vis-à-vis other groups or excluded others. Ritual secrecy works like an elementary form of copyright protection, an embodied intellectual property of ways through which the secret rites change the body or preserve it. Blood-letting and insemination rites are the most powerful of such dietetics among the Baruya and Sambia (Herdt 1982b). The sense of infringement upon ritual property was pervasive in precolonial culture and commanded significant energy in protecting against theft or loss of ritual custom through some other means. The secrecy exists for the protection of one's most precious assets, the ways of becoming and being: alive, healthy, productive, fertile. Ritual practices are the support of such being in an imperfect world of war and political assassinations, where enemies would rob the "soul" of the individual actor and thereby deprive the collective polity of the strength of another member of the men's cult.

In keeping with a neostructuralist Marxist approach, Godelier anchors the social economy of ritual secrecy in the material structures of life. His key question concerns how domination can be achieved in a classless society such as the Baruya. Unlike prior writers, Godelier examines a variety of concepts of power and compares rule with authority, particularly by his detailed conceptual model of the Great Man. He does not directly interrogate ritual secrecy, as his parenthetical treatment of the subject engages a series of spaces or lapses in the symbolic structure.

Yet Godelier's approach is perpetually cynical about the sources and meanings of secrecy, as we shall see, and it retains the antisocial conception of ritual secrecy as a tool of oppression to exploit women and children. "In male power, violence combines with ruse, fraud, and secrecy, all of which are used consciously to preserve and widen the distance that separates and protects men from women, as well as ensuring their superiority" (1986: 232). To place violence on the same footing as the system of ritual secrecy is to conflate two quite distinct orders of things, public affairs and secret reality, as we have previously seen from the critical reinterpretations of the Gahuku-Gama and the Baktaman. In addition, the paradox of conditional masculinity takes a more pronounced form among the Baruya, for the secret ritual embodiments of insemination of boys are here a means of negotiating gender relations differently than elsewhere.

Nevertheless, Godelier clearly understands that gender relations are all

about the politics of creating and contesting reality among the Baruya:
here we are in agreement. "Male/female relations emerge under a somewhat different light, as the opposition between two realities each of which
has its limits in the positive characteristics of the other" (1986: 53). Agreed;
while Barth was inclined to this direction, he never fully grasped, as does
Godelier, the immense import of these gendered realities for sociality.

The basis of Baruya gender relations begins with inequality but pro-
ceeds to complementarity in a whole variety of domains (Wagner 1975). In
general, however, women are prevented from controlling food production,
while they are in turn uniquely perceived to be in control of the production
of babies. As Godelier notes, women are excluded from the ownership of
land, the manufacture of tools, and the use of weapons, either for hunting
or war. Nor are women permitted to produce the local vegetal salt bars for
which the Baruya are famous (Godelier 1971). None of these restrictions is
based upon "biology"; they are the social controls and dictates of the men's
house. Men fill the more glamorous roles of society, produce game from
hunting, and participate in all aspects of the prestige system and warfare,
which funnel into the production of outstanding charismatic leaders. Great
Men, Godelier argues, are blessed with the rugged, masculine qualities of
courage, valor, physical strength, and spiritual power through knowledge
of myth and ritual lore, along with a variety of other attributes that provide
renown.

Women are physically constricted in many ways, particularly by spatial
movement, the choice of footpaths, and comportment toward men, especially their husbands. On the cosmological level, women are "excluded
from the ownership and use of the sacred objects which . . . allow the production of social order" (1982: 8; see also 1973, 1986). Domination
extends, according to Godelier, through marriage exchange, although
women have some say in these arrangements. However, once they are married, they cannot leave their husbands: "Baruya women are thus subordi-
nate to men materially, politically and symbolically" (1982: 11), and they
always consent or do not resist. Furthermore, ritual initiation generates
inequality and "legitimizes the apparatus of socialization of individuals"
through the ritual system. "But we must not forget that Baruya women
have their own secrets, protecting them from the men and constantly
reminding them that women have powers too" (Godelier 1986: 231–32).
Indeed, we must credit female secrecy as being the source or base of the
women's ontology, not to mention the suspicions that men have about the
diffuse power in the menstrual hut.

Men thus treat women as politically suspect and supernaturally dangerous pollution-carriers, as well as being the secret generators of divergent power and reality. Baruya men always regard sex with women as "dangerous because it pollutes, and the pollution weakens, corrupts, and endangers strength and life" (Godelier 1986: 18). Male attitudes about women's fertility and procreativity reveal the deeper project of secrecy among the men. Godelier tells us that the Baruya men seize "every opportunity of minimizing the importance, or even denying the fertilizing powers that apparently belong only to women" (69), a theme noted in the prior case studies. Thus, for example, men believe that women's milk comes from the men's "semen." Godelier remarks, "There is thus some play, some contradiction even, in certain parts of the Baruya . . . ideological edifice" (69), but not so much as to overthrow their primary aim: to create an entirely self-contained utopian world without women, capable of socially reproducing male reality. This is the primary tenet on which the Baruya social economy of ritual secrecy thrives.

Certainly, concepts of creation and concealment are necessary elements of many Melanesian theories of domination, as previously argued, but these take on a sharp profile among the Baruya. As Godelier has noted, Baruya myths and rites "serve to interpret and justify the social inequalities between men and women" (1986: xii). To be effective the means and ends of symbolic domination must be explained in the origin of things and hidden to mobilize voluntary human action (Gillison 1993; Keesing 1992). Again and again Godelier returns to the problem of symbolic reproduction by men; thus, the secret male reality abrogates "the principal role in the making of the child," extended through a "series of symbolic gestures, rites and practices . . . to demonstrate men's dominance in the process of reproduction of life" (1986: 228). Pascale Bonnemere (1996: 375) has written of the Ankave people, near the Sambia and Baruya, in a way that favorably compares this point with respect in the creation of gendered realities based in ritual secrecy.[2]

Godelier sees "male domination" as "the primordial basis of all social organization and cultural identity" in Baruya society (1982: 34). Here we face the fundamental issue of how sociality is made out of the "false consciousness" of male secrecy. The Marxist notion of "false consciousness" in this approach suggests a form of class oppression that is "naturalized" and uncritically played out in social reality. The experience of Baruya is a kind of false consciousness, implanted through rituals, that exists within the intimate and supposedly classless state of these societies. Such a view is consistent with the long-standing bias that regards secrecy as antisocial in Western bourgeois society. In a lovely passage toward the latter part of his ethnography, Godelier shows a subtle and deep understanding of the role of truth, illusion, and secrecy in relations between the genders:

> In erotic songs there is a bawdy exchange between men and women . . . but the songs pose no threat to the foundation of society. On the contrary, they demonstrate that each sex knows a good deal more about the secret of the other than is officially acknowledged. But is not the main thing, surely, their mutual complicity in keeping silent about what they know in order to keep up appearances, safeguard the social order, and hand it down to the next generation? Surely too, is not this solidarity between the sexes a sign that both acknowledge the necessity of male domination? (1986: 160–61)

Thus the suggestion of duplicity and accommodation by women to the men must be seen as a distinctive theory, part French and part New Guinean.

The whole notion of different classes of beings, the one that produces life from its body, the other that re-creates life from its rituals, becomes self-evident, like a "fact of nature" that may be used to dominate and justify secrecy. Here, the key image is of men giving birth or rebirth. Gender is ritually produced, garnered into oppositional social categories, socializing people into gender-distinctive desires and intentions that match those oppositional categories. Hence, men usurp all prior subjectivity in the boys in an effort to create trust and intergenerational alliances as the basis for future sociality. Soon enough, ritual socialization into male rhetorical ideology directs boys to see diffuse power as embodied through ritual and planted in the budding boy-agent, rather than as being born with them "naturally," as attributed to women.

Male initiation is therefore the basis of all knowledge and power. Initiations for boys begin at an early age and structure subsequent development leading up to fatherhood in the early twenties. Girls have initiations beginning with the formal marriage, followed by the menarche and birth ceremonies. According to Godelier, there are two "secrets" of Baruya male initiation. First, that semen bestows "life" and is given as nourishment for strength to a wife before vaginal intercourse can produce breast milk and a baby is created in her. Second, more sacred still (and no woman must ever know it) semen through fellatio is what gives men the power to "rebirth boys." Baruya men, like Sambia, need semen to complete their development. And like the Sambia, Baruya wives also fellate their husbands at the beginning of marital relations. Moreover, there is "the fact that men are the (more) beautiful sex" (Godelier 1982: 7). We shall return momentarily to the construction of the Ideal Man as the sexy and attractive object of desire.

It is important to note that the same processes of domination are directed toward children as to women, including boys before they are initiated, since the latter are viewed as extensions of their mother's bodies and sociality. Physical threats are exerted toward boys at the beginning of their sexual "domination." Godelier describes how boys are required to "accept the penis thus proffered" by older, unmarried youths, and if they refuse, they are "coerced" (1986: 53). Those who totally resist, according to male secret lore, were killed, and the "true cause" of their death was hidden from their mothers. There is no mention of their fathers; one wonders whether in this case, too, the boys' clan and patrikin are prohibited from seeking blood revenge or compensation for the death (see chap. 3 on the Sambia). I think it unlikely that the Baruya would kill a boy for refusal to suck the man's penis; no comparable cases are known for the Sambia (Herdt 1981, 1982b, 1987a). However, were the boy to reveal the secrets of initiation to his mother, especially his idealized rebirth through semen ingestion, this would surely be grounds for his assassination.

Perhaps it might be argued that anticipation of their positionality as adult men makes the boys and youth desire insemination and motivates them to play their part in semen transactions. Such a complex sexual subjectivity is as political as it is erotic. As regards the role of homoerotic meanings and practices in the domination of women and boys, Godelier has recently offered the following opinion:

> Homosexuality is thus in this case, fundamentally the affirmation and the construction of relations of power, relations of forces between the sexes and between the generations. Before being erotic, it is a particular way, a political practice, because the boys cannot refuse the semen given them, otherwise the adult men will kill them by breaking their neck and they will pretend their death was an accident. (1995: 121)

This is a bold position that is plausible but also conceptually flawed. We are not, of course, dealing with "homosexuality," as no such category exists for the Baruya or any other Papua New Guinea people (Herdt 1991b). It is half right, but only the half that deals with the creation of power relations and the coercion of boys. What is half wrong in Godelier's model is the failure to deal with the sexual subjectivities of boys and the youths who inseminate them. What is each party seeking? Neither of them, I will claim, is an agent. While I agree that the homoerotic act is a broadly "political practice," its presence within the homosociality of the men's house, and the intimacies that impel men to create trust to secure reality, make this particular "political practice" one of the greatest intimacy and embodiment, transforming the political into the erotic, and vice versa, before our eyes. In other words, the erotic is political, much as the political is erotic. As David Halperin once remarked, there can be no orgasm without ideology. Baruya boys gain agency through this insemination; the men believe that this subject can become an object only in this way. And as we know, the men cast stones at the untidy, unstable social world, and prefer a utopian but secret one for their own reproduction. On another point, I am in agreement with Godelier: The separation of sons from their mothers "is at the heart of the issue"; and what men do "in the imaginary world" is "to dispossess women of their creative powers and to transfer these to men" (1986: 146).

Now we are led back to the question: Is ritual secrecy to be explained in this conceptual approach? Is it treated authentically in the creation of cultural reality, or is it treated as a fraud, a hoax, a fiction, or a kind of performative game, biding the time of the men and women as they attempt to come to grips with each other in public affairs? Ultimately, Godelier cannot escape the sense that male secrecy is inauthentic. Godelier's work takes the issue of secrecy much more seriously than prior scholars, and he anchors it in the production of cultural reality. However, his observations are brought to bear on describing and explaining the domination of women, which cannot explain the fundamental question as to why men need ritual secrecy to accomplish domination.

A story is told of how a woman "suspected of having questioned a young initiate about the secrets of male initiation rites was put to death, and the boy as well. Her lineage was not permitted to exercise its right of vengeance . . . there was no pay back. . . . The laws of lineage vengeance were thus waived for the sake of the general interest . . . which were thus assumed to be identical with those of society at large" (1989: 179). Godelier suggests furthermore that the betrayal of ritual secrets creates such a threat of chaos to the social order that no refuge could be offered to someone sanctioned and fleeing their own society. Moreover, in the parallel case, if a woman discovered the men playing the flute she was also put to death and her clan could claim no right of blood revenge (152).

> This kind of betrayal haunts the imagination of the Baruya to the point of obsession, as well as those of their neighbors that partake of the same culture. One can see why anyone guilty of so heinous a crime cannot, and must not, be given refuge outside his tribe, for all the neighboring tribes, whether friend or foe, are threatened to their very foundations by the subversion that such betrayal implies. (1989: 179)

These structures of domination, including ritual, do not sit well on the folk psychologies of the Baruya, including their Ideal Man imagery, for these are part and parcel of how they constitute reality. The men use this public rhetoric to contest what the women do, and rein them in, for they suspect them of being political subversives loyal to their enemies. Moreover, the power women contain in their bodies, along with how the women's bodies are a proxy for the power of other competing social groups, is a political football in the intergenerational relations of boys and men, fathers and sons. While I agree with Allen's point that high-status women in some societies constitute a "threat to overt male dominance" (1967: 26), what does "high status" mean in intimate societies like the Baruya? Baruya women are perceived to be a substantial threat to the men, which suggests that they have higher status than might have been thought. Indeed, in terms of tuber production and the affections of children, they are not without leverage. Godelier does not entirely deal with this symbolic issue (but see M. Strathern 1988: 207–19, especially 219), since he relies upon the neopsychological essentialism of Baruya men's narratives. Thus, Godelier (1986: 229–30) suggests that it is women's reproductive powers and suckling of children that undermine men's hegemony and rule, leading men to resist or even "abolish" their reliance upon women.

Having started with the ontological approach that there were two realities among the Baruya—the public world and an alternative homosociality created through ritual secrecy—Godelier lapses back into the cynical model:

The women and children are led to understand that these are the voices of spirits come to mingle with their brothers and fathers. In male power, violence combines with ruse, fraud, and secrecy, all of which are used consciously to preserve and widen the distance that separates and protects men from women, as well as ensuring their superiority. But we must not forget that Baruya women have their own secrets, protecting them from the men and constantly reminding them that women have powers too.

   In societies where men do dominate women and permanently subject women to particular forms of ideological, social, and material violence, sexuality is constantly called in to prove to the men who commit it, and to the women who are subject to it, that this domination is "legitimate." We all know that, when it comes to oppression, the domination of one section of society by another is fully justified and legitimate only if the victims themselves become the guilty parties, those primarily responsible for their own fate. (1986: 232)

In short, Godelier relies upon Baruya "difference" ideology and a general theory of male domination to interpret a false consciousness and sexual legitimation. He seems in the end to have realized that in secrecy one is dealing with the absolute bedrock of symbolic reality. Yet, given that masculinity is conditional, and through it men create a parallel, divergent reality, to promote trust and loyalty among peers, I think it follows that ritual secrecy is vital to male efficacy and agency beyond what Godelier suggests. In short: ritual secrecy protects the men from themselves. By this I mean that the men might be led, by conscious or unconscious motives, or through accidental slips of the tongue and other modes of "forgetting" and "revealing" the intimacies of the men's homosociality and secret clubhouse, to destroy their social solidarity as a fighting unit. Godelier anticipates the possibility by saying that "sexuality is viewed as a permanent threat to the reproduction of nature and society" (1986: 18). But the insight is not applied to the data.

   However, again it is remarkable that Godelier offers the other perspective so often omitted from the literature—that ritual secrecy actually works as an instrument of oppression in people's material lives. "Suspicion, denigration, denial, dispossession, expropriation by means of theft, murder, or imaginary forms of violence," Godelier says: these are the "formidable barrage of conceptual and ideology violence aimed at women" (1986: 148). We should not imagine that the women do nothing in response, nor that they "consent at all times and in every way to male domination" (149). Women resist in many ways, passive and active, and they really mean business. But there is a limitation:

> They resist male domination in thought as well as in deed, but their resistance does not necessarily mean that they have any quarrel with the actual principle of such domination. They resist . . . but so far as I know no female counter model has ever been offered to the reigning social order. (1986: 151)

Godelier's unique contribution to the study of secrecy and gender in New Guinea is based upon a fundamental difference that divides the formula of power and class exploitation in Western cultures from that of the Baruya model of sexual domination.

> In [Western culture], the procurers are socially and materially separated from the conditions of production, just as the essential part of the products is concretely expropriated from the producers. In [the Baruya], women are separated from their procreative powers by thought and in thought alone. But the way in which they are separated from certain of their products, namely, their male children on a given day, when men come to fetch them to re-procreate them and turn them into men, is perfectly concrete and real. Essentially, then, the transformation, the new procreation is not imaginary, since it is intended to turn these boys into men, who will one day concretely occupy the leading positions in the relations of production. (1986: 146)

By taking this interpretative step—viewing Baruya folk psychology as a necessary dynamic of cultural production, rather than an "imaginary" fantasy—Godelier has parted company with all prior structural-functional studies as well as with neo-Marxism.

Ritual secrecy can produce culture—or what I would here call the folk psychology of sexual and gender difference. I am particularly inclined to agree with Godelier that "these myths are undeniably the dominant ideas of the dominant sex" (1986: 74). The men create a distinct cultural reality that distances themselves from women, who become such an exotic Other, and the men set up systems of ideas that must be seen as justifying their own situation of domination. This is the insight that was missing from Barth's analysis. Whether conscious or unconscious or probably both, as Freud or Foucault might argue, is really beside the point. Ritual secrecy has embodied the reality in daily life.

The ritual systems of men in precolonial New Guinea were highly dependent upon secrecy as a means of defense, as well as for the constitution of reality itself. Ritual secrecy provided a sort of "concealment" of their intentions and meanings in these intimate societies with war and publicly contested realities. Concealment for men was a means to preserve the sanctity and rule of the men's house. To move the imagination a step further, secret images of "creation" drew upon the raw imagery of birth, menstruation, sexuality, death, and rebirth for the content of cultural production in ritual. No more mysterious processes than these exist in the human condition for the making of reality (Jay 1992). What this reminds us of is the imperative to understand social life as complex and multilayered in social consciousness. The realities of men and women, lived and practiced in New Guinea, are no different.

When all is said and done, the cynical French neo-Marxist philosopher-anthropologist Godelier has done more than any scholar since the time of Kenneth Read to illuminate the meaning of ritual secrecy and gender relations in New Guinea studies. Domination can be achieved and maintained in the absence of classes, Godelier suggests, through ritual reproduction: the rebirthing of boys by men through the fluid fetishism of homoeroticism. There is good reason for this focus. According to Baruya male ideology, men play "the principal role in the making of the child" and then continue this through "symbolic gestures, rites and practices . . . to demonstrate men's dominance in the process of reproduction of life" (Godelier 1986: 228). There is no way to rescue this knowledge from the meaning of the particular and peculiar folk psychologies of the Baruya and the Sambia, for this way of reckoning difference and desire is part and parcel of how they constitute their reality as a homosocial group.

Conclusion: Secret Masculinity

Conditional masculinity was a delicate balancing act situated halfway between chronic warfare and internal strife. The homosociality of the men's house tradition has not been thoroughly explored, however, particularly in its desires and sexual pleasures. Phenomenologically, intimacy, including living and sleeping in the same household, created perpetual torment between the genders and the generations in precolonial New Guinea societies. Ultimately warfare and pervasive mistrust are at the root of this process. Ritual secrecy was the attempted solution, however inadequate, in making secret masculinity as the historical solution to these challenges. But if ritual secrecy cannot be reduced to rational-based knowledge systems, how should we think of these elaborate forms of reality-making?

The anthropological study of secrecy has generally omitted the ontological perspective and what it may contribute to our understanding of self and cultural processes in time and space. Among these contributions is the basic point that ritual secrecy was the means of creating and maintaining internal coherence and the intimate social relations necessary to maintain a power system. Secrecy is thus a striving for an idealized and golden purity—ideological in the effort to accept only "masculine" but not "feminine" desires and relationships in the men's house. Like utopian cultural systems in the West that are constitutive of all essentializing classification systems—whether racial, gendered, religious, or generational—these projects all too often typify masculine hegemonies aimed at consolidating power and rule under a singular sacred ideology. Like sacrifice ritual in its ability to maintain and even promote patriliny through lines of father and son descent (Jay 1992), secrecy is a powerful means of uniting fathers and sons, and age-groupings, across diverse or even oppositional social boundaries. However, in the system of ritual secrecy, there is a process of imagination that provides the canvas for an expanse of the self to merge with the other in the smaller quarters of what is hidden.

Recall the paradox of male ideology, continually repeated above: Men portray themselves as superior and strong in public, and weak and harmless in secret, vis-à-vis women. Now, in ritual experience, this is only a seeming paradox. Social relations and subjectivity were highly fragmented when it came to men's positionality in public affairs, the women's domestic houses, and the secrecy of the men's house. As soon as it is realized that the purpose of ritual secrecy is to coordinate male agency and action with an intentional secret reality in the men's house for the duration of the life course, then it is patently clear that secret masculinity fulfills the teleological aim of merging male subject and object within a closed system of "male" or "masculine" precepts and concepts. By reordering sensory perception of phenomena in the time and space world (a process of "interpretative drift," for Luhrman 1989a), reality created in the internal discourse of secret knowledge reorders external relationships. This "ontological approach" to collective secrecy not only refers to hidden knowledge and practices, but also to hidden systems of desires, in order to understand a radical hiatus or break that exists between social relations and subjectivity in public versus secret domains. Ritual secrecy can be viewed as a special means of creating reality in highly contentious, unstable social systems characterized by decentralized networks of intimate relations. Ritual secrecy enabled men to consolidate their trust in the men's house, wage war, intermarry with hostile villages, and participate in wider networks of social and trade relations, all of which were dynamic and inherently unpredictable arenas of social life—arenas in which male agency was limited or dependent upon the trust of other men. It might be countered that the men married and experienced lifelong durable relations with their spouses in spite of the instability (Langness 1967). While I would not disagree that this indeed characterized certain individuals, others had multiple wives and experienced divorce and separation, wife-capture in warfare, not to mention the death of their spouse; such occurrences enhanced the contingent or conditional nature of male agency.

The exploitation of secrecy to negotiate social and personal conflicts through the creation of hidden and duplicitous public systems of knowledge and feelings in public and private domains of action and discourse seems so thoroughly modern, and perhaps so strongly based upon self-interest, that we are surprised to learn that this is common to a culture area such as New Guinea. The difference, however, is that anthropologists and other scholars have often thought of the form (secrecy) only in the presence of a particular content or institution (initiation rites). While initiation rites are of great importance in understanding collective secrecy in New Guinea, they are only half of the equation in conceptualizing how ritual secrecy fans out to become a worldview and alternative mode of creating reality in such places.

The developmental perspective, so beautifully illustrated in Simon Ottenberg's (1989) work on the Igbo of West Africa, has largely been neglected in New Guinea studies in understanding the creation of trust and distrust through secret systems of reality-making. What people know and what their being is like, or rather unlike, at a particular moment in the developmental cycle, are surely formative of the issues confronting gender and "sexual difference" theories in New Guinea folk psychologies.

As we have seen, Godelier interpreted the homoerotic age-structured relations among the Baruya as an expression of domination. Boy-insemination is an "affirmation and the construction of relations of power . . . between the sexes and between the generations." He also suggests that "before being erotic, it [homoerotic insemination] is a particular way, a political practice, because the boys cannot refuse the semen given them, otherwise the adult men will kill them" (1995: 121). The coercion is undeniable among both the Baruya and Sambia. But I think that Godelier's view that the politics precedes the "sexual" sets up a false dichotomy between the erotic and the political, and it ignores the local or ontological qualifications and functions that the boy-inseminating is for "growing" and "strengthening" the boy. In fact, it is difficult to disentangle the first factor as between the political or the sexual in social relations in many societies around the world, including our own, as feminist critics of this corpus of comparative ethnography have long argued (Gillison 1993; Sanday 1981; M. Strathern 1988). This statement can be used as a justification or rationalization of the men's behavior, of course; that is not my intention, but neither must I ignore the insinuation in Godelier's view that the men are mostly utilitarian about their sexual relations with boys. He implies that whatever the merits of their belief and secret ontology, we must first recognize their actions as being political. Yet, as Gillison (1993: 334) has noted for the Gimi, a subtle and perhaps secret notion of "homosexual heat" that bonds the relations between men in the clubhouse is so diffuse as to combine comradeship, friendship, and politics in opposition to women. For the Sambia, of course, the secret ontology of the men's house teaches that their inseminations of boys "grow and feed them," but also that the boys themselves can never attain power (politics) or sexuality (reproduction)—become agents, not subalterns—unless they first take the high road into the men's house and liminality for sexual relations with their seniors.

What Godelier's perspective fails to adequately explain is why—in view of the superior power of Baruya men, as Godelier has described it—the men require secrecy to accomplish the task of inseminating boys. What is left out of his account are the two special characteristics of ritual and secrecy. When we analyze the Melanesian archives from a similar perspective, it is hard to escape the conclusion that secrecy is not necessary or sufficient to do this (Herdt 1989a). A few cultures, such as the Big Nambas on Malekula Island (Allen 1984), the Marind-anim (Van Baal 1966), and the Kaluli (Schieffelin 1976) all practiced boy-inseminating practices in precolonial times but without secrecy. Therefore, if politics precedes the homoerotic as Godelier claims, it is difficult to understand what would precede the homoerotic in these societies if male domination does not need it. A glance at Kaluli culture suggests the larger reason why homoerotic bonds depend upon secrecy for the creation of reality:

> Despite its benefits, however, men's homosexual relations with boys are a vulnerable point in the male image of strength and consequently a subject of considerable embarrassment in relation to the women. . . . For their part, men profess (clearly falsely) that they do not know where babies come from. "This [pederasty] is our thing," I was told uneasily by one informant. "What happens when women go to the forest and bring back a child is their secret." (Schieffelin 1976: 124)

From this assertion, Kaluli ideology seems to claim the power to produce or "rebirth" boys as part of its enchantment. Schieffelin reports that the Kaluli believe nature, society, and the cosmos, including the productivity of the gardens, health, hunting, and success in warfare, "are affected by the potencies embodied in maleness" (1976: 125). This statement reminds us of the Gahuku-Gama ideology studied earlier, and it suggests an epistemology that supports the inculcation of maleness/masculinity similar to the Baruya and Sambia. Because of the men's insecurity we might predict that ritual secrecy would be sanctioned to support the cause.

Sexual subjectivity, dependent upon male ritual secrecy, was the great mediator in these systems. The character of disjunctive sociality made trust very difficult. The "vulnerable point," the paradox of the men's house, was the inability or even impossibility of achieving agency and power among younger males without ritual treatment. Homoerotic relations was but one of several strategies to create trust, agency, and power while producing social reality in the men's house. The paradox remained in spite of the power and illusion of this extraordinary means of building secret masculinity. Only with the destabilization by colonial authority did the unity of the men's house begin to unravel, which is the subject of the next chapter.

CHAPTER 5

Colonialism & the Dissolution
of Secret Reality

✳

SINCE SECRECY HAS LONG BEEN SUSPECT—a source of subversion, abuse
of power by brokers and nefarious agents of the state, and social ill—we
should not be surprised to discover that precolonial male agents of ritual
secrecy and colonial agents from Western powers competed for hegemony
in Melanesia. With endemic war, troubled relations between the genders,
questionable subversive activities in secret cults, and weird stories of cargo
cults prevalent following first contact, the view evolved among colonials of
a civilization at war with itself—a worldview reminiscent of the cynical
attitudes noted in chapter 2. There seems little doubt that this political
perspective supported the colonial policy of intervention at certain times
and places, as we shall see. Especially in matters of suspicious secret ritual
practice, colonial agents provided force when necessary to support missionary zeal in the destruction of secret cult objects and practices. As these
things go, the "problem" of secrecy was not a very large one for the colonial powers. However, long after the male cults and cargo movements had
begun to dissolve, the antisocial cynical and romantic views of male ritual
secrecy in these societies continued to belabor and undermine their cultural historical interpretation.

When social relations are built upon the contrast of public and private—and considering that trust between males was created through the
homosociality of ritual secrecy in the men's house, as it was in precolonial
New Guinea—what happens with the introduction of colonialism? In a
word: secrecy dissolved as the social order was radically breached from
outside. Warfare was typically suppressed, and missionaries followed. As

173

ritual secrecy was a counterforce to the instability of warfare, its demise undermined the men's house and defused attempts to regulate gender and intergenerational relations. Radical change forced men to redraw the lines of their reality precepts. With ritual gone, what remained was the rhetoric and morality of public affairs—the other side of the public/secret duality. However, those discursive controls were not up to the task of managing intimate relations, including those between the genders. Increasingly, individuals were left to their own devices. Hence, a new subjectivity began to unfold, characterized by the development of the concept of a "jural individual," harboring notions of "privacy" and private property, where once the tightly bound clubhouse territory of ritual secrecy reigned supreme. This change is the focus of this final chapter.

The study of secrecy must always highlight the analysis of unfaith—of what is challenged and incoherent within cultural traditions that relied upon the uneasy truce of ritual secrecy. And this unfaith is a difficult arena for the operation of Western science, and no less so for anthropology. Indeed, the very fabric of faith and fundamentalism is made from deeply seated beliefs and ritual practice of the person, and not just in the politics and public appearance of the cult. Faith in a sacred core of ritual is as significant for what it extols as for what it forbids. We have seen this repeatedly demonstrated in the exclusions of ritual secrecy and the means by which coherence is created in a hidden world that rejects secular ideas and sentiments as inimical to it. As the late Ernest Gellner put it, "Fundamentalism is best understood in terms of what it repudiates" (1992: 2). Nowhere is this insight of more value than in understanding male ritual secrecy in New Guinea and its postcolonial dissolution.

The Last Governor-General's Confession

Seldom are we granted the testimony of the chief colonial officer who assisted in the dissolution of an entire tradition of ritual secrecy, and for this reason alone the account of the late Jan Van Baal's time among the Marind-anim is unique. For in the colonial history of Dutch New Guinea (before it was annexed by Indonesia in 1961 and became Irian Jaya) we have been given the gift of how Marind-anim secret practice was curtailed. Van Baal's story is troubling and incomplete, being the sole surviving record; indeed, this is the testimony of the highest authority of the colonial administration, since he would become the last governor-general of the colony, and the last surviving viceroy in the world, facts in which Van Baal took glee. Beginning in the mid-1930s the great Dutch anthropologist was charged with administering a vast and wild territory, a task he relished alongside of his deep interest in Marind-anim society.[1] Van Baal was not only a man of iron will (the Japanese during the war interned him for a long time but could never break his spirit), but he was also an impeccable scholar and a Calvinist with a lifelong interest in what he called the "partnership" between God and man (Van Baal 1981). The combination of this and his politics (he once was a member of the Dutch Parliament) make his account all the more remarkable in its confession.

There is no doubt that Van Baal (1966), who was a tolerant and worldly man, was concerned over what he refers to as the metaphysical "dark side" of Marind-anim ritual sexuality. He might have been able to accept the heterosexuality of the rites, but the homosexual anal intercourse (involving "very young" boys, no less) and heterosexual defloration (perpetrated upon "very young" girls by groups of men) were practices that stunned colonialists, even the sympathetic ones. Certainly they must have shaken the heart of a liberal young Calvinist colonial officer from Utrecht, in spite of the preparation by Van Baal's professor, the Swiss Paul Wirz, who reported cannibalism, head-hunting, and sexual orgies as if they were so very common ("If ever there was a scholar who went for the dramatic, it was Wirz," Van Baal, personal communication, 1982).

Nevertheless, Van Baal was a dedicated ethnologist who soon discovered the centrality of ritual sexual practices in Marind-anim religion. So vital in the formation of the cosmos and in the cultural ontology of the body, fertility, and the soul, Marind-anim mythology was "obsessed" with these matters, Van Baal reported. For instance, Diwa, the great culture hero of the Marind-anim, is mythologically represented as carrying his long penis over his shoulder, an image that threatened the virtue of women and was not unconnected with warfare. "In fact, the myth is but seemingly a dirty story. Diwa's molesting the girl is not merely an act of copulation but one of head-hunting as well," Van Baal tells us (1984: 158). Whatever his private attitudes about sex, Van Baal suggests in this semiautobiographical essay that the mythic charter of Marind-anim heterosexual practice was immoral and bad, and needed to be stopped.

Of course, as a colonial officer, Van Baal felt an obligation to worry over such matters, particularly as he was charged with the pacification of the Marind-anim. Beginning in 1911, the Dutch had managed to rein in the famed Marind war-raids upon their neighbors and distant tribes, conducted to capture children and women. Even so, the Dutch permitted the initiations that symbolically supported the continuation of these raids. Van Baal was, by his own admission, personally disturbed by these practices, especially the "ritual homosexuality" and "promiscuous" heterosexuality of the Marind-anim. It was not simply that Van Baal was antihomosexual, though perhaps at the time he had his compunctions about it. It was rather the idea that sex was done in ritual, a compulsion of dark passions stirred up by forces beyond the control of the individual agent, in the sense that an "orgy" was going on. Indeed, Van Baal (1963, 1966) uses the term *orgy* often and without apology to refer to the rites, and this trope provides a critical clue to its meaning for him. Sex, in the Calvinist worldview, was supposed to be a matter of marriage contracts and church weddings that preceded individual desires and charted its splendor, in the Old World view. This was nothing of the sort.

By the late 1930s, Van Baal had grown increasingly disturbed by the reemergence of the ritual practices from years past that represented "orgies." He tells us that he played a critical role in thwarting them:

> The Marind-anim male is a kind and highly sociable man, but aggressiveness lies at the bottom of his heart. It can be overheard in the sonorous songs accompanying their great, olden-time dances. I attended one on the last day of August 1937. Two solemn circles of men sang and danced in opposite directions. They were surrounded by a wider circle of torch-bearing women lighting the colorful shapes of their males so that everyone could admire their magnificent attire and dignified demeanor. It was beauty itself. Yet, well after midnight, the psalm-like sonorous singing took on an undertone of threat which gradually became stronger and stronger until, around four-o'clock in the morning, I became aware of a savage aggressiveness about to be unleashed from the hearts of these otherwise kind and jovial men. Half an hour later I intervened. (1984: 164)

Intervention meant using armed troops and suppressing the rites forever. This ended—or should we say presaged the end of—one of the remarkable cults of ritual secrecy in Melanesia. Their rituals of boy-insemination, once greater in scope and longer in duration within the scope of the life cycle than those of the Sambia, died with the cult (Herdt 1984a).

In whose name was the last governor-general acting, his own or that of the Dutch empire? The answer to this question leads us into the rhetoric of colonial intrusions into such practices, a matter with which we are now well familiar, due to the opening story of Lewis Henry Morgan, and his ethnographic dealings and then progressive campaigns on behalf of the Iroquois. He was troubled to some extent by the existence of the secret societies among the Indians, as we saw, and the reasons for his concern are relevant to the dissolution of ritual secrecy in Melanesia today.

The political ideology of colonial authorities such as van Baal typically depended upon a public/private rhetoric that imagines but one society or valid civic group, equivalent to a state, or nation, inhabiting the same time and space. As we have seen, the Norwegian anthropologist, Barth, appealed to this imaginary in his ethnography of the Baktaman. The notion of a secret force in the same spatial and temporal field could mean only one thing, subversion, and this could only spell trouble for administrative agents responsible for "keeping the peace." All the other contestants for a voice are then perceived as subversive to authority and legitimate power. K. E. Read's account demonstrates this view. There are numerous examples of the process in Melanesia, but consider the following report from a key informant to the late Roger Keesing (1992). He is explaining the actions of himself and his fellow Maasina Rule Chiefs in the famous Marching Rule movement suppressed by the British (under the Sedition Act of 1798!) in 1947 in the Solomon Islands:

> They charged us with holding seditious meetings. That was the kind of law that was used by the Romans when the Jewish priests turned Jesus in. We were imprisoned for holding secret meetings . . . But we didn't hold secret meetings. How can meetings be secret when people come from all over the island to attend them? We were on our own island, trying to follow our own customs. (Keesing 1992: 117)

One can imagine such a complaint by Thomas Paine or another American patriot about the British during the eighteenth century! It is no accident that many of the American revolutionaries were members of the Freemasons. There was a kindred complaint, generations later, by the Iroquois who were forced to set up the False Face societies, vis-à-vis the followers of Handsome Lake, as interrogated by Ely Parker and his friend Lewis Henry Morgan. It is extraordinary to think of Morgan taking down field notes on a secret society whose existence was only partially desired by the Native Americans themselves in antipathy to the colonization by a civilization that Morgan sufficiently disliked as to form his own secret society to escape from it!

And so on: what is subversive to colonial authority or authorities on the margins of society shifts with history, in the geography of conquest. The contradictions are perhaps always clearer in hindsight—and to outsiders. The difference is, of course, that colonial powers could not imagine unruly Melanesians engaged in ritual secrecy as being "equal" or agentic in the same way as our Founding Fathers or Morgan and his collaborator Parker. For there was no viable concept of the jural individual or cultural category of privacy in precolonial Melanesia (Simmell 1950).

From Ritual to Contracts

The particularizing cultural metaphors employed in understanding these distinctions are critical, since, as we have seen, the form of ritual secrecy is obviously divergent from contemporary Western models of jural individuals and metaphors of their contracts. The public/private distinction drawn in these matters is insufficient; as Marilyn Strathern has written, "The Western equation between personal subjectivity (and its exercise on others inert in respect of it) and the creation society/culture tends to regard the public realm/political life as an exercise of an enlarged subjectivity" (1987: 288). Indeed, precisely the opposite is true of ritual secrecy: Subjectivity is expanded in the hidden discourse and ontology of the men's house, not in the public domain or its affairs. Ritual secrecy as ontology cannot be divided between "society" and "secret society" (Read 1952; see also Tefft 1992; Keen 1994), as we have seen, for this duality evolved from false impressions of primitive and modern, central state society versus "nature" society, evolutionary leftovers from the age of Morgan and Simmel.

New Guinea meanings of ritual secrecy center on the contrasts initiated/uninitiated, male/female, old/young, revealed/hidden, and—more global—inside/outside, as noted from the case studies in chapter 4. An ethnography of local politics among the Kwanga of the Sepik River has well shown the secular inadequacy of the public/private dichotomy: "Kwanga social structure creates a situation in which people always have reason to suspect a hidden meaning behind every remark or action" (Brison 1992: 140). Moreover, as Strathern and Strathern noted of body painting and self-decoration in Mt. Hagen and across New Guinea, an "opposition between dark and bright elements is linked to the opposition between men and women" (1971: 172). Other social values, such as aggressiveness for males and fertility for females, they suggested, can be understood as diffuse signifiers of gender embodied on the skin surface via body painting.

These examples of meanings are constitutive of what we might call "ethnotheories of difference" in New Guinea: essentializing classifications and rubrics, typically the stuff of signifying differences between man and woman, and older and younger males, and at a higher level of abstraction, between self and Other. While the gendered differences have been most studied in New Guinea (M. Strathern 1988), age hierarchy and generational conflict have been less frequent in theory (Flanagan 1989; Foder 1984; Mead 1956).

Where the traditional schemas are shaken up badly and rapidly, as in the many examples of historical millenarian movements and cargo cults in Melanesia, it has been found that gender and age differences are reconstituted, but not necessarily undone (Lindstrom 1993; Mead 1956; Williams 1924; Worsley 1957). As Victor Turner once wrote of Melanesian millenarianism, "There is strong evidence that religious forms clearly attributable to the generative activities of structurally inferior groups or categories soon assume many of the external characteristics of hierarchies" (1971: 190–91). Turner noted the famous case of the prophet Yali, in Peter Lawrence's *Road Belong Cargo*, as illustrative of how colonial ideas got wrapped around traditional beliefs and practices. Again, however, such a view threatens to normalize and homogenize a vast array of distinctive processes under a general umbrella (Lattas 1999). "A variety of desires for collective benefit coupled with apparently irrational strategies to attain those desires have attracted the label cargo cult," Lindstrom has recently written (1993: 189).

Space does not permit detailed examination of the transformations that have occurred in the colonial period, but we should reflect upon a few points of interest in this matter. As we have seen, throughout New Guinea, systems of ritual secrecy rely upon notions of collective substance, metaphors of the body as polity, hidden dependence upon ancestors, spirits, gods and the like in defining the nature and being of ontology and the practices necessary to achieve this. As noted earlier, the cultural secrecy I classify as contract secrecy occurs in Melanesia as well. Typically, however, ritual and contractual secrecy tend to be mutually exclusive as symbolic modalities within the same cultural-historical tradition. For example, boy-inseminating rites, as known from an ancient ritual complex in South Coast Lowland groups (Herdt 1993), are distributed within systems of ritual secrecy, while large-scale forms of ceremonial exchange systems in these groups are generally absent or poorly developed (Knauft 1993). Ritual and contractual secrecy may also occur within the same social field, though seldom within the same tradition, and, even more rarely, inside the same social actor. For example, the Gahuku-Gama and the Paiela (Biersack 1982) have secret ceremonies that lead, at least on their fringe, into contractual systems of ceremonial gift exchange, while peoples such as the Mae Enga (Meggitt 1964), with large-scale pig and shell gift commodity systems, institutionalized a bachelorhood cult that suggests male/female themes of the kind commonly found in systems of ritual secrecy.

Parallel cases concern the large-scale ceremonial gift exchange systems, such as the *kula* (Malinowski 1922), *moku* (A. J. Strathern 1971), and *tee* system (Meggitt 1971), which have long been known to involve elaborate codes of etiquette and incorporate aspects of ritual secret practices (Godelier 1999: 95–99). The latter are probably best understood as incipient forms of contractual secrecy, a context for negotiation and hidden understandings between individual actors as trading partners and, by extension, from one jural group to the other.

However, in the form of ritual secrecy, which appeals to idioms of nature and spirits as inherent in the order of the cosmos, conditional masculinity is paradoxically viewed as immutable, inherent, and fixed. In this sense ritual secrets are not a gift, as they cannot be "given away" or "exchanged." Such ideologies and their contradictions were constitutive of personal and cultural reality in precolonial times (see chap. 4). Contractual secrecy is more discrete or immutable, and it appeals to self-interest—with justifications and rights a matter of secret contracts that facilitate these interests. Though all systems of contractual secrecy in technologically complex societies such as the United States appeal to the private and solitary actor in concert with his or her broker, such a conception is obviously culture-bound and too limiting for New Guinea systems. Again, Melanesian systems of *kula* trading, the *moka* and *tee* systems in the Western Highlands (M. Strathern 1988 reviews these in a parallel light), and possibly systems of sorcery, witchcraft, and shamanic practice (Herdt and Stephen 1989) are sophisticated but divergent forms of contractual secrecy based upon hidden meanings and networks of partners, brokers, and interest groups. This latter model of sociality merged with group identity transcends the lone-child model of Western jural individualism. Both of these systems, however, appeal to divergent models of time, with the form of ritual secrecy typically based upon cyclical images of time, not the apocalypse of cargo cults.

According to this model, social formations of contractual secrecy do not emerge as historically salient until such time as the concept of a "jural individual" is established in a historical culture. While we cannot enter into all of the reasons underlying this claim, I would note that the concept of the jural individual is distinct from the notion of individualism as a principle in neoliberal democracies. A "jural individual" is a person-construct implying agreements and contracts as a semiautonomous agent, either in pursuit of self-interest or as a representative of a class or groups. Here, the individual as a separate ontological entity is critical to the enterprise of establishing how change occurs in cultural systems, and what the concept of agency implies for the transition from one form of secret exchange to another, based either upon embodiment and ritual secrecy or jural contracts.

Cargo Cults That Undermine Secrecy

Whatever the meaning might be of cargo cults and millenarian movements, many writers have interpreted these to inaugurate a new social reality—possibly a divergent or competing reality system, as we have defined it in this book—in reaction to colonial agents, sociopolitical oppression, and other sources of real-life challenges to the epistemology, social structure, power, and social practices (Lantenari 1959; Worsley 1968). As a means of defining cultural reality or hidden ontologies, however, the study of cargo cults was underanalyzed (Lindstrom 1993) until the recent work of Whitehouse (1995) and especially of Andrew Lattas (1999).

The tenets of a new order, the delights of new materialism, the pleasures or horrors of new social relations or rebellious sexuality, are all implied in these sensational and sweeping movements, which were typically opposed by the colonial administrations. The cargo cult may be construed as an emergent new form of agency with the potential for imagining the jural individual in colonial contact encounters. For the traditional power base of the secret society, the potential disruption that came from these cults was very great. The cargo cults neutralized factions within the village or rendered status distinctions between the genders and generations relatively feckless. Male rule was thus overturned, sometimes quickly enough as to actually see the displacement of beliefs and practices from the one to the other. The change in sociality was also dramatic, being neither purely "public" nor "personal" (Lindstrom 1993). The vital lesson in this transformation can be so subtle as to elude us:

> Sociability changes serious communication to noncommittal conversation, Eros to coquetry, ethics to manners, aesthetics to taste. As Simmel shows, the world of sociability is a precarious and artificial creation that can be shattered at any moment by someone who refuses to play the game. (Berger 1963: 139)

The millenarian is fundamentally a political activist and a social worker, and, as with all vehement reformers, he or she must articulate an alternate vision of reality compelling enough to make the public overcome its fears of experimenting with the future or its suspicions of fraud. The most revealing examples emerge from the times in which ethnographers were able to chronicle the historical transformation of peoples undergoing radical change. For example, the strange cargoism of the Orokolo tribe is known to us from the great colonial Australian anthropologist Frances Edgar Williams's (1924, 1936) classic texts on men and bull-roarers in the Papuan Gulf, which contain fine examples of how ritual secrecy was breached in the throes of colonialism.

The Vailala Madness among the Orokolo was among the most striking and zealous of millenarian movements to come to the attention of the colonial authorities in New Guinea. It resulted in the complete destruction of the traditional men's cult houses of the Gogola and most of their sacred art (Williams 1924). So far-reaching was the cargoism of this extensive social movement that Williams's diary account gives the impression of a people swept up in a kind of "disease epidemic" of "nervous disorders" that infected bodies and minds (Schwimmer 1975). The prophets' new visions were overlaid on top of the heap of the destruction of the old practices and the material culture that embodied secret reality. The ritual icons of the new sacred order, once used to create an alternative secret reality of more or less the same order established among the Gahuku and the Baktaman among others, dissolved this concept of Otherness by replacing secret practices with public ones. This breached the requisite social relations between the genders and generations that had previously been kept immutable and separate. All this was swept away in order to ponder the urgent problems at hand: how to gain access to coveted material goods; what sorts of ideas to make of them; what rituals to implement these plans to secure the goods; how prophecy could reveal truth; and how to conjure magical power to take control of heaven on earth (Burridge 1969).

Among the Orokolo, two ceremonies, the *Kovave* and *Apa-heheve*, combined the fervor of ritual secrecy and the generosity of communal feasting (Williams 1930). The combination was not an accident, since the Orokolo were remarkable in sponsoring initiations of boys and girls simultaneously, and extending a degree of secret participation to women, that goes beyond any examined above. When it came to the matter of their traditional ritual sound instruments, however, this was not the case. The bull-roarer, an instrument of enormous power, fertility, and destruction in this area, and which surely designated forbidden desires and objects of intimacy and homosociality among the men, was kept especially secret from women. Both ceremonies aimed also to protect the secret of the bull-roarer, ultimately sanctioned by death threats aimed at women. While the degree of the secrecy and the threats remain open to question, the colonial situation at the time definitely complicated the extent to which the death threat could be carried out. Colonization, in short, compromised many things in the men's secret reality, most notably its conception of masculinity and its difference theory of gender.

Williams was both a government anthropologist and a colonist, and we have some reason to suspect that he was not entirely impartial in his interpretations, though few would dispute his seminal contributions to the comparative ethnography of the Papuan Lowlands (Knauft 1993; Schwimmer 1975; Van Baal 1966). Williams was a pragmatist; his views of the bull-roarer were down-to-earth, perhaps the result of having spent too many years slogging through the Papuan bush on practical missions and medical patrols. "It is possible to unearth some esoteric meaning in the bull-roarer," Williams asserted. "But I would state with all possible emphasis my own view that mundane, secular interests are uppermost in the minds of most of those implicated in the ceremony" (1976: 87).

The men guarded the secret of the bull-roarer, a utopia that made possible performances of conditional masculinity and expressions of sexual control. "The women must not pry into it, and they are made to understand that prying will be punished by sorcery" (Williams 1976: 105). Indeed, these threats against women and children were constant, and the men were sometimes cruel and mean-spirited about them. Williams reports that men found "some fun" about their threatening aggression, and the younger men in particular enjoyed "hoaxing" the women and children (103). The playful/cynical meanings of the term "hoaxing" in this construction imply a kind of buffoonery tinged with hostility, all throughout the men's secret initiation ceremonies.

How much did Orokolo women know of the bull-roarer? Faith and unfaith: "The effect of this standing threat . . . is to make the women avoid all possible appearance of knowing the secret." The charge of duplicity and complicity, so common in systems of ritual secrecy (Herdt 1982a), would have it that women were assigned and played a role in the performance of every ceremony—appearing and disappearing "at their appointed time." Hardly the image of "rituals of rebellion" described by K. E. Read (1965) in his poignant account of a similar process among the Gahuku-Gama. But the Orokolo women would exit the village "in high good humor" to allow the parade of secret bull-roarers by men (Williams 1976: 104). "And when, in about 15 minutes, all was over, they returned as noisily as they had gone and resumed their cooking for the feast which was to end the day." The ethnography reports that the women "do not resent" such inconveniences. I wonder. At any rate, considerable resentment seems to have occasioned the advent of the Vailala Madness two years later.

As the cargo cult got into full swing, male rule was systematically undermined and began to change the working of the women's role. In particular, the women's adherence to the ritual secrecy and its threats of death seemed to fade or wane. Colonial and missionary agents were absolutely instrumental to the effect.

> It appears that a former missionary was preaching to a congregation composed of women and girls, whose minds he wished to disabuse of groundless fear. Intending therefore to drive home his point by practical illustration, to show them in fact what the *hevehe* really was, he produced one from his pulpit and swung it before their eyes. The result may have filled him with astonishment. For the female part of his congregation rose panic-stricken to its feet and in one wild scramble fled the church. (Williams 1976: 104)

Women at one time feared the bull-roarer, Williams remarked, and not just because it is was "intrinsically dangerous" and a devouring monster. As the Vailala cargo cult spread through the neighboring culture (Williams 1924), ruining the rituals and sacking their cult houses, all of the Orokolo ritual secrecy was still not spent:

> When during the Vailala Madness the bull-roarers were exposed at Arihava while they remained secret in the conservative Orokolo next door, many women of the latter village were supposed to have learned everything in their visits to the former, and to have been talking and laughing over the secret in their homes. Then it was that they began to die off: the old men of Orokolo were taking their revenge. (Williams 1976: 105)

Even this revenge sorcery was supposedly not objectionable to most Orokolo women, Williams insists, because of their "low" social status. It is likely that his informants were in a position to know. However, we must still wonder if he might have been wrong and simply guessed. We cannot be sure, either way: there are no other notes on the cultural reality of the women. However, a more recent report among the Kwanga, involving missionary revelation, may cipher a similar difference. Karen Brison (1992: 152) reports that the revelations "undermined the authority of initiated men." But in a further twist, now familiar but still useful to add, she tells us: "It is not important if uninitiated men and women know the secrets, as long as they do not claim the right to know them by speaking of them in public." Such a distinction is illuminating and may go a long way in explaining the situation of the Orokolo described by Williams. Yet the account of the situation of Yagwoia men (see chap. 3) also suggests that knowing the secrets and stories is sometimes desired but thwarted; not just as a "language of claims" (Brison 1992: 152), but as a system of being and masculine conditional agency.

Williams has demonstrated how women's adherence to men's ritual secrecy encompassed two distinct, even competing, situations: the assumption of a ceremonial role, and the secrecy behind it. He tells us that the women did not hold a grudge but I think this is just a bystander's opinion. It is more likely that men's threats and sorcery made them hold their tongues. It would be too simple, I think, to divorce the men's authority to enforce their secret reality from the women's "lower" social status or the colonial authorities impinging upon male rule. The men's ceremony is more than "deception" or "domination," to use the pejorative moral tropes studied in this book, and the women's role represents more than fear. That the colonial authorities treated the whole matter as a "disease" or a "nervous disorder" is perhaps not only an expression of the assumptive medical ideas of the times, particularly vulnerable to gender and sexual stereotypes (Herdt 1991a); it is diagnostic of how vehemently the village secret cult was in opposition to its encapsulation by the government. Whatever the case, as rapid change comes along, traditional regimes and systems of secret desire may unravel quickly. Change disrupted communities in which the balance of power was already loaded in one direction or the other, as Williams suggests in the cargo cultism of the Vailala Madness. The result of that adventure, the apocryphal myth tells, is death and destruction to the interlopers.

In such places—where male ritual secrecy was their central means of connecting male authority to public affairs and domesticity—is embedded what Murphy referred to as the "functional diffuseness" of social relations (1971: 144). To undo the diffuseness—the knots that bind public and secret into an extremely rich and untidy cultural reality—siding with the outside preacher, listening too much to the rebellious neighbor woman in her attempt to destroy the bull-roarer—is to unravel the entire civilization. Cargoism has become such a popular metaphor for these processes that we should not only call into question the basic construct, but also the problem of how we might construe the implications for reality-breaking. As Lindstrom (1993: 189) has argued, "The closer cargo cult comes to the self, the more the tone of such extended usage slides from melancholy to mockery. Comic book cargoism returns." As a new form of male agency for emerging jural individuals, cargoism destroyed what was formerly "sacred" masculinity to achieve a new private-property materialism consistent with a new theory of agency: an individualistic soul that is more gender-neutral and is less dependent upon the collective, drawn into messianic Christian afterlife.

It is this threat of the collapse of male ritual icons and their utopian ontologies that is the greatest result of social change, and in New Guinea we see the anthropologist involved, as well, which links up to other examples of transformation in ritual secret collectives across the island.

Fall of the Tambaran

"Every anthropologist has some share in the experience of a prophet," Burridge once wrote, "and every prophet must have something of the anthropologist in him" (1969: 160). The idea is helpful in introducing the last ethnographic case study of rapid change in systems of ritual secrecy. To bring the argument for an ontological approach to ritual secrecy full circle, we need to train our sights on an ethnographic project sufficiently rich that the unraveling of secrecy under intense messianic pressure becomes visible. The trilogy of Donald F. Tuzin's work (1976, 1980, 1997) on the Ilahita Arapesh is rich and comprehensive, and it is close to the story of change in this corner of New Guinea, not far from Margaret Mead's field site. Not only does it illustrate the intrusion of the outside to inside—when doubt and skepticism of the Other infects the men's house, shattering its secret reality and thus the trust of men—it also reveals the fascinating shift from secrecy to privacy, and from ritual reality to the private contractual arrangements of individual jural agents, men with men, and men with women.

The role of the anthropologist-as-witness becomes quite critical in understanding these highly contested controversies and revelations on both sides. Of course, we have observed in the studies of Read, Langness, Barth, and Godelier, and others, as well as my own, the contradictions of more stable pre- and postcolonial systems. Moreover, the situations recounted by F. E. Williams on the Orokolo, and Margaret Mead among the Arapesh, reveal the challenge of understanding the change from ritual secrecy to something else. To return to Burridge's comparison of cargo cult prophets and anthropologists:

> Both must pare their experience into what is communicable. An anthropologist is trained to appreciate just this shift from one mode to another. Nevertheless, in the event he is never quite ready for it. How much the greater, then, is the shock and turmoil in one who is not wholly aware of the nature of the transition in which he is involved? (1969: 160)

The Ilahita Arapesh of the Middle Sepik River (studied by Tuzin from 1969–70, and again in 1986) provide the kind of fine-grained ethnography necessary to meet the interpretative challenges of the task. In a series of ethnographies, Tuzin (1976, 1980, 1989, 1997) has built upon the corpus of Margaret Mead decades before to provide one of the most exhaustive descriptions of religious culture and secret initiation ever to emerge from Melanesia. The high point of this work is *Voice of the Tambaran* (1980), a masterpiece of religious anthropology, and the primary text on which to rethink ritual secrecy in precolonial Arapesh society. The incursion of a messianic Christianity provides the context for understanding what such a system looks like in decline; how the cosmology and ontology create unimaginable problems when the ritual secrecy system dissolves; and how a fundamentalist Christian cult displaced male secret intimacies, though it should not be thought of as a replacement in any simple sense of the term. Not quite old wine in new bottles, as Mead might have said; but certainly a perfume and bitter taste that lingers from the past. In brief, the Ilahita ethnography reveals how ritual secrecy gave way to messianic fundamentalism, which in turn boosted the idea of the jural individual among the Arapesh, embodied through individualized moral guilt.

The Tambaran men's secret cult is a venerable institution that has long been known to historically link and typify features of the Sepik River societies of New Guinea (Mead 1933, 1935, 1938, 1977). In her first article on what she called the "*Marsalai* cult" among the Arapesh, Mead called the *Marsalai* a "localized supernatural," which was "usually embodied in a water creature" (1933: 39). It had the power to change its form into ghosts and to become a variety of other forms, including snakes. The spirit was "male," and it seemed to dislike women, especially menstruating women, since it was "offended by the body odours involved" (43). The *Marsalai* would punish offenders or trespassers bold enough to enter its haunts. The area-wide Tambaran men's cult as a system of power relations spread through most of the Sepik River area and invoked "the innate incompatibility between *Marsalai* power and feminine functions" (45). The cult houses and men's houses that paid homage to this spirit were everywhere, often topped off by the inexplicable sight of the wooden statue of a woman, spread-eagle. In fact, at the end of her career, Mead (1978: 70) suggested that the *tambaran* spirit and the Haus Tambaran were surely Sepik-wide culture traits (Bateson 1958; Forge 1979) foundational to cultural reality. Mead suggested that the spirit "and his many attributes are felt as continuing realities" (1933: 50), though this was soon to change.

Mead (1935) of course studied the Mountain Arapesh, while Tuzin later worked in the Lowlands, nearer the river, among a people historically distinct but related to them. The Mountain Arapesh, as is well known, were generally peace-loving, communitarian, and fond of children. They engaged in hunting and shifting horticulture, dwelt in small hamlets, and were no match for larger, more aggressive groups along the Sepik. The

Mountain Arapesh had a Tambaran cult (or at least their version of it) situated in the men's house, complete with spirit masks and initiations and the other accoutrements as noted previously in Mead's attempt to photograph the ritual sacra (see chap. 4). Throughout male development, the initiations into adulthood used secrecy and ritual ordeals in the confrontation between the boy and the Tambaran spirit.

Among the Arapesh, the *Tambaran* is the embodiment, in some noise-making devices, of the spirit of the male rituals. Adult men assert their solidarity, reaffirm their masculinity, and produce growth and welfare for all the people through these spirits. Women and children are thought to hear the *tambaran* as a being and the noise-making devices, flutes, or bull-roarers, which present its voice. But to the initiated men, the word is a sort of shorthand reference to the whole ceremony. The *tambaran* is called *wareh*, sometimes used to describe the cassowary incisor, sometimes applied to the flutes, while at other times referring to the masks now going out of style but that once formed part of the esoteric material (Mead 1940: 429).

Mead was unusual in her ability to accept the secret practices of the Arapesh more or less at face value. Was this the product of her cultural relativism? And what role did her gender play in this perspective? Certainly, Mead was able to make cynical interpretations in her New Guinea studies (e.g., her largely unsubstantiated claim that "the Mundugamor had no viable male cult"; 1935: 182). It might be posited that Mead was just partial to the Arapesh, which was true (see Mead's Preface to Tuzin 1976). However, Mead's inability to deal with the complications of secrecy seemed to come from her objections to how gender relations were handled. Secrecy existed as a necessary part of the men's cult in the creation of masculinity, Mead believed; its contradictions or duplicity did not particularly trouble her. Indeed she seemed to understand the contradictions as vital and necessary, in spite of the fact that the cult ordeals of ritual initiation challenged her picture of a relatively happy, peaceful, and nonhierarchical culture such as the Arapesh (Mead 1972, 1977). Again, by comparison, she had a lower estimation of Chambri culture, whose men's cult she once called "a sham" (1956). Ironically, Mead seemed to turn cynical in these cases only when the men's secret cults produced traits that were so self-preoccupied, aggressive, and quarrelsome as to undermine solidarity of commitment to the village. Mead was of course a woman of strong opinions, as much as she was a brilliant ethnographer; we can surely accept many of these statements as artful characterizations. Years later she could formulate area-wide features of the Tambaran in historically interesting ways that showed a keen attention to contrast the cognate traditions.[2]

In 1969, when Tuzin began his studies, the Ilahita had a historically expanding and complex tradition of dual organization that was remarkable mainly because of the large size of the village and the tenacity of its Tambaran cult. Localized patriclans articulated with high village endogamy to create conditions of warm and felicitous domestic life for families (Tuzin 1976). The dual organization, however, existed alongside of the area-wide Tambaran men's cult; a complex, age-graded initiatory system based upon collective secrecy of the kind that Mead had observed earlier among the Mountain Arapesh. However, the combination of all of these institutional forces, as Tuzin wrote at the time, created dynamic but unstable social conditions. While colonialism was not at first a part of this picture, it enters later, as Ilahita village transformed from being a regional center of the Tambaran cult "to being a regional center of the Christian Revival" (Tuzin 1989: 206).

The Tambaran was a "champion of village wars," Tuzin (1980: 319) has written, and the "president of a cult of war." To see the link between warfare and the institutionalization of ritual secrecy so clearly is critical not only to understand the precolonial basis of secrecy among the Arapesh; it also illuminates intertribal relations that ramified violence and contestations via exchange, ritual, intermarriage, trade, and expansionist warfare throughout the Middle Sepik area (Gewertz 1983; Harrison 1993). The stakes were thus high in how secret ritual could be used to gain or lose ground in territorial contestation and intertribal poaching (Forge 1990). When the colonial authorities began to make their presence felt in this particular area, beginning in the 1920s, tradition began to dissolve quickly. But the government was unable to effectively suppress warfare until the 1950s (Tuzin 1980: 288), suggesting that the Tambaran cult among the Ilahita Arapesh was able to sustain much of its sociopolitical and ontological force until seventeen years before the arrival of Tuzin in 1969. Where Margaret Mead had operated within the context of a functioning and only recently colonized men's house, at least among the Chambri (and this surely tempered her opinions of it; Gewertz 1981, 1984), Donald Tuzin's arrival was sufficiently later that long-term changes, intended and unintended, conscious and unconscious, had already begun to dissolve in the silent barn dance that is ritual secrecy.

The anthropological story of this society suggests that among the Arapesh the Tambaran ritual secret formation was a military organization with religious features of a spirit complex and, unusual for Melanesia, a kind of high god. The same construction can be made as well for their neighbors, the Iatmul, and also for the Abelam, at least in certain of its symbolic features (Forge 1966; Juillerat 1990; Mead 1938; Tuzin 1976). The highly expansive Iatmul called forth a degree of secret ritual organization that was unmatched but had reached its logical apex and was perhaps already in decline, as can be inferred from the problems of schismogenesis that were central to Bateson's (1958) analysis of the famous *naven* ceremony—part of yet another Tambaran secret complex (see also Herdt 1984a: 44–46). Indeed, masculinity—its name, its silence and glory, especially its vulnerabilities—were always at stake in these ritual acts (Silverman 2001).

Thus, I would claim that the creation of elaborate initiation rites must be understood among the Middle Sepik River cultures as adaptations of conditional masculinity, particularly to the political requirements of filling and training the warriorhood, as previously studied among the Baruya and Sambia. The Arapesh opposition between the genders is in this respect quite typical (Herdt and Poole 1982; M. Strathern 1988). The elaboration of male secret ritual practices may be understood as a sort of progressive cultural increase across time, in response to these historical conditions of war (Bateson 1958). "Even in organizations where membership is compulsory, such as the military, great emphasis may be placed on rituals of induction . . . the greater the transition, in general, the more elaborate the rites" (Kertzer 1988: 17). The succession of initiations among the Ilahita was indeed impressive, even by the standards of the Baruya and the Sambia, matching their symbolic richness, but surpassing them in mythological narrative and architectural beauty. Tuzin's study of the Tambaran cult is especially remarkable in showing how physical form, ritual, and myth are seamlessly woven into a system of revelations throughout the male life cycle to create permanent subordination to the spirit *Nggwal* (Tuzin 1980).

Tambaran representations in these Sepik River systems varied in their perceived political power, mythological greatness, and supernatural authority. Among the Ilahita their supreme Tambaran is *Nggwal*. He was no ordinary poltergeist. *Nggwal* was both a great god and a monster, and omniscient—all-knowing and all-seeing. *Nggwal* was also capricious and devious; he liked to punish and seemed to savor the taking of human life as punishment for many wrongs in village life. He especially liked to punish women. Initiates could impersonate him on certain ritual occasions, but only so long as they behaved themselves and were faithful to ritual rules and dictates; if they got out of line, he would punish them, too. This custom of impersonation made him into a being that disrupted village life. Neither Sambia men nor Baruya nor any other group previously studied in this book achieved such a pinnacle of religious hierarchy and spiritual violence. *Nggwal* was not opposed to unleashing an occasional reign of terror by taking possession of men's bodies, as they would don his ritual masks. He likes to incite "brutal hazing" (Tuzin 1980: 319) on the boys who are initiated into his cult. So institutionalized and notable was this cult of ritual violence that Mead (1933) and Tuzin (1980) viewed it as a formal custom, called *laf,* or "ritual murder." It is said that in this trance and guise that the men could honor the village by killing its enemies in other villages. But sometimes they also went in pursuit of their own kin. Any man who dons spirit masks is subject to the will of *Nggwal.* Such a man, it is believed, is no longer himself, having a divided consciousness and personal identity, half man, half Tambaran. This identity state as a part of the precolonial system is remarkable in its own right, suggesting the inkling of a secular social self (Tuzin 1997). The merging of the desires of the god and of the man, outside and inside the body, is a remarkable feat of the secret system in these parts. Being no longer themselves, but rather the god, they are empowered with the assassin's secrecy provided to them by the Tambaran spirit mask. The god *Nggwal* thus substitutes his reality for theirs.

It is hard to see in this dramatic and destructive custom the source of social solidarity in community and society that both K. E. Read and later Fredrik Barth imagined long ago as the function of the men's ritual cult. Read, Hogbin, Langness, and others tipped their view to one side and concluded in the end that these practices all amounted to a hoax. Nor is it easy to fathom this kind of ritual murder as a sort of failed search for Platonic Truth, as Barth has suggested on the more romantic side of the equation. Much easier to accept is a rather pure form of the male domination hypothesis extolled by Langness, but later documented by Maurice Godelier. All of these accounts, however, generally omitted the historical effects of colonialism on the particular place and time. The complicated shift from a precolonial to colonial system that shattered the sharing of a system of desires and objects that left the men vulnerable, divided, and alienated was told in chapter 3's comparison of the Sambia and Yagwoia. However, what none of these examples has done is to deal with the presence of cynicism *within* the men's own subjective experience of their rituals, and this is the special gift of Tuzin's ethnography.

In a poignant essay in 1982, Tuzin initiated discussion of the problem of ritual violence and moral skepticism among the Ilahita in a particularly American way: "Why do good people do bad things to one another?" (322). He noted the reticence of anthropologists to enter into the problem as a result of their understandable reaction to the moralistic evolutionary notions of the nineteenth century (reviewed in earlier chapters). Classic social theorists might be inclined to answer unabashedly as a product of their own folk views of human nature: Marx and Weber cynical, Durkheim optimistic, Freud darkly pessimistic. While there is much to admire in Tuzin's account, as in many other cases we have studied in this book, it does not ultimately lead us to formulate an answer to the question, Why secrecy? Why did the Arapesh require the addition of ritual secrecy in order to achieve the ends of the Tambaran or to do "bad things"?

All of the elements that Mead and Tuzin incorporated into their ethnographies are important to interpret the cultural reality the Ilahita created out of necessity to deal with warfare in the past. However, history and colonialism were largely ignored, and here is where the later part of the story of the Ilahita makes no sense without the addition of the new colonial Other, which shaped the "double reading" (Lattas 1999: 314) of resistance and reuse of ritual secrecy in changing times. Once Australian authorities entered the Sepik to curtail warfare, their presence resulted in critical social changes. Among these was the increase of sorcery and ritual murder within the village itself—where formerly it had been directed to distant enemies, now it was turned against the village itself. *Nggwal*, castrated by the colonial authorities, turned bleeding and angry to prey upon his own people. We can now understand this unintended outcome as yet another manifestation of conditional masculinity gone awry.

The Tambaran in the traditional system imposed many burdens upon the men, even if he also offered them purification of their bodies and protection from their enemies. *Nggwal* constantly introduced conflict within the village. And his intense misogyny, registered in the hatred of menstrual blood and the willingness to do bad things to women while the men were possessed by the spirit, signified a profound gulf of internal differentiation within the village, especially regarding ideas about gender and the meaning of women. But Tuzin saw this as a personal and social burden for the men, and rightly so, since they generally liked and had cozy relations with their wives and greatly desired intimate sexual relations with women. (For those skeptical of the men's desire for women, consider Tuzin's 1994 report that Ilahita men practice cunnilingus on their women; for, as Godelier [1986: 61] has said of the Baruya attitude toward this practice, "the very thought is unthinkable" in many other cultures of New Guinea!)

A problem of terrible conflict and contestation opens up in the dialectic between what men do, say, and think in the men's house versus what they feel and do with their women in domestic settings. As Margaret Mead reported, Mountain Arapesh men love their children and enjoy playing with them, though later they have to initiate them, which causes great pain. The fathers can hardly bear to carry out the instructions to ritually bleed the boys or make them cry. Besides the tremendously trying ordeals of all the initiations that are required of all boys, there is another problem: the systematic hoarding of pig meat by men. This is even more difficult to explain as a necessary social practice, since the men never share this pork with women. Indeed, men say that the Tambaran has instructed them to feed only the boys and themselves, never the women. Knowing the god's dislike of women, the women seem appeased by this account. Or do they?

These are surely the collective torments of secrecy. Tuzin documents the pervasive existence of indigenous doubt about the ritual cult practices of the Tambaran, not among women—that particular barrier we have seen before—but rather among the men as they narrate their secret reality. And this is what is remarkable about his study: Ilahita men are skeptical about the actions of the Tambaran and the ritual violence used to reproduce their secret collectivity. Tuzin was the first anthropologist of his generation to introduce into the picture of the men's clubhouse an explicit concept of masculine guilt, which men confess about their secrets—a long-unreported phenomenon in Melanesian secret clubs (cf. Read 1955; Tuzin 1982: 332–33).

I must confess that I once was skeptical about this report, for the correspondence between the Ilahita account and my sense that it conveyed a kind of American reading of the emotions involved, though one not entirely out of keeping with Mead's own moralistic emphasis in her earlier work (Gewertz 1984), was fairly strong. But my reaction was formed before I began to puzzle over secrecy and then sought patterns to explain the maddening complexity of secret ritual in New Guinea cultures. Not until I had begun to read the larger anthropological literature on West African secret societies (Bellman 1983; Horton 1972; Ottenberg 1989) was I struck by the parallels to Tuzin's view of the Ilahita (remember, West Africa's colonial history is much longer than that of Papua New Guinea). Colonial change, as noted in the circumstances reported by Tuzin, also make "sense" of certain expressions, such as "guilt" and individual doubt—but only as long as these ontologies are placed within the dynamic of disrupted ritual secrecy which had destabilized the Middle Sepik area.

Now we can begin to understand these male subjectivities as precisely the reactions that would be predicted of men in the throes of the collapse of their secret cult, which previously defined collective reality, but now eroded with the emergence of the jural individual as a part of the systemic change. Tuzin has argued for demographic and social changes situated within a historical context, such that the Tambaran was introduced from outside of Ilahita culture and then was merged with existing structural social formations, albeit uneasily. As Tuzin (1982) reminded us, the Mountain Arapesh also disliked hostility between the genders, creating an internal contradiction: "a cult that stresses hate and punishment [is] out of place" (Mead 1935: 67–68). The Ilahita, however, went far beyond their mountain cousins in the torment of their contradiction. Where once they directed ritual murder to outside enemies and reserved masculine secrecy as a means of defending the inner sanctum of the Tambaran, the Ilahita transformed the violence and projected it upon the village—even toward their own families. Thus, Tuzin concluded that polarity between the domestic "spheres" or "ideologies" of men and the Tambaran secret cult generated out of itself created an unparalleled moral crisis: fabrication, lies, and the miserly hoarding of pig meat by men. All of this made the men feel bad, and hence, "guilty," a sentiment reminiscent of Western middle class emotional constraints.

Two elements of precolonial culture do not square with this view, however. The first concerns the practice of ritual murder, while the other conditions the creation of homosociality and masculine rebirth of boys through initiation. Traditionally, a category of young warriors, called *hangahiwa wandafunei*—which meant "violent" or "hot-blooded man"—was "universally feared throughout the land. . . . Nothing can vacate a hamlet so quickly as one of these spooks materializing out of the gloom of the surrounding jungle" (Tuzin 1980: 50). The "spooks" in question were men in secret drag; the warriors donned the masks of the Tambaran to become possessed by the indwelling spirit. Notably, one in ten of these masks was known to be "angry" and "blood-thirsty." How much the man was aware of this possession and its accompanying destructive emotions is not clear. He could take as fair game his own wife or child, if necessary, though obviously this was a manifestation of *particular* circumstances, individual choices. Always, the women could be victims, but dogs and chickens would substitute if neces-sary. It was a matter of "honor" to kill in this way—indeed, it was funda-mental to advancement—though originally, ritual murders were meant to wreak havoc only on enemies. Pacification by colonial authorities changed the situation, presumably in the 1950s. After the killing, men would hide the mask and return to the village, feigning innocence, seemingly as sur-prised by the violence as the others. "To this extent, the men are not entirely deceiving the women when they tell them that the *hangahiwa* are spirits incarnate" (Tuzin 1980: 50–51). Such an interpretation is surely con-ditional. Tuzin's reluctance to engage in cynicism about the men's violent performances is a product, we might speculate, of his insider knowledge that the men are apparently without choice in the matter of being possessed and must conform to the dictates of the Tambaran. A smidgen of doubt remains; might these particular males have actually enjoyed or found plea-sure in their violent attacks upon women and children?

The use of ritual masks to disguise the social identity and probable motives of ritual actors is a common practice in Melanesia, wherein it is culturally understood that male couples are the minimal social unit (Schwimmer 1984), and skin has the meaning of being the surface of the self (M. Strathern 1979). Ritual impersonation of spirits was especially significant in cultural systems that required the ritual leader to stage haz-ing or farces in order to "test" the violent capacity of initiates, toughening them (Allen 1984). Indeed, it was even truer when ritual secrecy demanded men to hunt for the heads of distinct enemies, as among the Marind-anim (Van Baal 1966). Here, ritual secrecy was perceived to be evil and perni-cious, and was, of course, the most intensely suppressed of practices by the colonial authorities, as noted earlier.

The idea of ritual cult masks used by a secret order to conceal the iden-tity of aggressive or homicidal actors was by no means restricted to Melanesia. As Robin Horton once wrote more broadly of the "majority" of West African societies: "Execution of the society's decisions is typically by junior members whose identity is concealed by masks" (1972: 102). He went on to elaborate a view of ritual secrecy that framed it as a "cluster of adaptations to the problem posed by the continuing presence in the com-munity of strong and rivalrous lineages." He identified properties of ritual secrecy that ensured the neutralization of lineage factions, that is, rupture in masculine solidarity. These secret measures, he suggested, were sanc-tioned by an appeal to the greater good of men's cultural reality, an insight that sheds lights on the Ilahita variety of ritual murder.

But what is this collective secret reality? At the time of the *Wafit'wi* stage of male initiation, when the yam vines dry, the initiation subclass sleeps in a special ceremonial hamlet far removed from the women and the children. The men here create a true liminal world—timeless and utopian-perfect—without the differentiation of gender in the time and space world, and absent the kin rivalries that mark other settings. The men take to feeding and caring for the boys in a most extraordinary way. "They are said to be caring for the 'woman,' feeding her by placing food in her mouth" (Tuzin 1980: 85). The older males are called "young adolescent girls," the name reserved for older women who sleep in the menstrual hut with a girl during her first period, a curious analogy. Toward the end the men take on transvestite appearance to represent in secret both "genders," most unusual for the Ilahita, though reported for the Iatmul (Silverman 2001) and not all that rare in other New Guinea initiatory systems (Allen 1984). These transvestites mock-attack or castrate the boys with digging sticks and generally act in vicious ways toward them. The initiates' ordeal culminates in their embrace of the "corpse" of a victim of sorcery. At this frightening moment, then, the boys are told "that if they reveal the secret of what went on inside the house, their future will be that of a corpse's" (Tuzin 1980: 85).

It is a strange set of images, to be sure, but the effect of demarcating boys from women as Other is obvious; when viewed in perspective, the imagery of Ideal Man and Woman/Other, with which we are now so familiar from prior analyses, reveals the utopian yearning of the Ilahita. Clearly, the Ilahita men are fashioning an ideal cultural reality in an effort to exclude the messy imperfections of their desires and object relations with women on the outside. They simulate a reproductively self-sufficient world that is used as a foil against secular society and become a secret ontology to hold onto in times of trouble when they might be tempted to betray other men. The imagery of the corpse surely warns them of the wrath of the Tambaran and becomes an internal signifier of the secret world at such times. The all-too-perfect world of the ceremonial village is reminiscent of the search for an unconditional order of masculinity that can never be realized in the time and space world. And this leads us back to ask how change disrupted these customs in the direction of the present.

The culture area of the Arapesh was dynamic and volatile in the dim past, as Mead hinted, resulting from the stress of "Middle Sepik tribes invading their territory from the south" (Tuzin 1980: 318). People gathered to form large village fortresses and adapted customs to meet the needs of demographically large communities. Initiation rituals were part of this adaptation. Mead tells us, for example, that during World War II, fighter planes bombed the Great Tambaran Haus in Tambunam, which resulted in "men being forced to show tambaran objects to the women and children" (1978: 74). Long before, however, European colonial encroachment had systematically opposed initiation customs, primarily under the guise of missionary activity (Roscoe and Scaglion 1990).

The record of this change is remarkable and shows the great extent to which each local culture and Tambaran cult responded differently to colonization in the area. In her original work, as is well known, Margaret Mead largely ignored this social history, consistent with the structural-functional theory of the times (Gewertz 1981). She was to some extent aware of the social change in Chambri, for example, but she did not utilize her own data on population decline, or the routing of the Chambri by the Iatmul years before, as evidence of change in her ethnography. The Iatmul were expanding aggressively, and they chased the Chambri off their territory and burned down their Tambaran cult house. Only after the Australians pacified the area and allowed the Chambri to return did the Chambri commence a feverish rebuilding of their own Tambaran cult. Arriving in midframe, Mead mistook this activity for a kind of timeless expression of female power among the Chambri, portraying the men as narcissistic and more preoccupied with art and religious dances, rather than assuming the "dominant" role of warriors or hunters. For their part, the Iatmul had undergone so much change under colonial rule that, by 1932, Gregory Bateson reported that their initiations had broken down because "all the available young men had left the village to work for Europeans" (1958: 275). Mead was cognizant of the change in Arapesh (1938), as hinted before in the story of her request to photograph cult objects (chap. 4). However, she never understood how truly compromised was the local security of men and how their masculinity reeled under the introduction of radical new gender relations.

Decades later, when the neighboring Abelam had abandoned their traditional Tambaran cult—which was remarkable in view of the advance of their sacred art and the role of the artist among them—they became enmeshed in problems of culture change. Indeed, Forge (1990: 169–70) remarked on the politics of reenacting traditional ritual among the Abelam. It is clear that the intervention of colonial authority and religious missionaries was of concern to the Abelam in this history. Forge describes how the Abelam denied they were reviving the Tambaran cult—obviously raising the question of the audiences and discourses to which such denials were being made—a nod to the fundamentalist Christianity and prophet or cargo cults sweeping through the area already. Even further afield the Kwanga are said to have practiced initiations only sporadically for the last thirty years (Brison 1992: 40). All the while, of course, the Ilahita were not standing still, and time moved on. Tuzin's (1997) latest account of messianic Christianity adds another chapter to this history of shaken and ultimately failed ritual secrecy.

By their transformation, the Ilahita serve as a pivotal example because they epitomize Simmel's (1950) idea that the secret is the "moral badness" that wounds society. The messianic Christianity among the Ilahita seems to have wrought such badness. The natives themselves heap abuse on those who cling to ritual practice, and a counterhegemonic ideology of "threats, oppression, and domination" emerges among women, children, and lower-status or uninitiated men. Women, in particular, scorn men today because they feel they were "duped" by the "fictions" and "fraudulent" traditions of their men (Tuzin 1997: 161). Local evangelicals demystified the men's ritual cult and revealed it to be a "hoax," reconstructing the past from the pulpit, then staking the claim that men's secrecy was never more than a child's seduction by Satan (Burridge 1969). By his thorough examination of the ritual complex, Tuzin enables us to understand how colonialism undermined secret reality and to look at whether Simmel's cynical idea really works in New Guinea.

Throughout the Sepik River area the existence of gendered ritual practices was a historical-cultural reality, including residential gender segregation and strong ideas about the differentiation of the sexes and their bodies. Mead (1933) early reported women and men could live in the same house among the Arapesh, but they had to part company during times of warfare and menstruation, plus whenever boys were initiated. Indeed, Mead never fully explained why such a loving and peaceful people found menstruation and menstrual blood so appalling. As her former husband once explained:

Then there is Margaret Mead's well known contrast between the Arapesh and their neighbors. Both cultures see an opposition between yams and menstruating women. Her Arapesh protect the women from the yams; the neighboring culture protects the yams from the women. (Bateson 1978: 78)

We know from the account of Scaglion (1986) on sexual segregation and ritual pollution among the nearby Abelam that the genders spent approximately six months apart each year (cf. Kelly 1976). When the yams were being cultivated, the genders had to separate and observe a variety of ritual taboos, including sexual abstinence. The spirits punished infractions, and we have seen the wrath of *Nggwal* at work in such matters. The reason is that the yam is a phallic symbol, a signifier of the man's anatomical identity, his virility and virtue; on this point a number of ethnographers seem to be in agreement (Forge 1966; Tuzin 1972). The spirits are particularly likely to lash out with ritual murder at women who offend their phallic pride (Silverman 2001).

But Tuzin's meticulous ethnography shows something else noted before—the presence of gendered ontologies emerging from initiation rituals. At least among Ilahita men, ritual initiation was constitutive of new subject/object relationships that displace the secular in favor of a secret reality, and this reality, in turn, imposed sweeping conditions to regulate interaction and intimacy with women. All of this is necessary for secrecy to "work" in situations where men's virtue might be compromised, where the construct of manhood could be breached.

When the men hold their secret pig feasts, the story given to initiates is that the gigantic, devouring *Nggwal* is present in the flesh—hence the impossibility of outsiders joining the banquet. Initiates presumably interpret this as a metaphor signifying attributes of the deity. Women are judged incapable of comprehending the metaphysical *Nggwal;* if told that *Nggwal* is invisibly present at the feast, they would not believe it and would insist on participating, thereby provoking wrath on a cosmic scale. For the men, *Nggwal* is present, eating the invisible essence of the food; when he "devours" his human victims, he does so either through a human agent—sorcerer or *laf* (ritual murder) executioner—or by striking directly, in which case the physical body displays no outward sign of having been "eaten" (Tuzin 1982: 348).

Nggwal does not just warn of the dangers of women, which seems to be the lesson of the teaching. The men are also being told that their separate reality is made necessary by the divergent natures and dispositions of men and women, and the utter impossibility of knowing what all of this could possibly mean. This rhetoric actually underscores how the man's separate reality is a condition of the masculinity, their agency. As we have seen in all previous cases, this rhetorical position led either to the substitution of boys for women (the homoerotic displacement) or the use of violence (displacement by domination), or both. The effect is the symbolic imposition of an Ideal Man and Woman/Other imagery, not unlike the mythopoetics previously studied.

Secret ritual predicates masculinity and the practice of male agency upon maintaining a separate, secret reality. The Arapesh crystallize ontologies of the genders that reach the logical extremes of ethnodifferentiation within New Guinea systems of ritual secrecy. I do not mean by this that their secrecy is more extreme or misogynist than the others. I mean that the Arapesh seem to suffer the torment of awareness, of knowing that there is a difference between their secret desires and their public ones; the contradiction between their subjective "guilt" and objective practice is resolved or appeased by violence. It is all too common a theme in New Guinea. The symbolic solution of creating homosocial coherence among all the males by the use of boy-inseminating is not present and seems only dimly reflected in the transvestite "menstruating girls" feeding the young initiates in the liminal state.

This is where the symbolism of rebirth enters as the overriding theme of the secret reality of the Arapesh. The election of a high god and that god's warrant for extreme sanction of difference outside of itself—even murder—implies its own mode of the production of cultural reality in the service of the creation of something entirely different: the utopian vision of immortality for the men. This is what ritual initiation and the feasting of the Tambaran promises. However, the men cannot reproduce their perfect world without women, and thus ritual secrecy must perform and objectify the roles of "menstruating girls" who can procreate and feed young boys. Men feel that "women are the bane of a peaceful society," Tuzin reports, but say that only in secret homosocial discourse. The men must not "compromise their masculine unity"; and thus they use ritual secrecy to create a "paradisiacal world devoid of women and full of life's pleasures." Women in this Elysium, we are told, need not produce babies, since men have taken on reproduction too. "A man's supreme loyalty must therefore be given to his sex group and to the important secrets they guard," Tuzin offers. "No devotion to family may override this, and man must be prepared to sacrifice—if necessary by his own hand—his mother, wife or child at the behest of the Tambaran." The men go off into the bush with younger initiates, there to create a "perfect world" devoid of women that corrects for the imperfections of real village life among Ilahita. Tuzin believes, "The case reveals with particular clarity the strict Durkheimian sense in which *Nggwal* is the symbolic epitome of social cohesion: 'the idea of society is the soul of religion.'" And from a different viewpoint, he adds, "The case exposes *Nggwal* as a corrupt deity . . . a judge suborned by the prosecution" (1980: 106, 304).

The Durkheimian appeal to the Tambaran as the ultimate symbol of Arapesh society is not entirely convincing. The Tambaran produced a perfect ritual secret world as an antidote to the imperfect village: society was wracked by internal competition and external war, forces that existed prior to colonialism. Yes, the Tambaran unified men; kept them apart from women and juniors; secured their cooperation in troubled times; and tended to suppress rivalries and the unfortunate spiraling conflict of an age-structured hierarchical system.

In another time, Bateson (1958) thought of this process as "schismogenesis," but that is another word for historical systems that destabilized masculinity and rarely allowed for peaceful coexistence. The warfare all around was the driving force in these systems; once violence was perpetrated, it took on its own subjective and material characteristics. After colonization, this system was all shaken up, and masculinity evolved into a darker and more troubling performance that remains to be explored. The Tambaran secrecy created a force—on one level political, on another ontological—under the guise of male prestige and ritual rebirth based upon a local theory of being that desires immortality but without recourse to the bodies and procreation of women. Men in many cultures have strived for this kind of nationalism; they like to think a utopian regime will last forever, but its exigencies reside in the moment, and not even for that long without the protections and commitments of secrecy. That men believed in the *Nggwal* and his power was obvious; that they also say women could not comprehend him, or his effects upon the secular order, was also clear. The women's motives, drives, feelings, and metaphysical conceptions differed from theirs, but perhaps not so much, or not sufficiently to create the homosocial solidarity they sought in times of war. Men's claims to power achieved through the Tambaran were mighty and probably difficult to defend all the time. Ritual secrecy—collective, embroidered with institutional and artistic forms, and distilled in a sophisticated pantheon, which forces men to obey it—is the protector of male rule. This total cultural reality bolstered a gender theory that was self-serving of this rule, as is true of virtually all theories of gender employed by men around the world. Thus does their secret ontology enable men to live in close quarters with those whom they regard as inimical to their being and welfare: the mothers of their children.

However, such an attitude burdens their village life in many other ways, introducing strife and ritual torment that is unusual in New Guinea but by no means unknown. Indeed, I suspect that it was just this sort of colonialism-induced state of affairs—with its strange incompleteness borne of the inattention to historical change—that Hogbin mistook for cynicism among the nearby Wogeo Islanders long ago in the 1930s. The Ilahita men are tormented to reconcile their worship of *Nggwal* with the family relationships and domestic bliss they feel most of the time. Such a social ethic is difficult to sustain and may frame the problem more in terms of contract secrecy and individualism, and less as ritual secrecy. The problem is that those sometimes-possessed young warriors take on the Tambaran masks and go out to do violent things. Their own local cynicism breaks through, reminding us of Simmel's insights about secret societies. Tuzin continues:

> The more senior and sophisticated initiates . . . are privately skeptical of these conventional metaphors. More than once it was intimated to me that just as the fiction of the physical *Nggwal* enables men to dominate women, so the invisible *Nggwal* enables the senior initiates to dominate the junior colleagues. The lie is itself a lie. Astonished upon hearing this, I asked my informant, "what then, was the truth about *Nggwal?*" To which he replied, "*Nggwal* is what men do." (Tuzin 1982: 348–49)

The anthropologist has here captured for us an extremely precious and rare historical moment of reflection by insiders about their own secrecy. Of course, it is a subjectivity constructed in dialogue with an outsider, but there is plenty to admire in the work that enabled its understanding. What I reject is the language employed—the universal concepts of "lie" and "truth"—which assume Western epistemology and an individualistic frame of reference, much like the reinterpretations of works by Read and Barth.

More important, the notion that ritual secrecy is empty—a kind of "lie" because there is nothing to it, being conditioned not by the gods but by men—is a fundamental misunderstanding of the cultural reality of the men. When Ilahita say to the ethnographer, "This is what men do," why should it be read in a cynical frame to mean, "This is a hoax"? I think it is much more plausible, in keeping with his own ethnography, for Tuzin to realize that he was shown what the men see. What they see is their cultural imaginal—a secret reality earned the hard way for years and years—which they now see reflected back to themselves in the tradition of the men's house. What Tuzin construes this to mean is something not entirely different, but his rendering is not the result of being an initiate, nor did he reside in the social relations of this village world forever.

The dilemma of the men, especially the elders, is plausible. The men's secret ontology was in double jeopardy. It has its own shared aesthetics of a secret collective: what is sensed as ugly or beautiful, graceful or sluggish, exciting or dull. The ontology of secrecy is thus a particular sensibility, based in sensing and touching, not just in knowledge, but in subjectivity and desire, too. It represents back to its participants that others outside the secret collective have contrary images, sensations, motives, and even innate drives (such as the sexual). In short, the excluded Woman/Other has a different sensibility, and thus another kind of communal purpose, than the Ideal Man. Among the Arapesh, ironically, ritual secrecy has embodied the Tambaran in acts of ritual violence, but ultimately the men felt that their Ideal Man image was not made sufficiently in the image of the Tambaran to do his deeds.

This is what ritual practice protects but also removes awareness of—until social change intrudes, reminding the participants of their mortality, the loss of grace, and exposing their cultural imaginal, not as grand, but as personal wish-fulfillment. As Bellman (1984) has suggested, following Simmel, the paradox of secrecy is that it cannot be discussed but it is so intensely "sociological." Secrecy creates cultural reality, just as social practice (read: ritual) re-creates secrecy.

The ritual secret formation of Ilahita men created an ontology that met the needs of their double lives: as domestic husbands and fathers, and as servants of the Tambaran. In the past, they engaged in this for reasons having to do with the historical integrity of their faith in their gods and the ritual practices devoted to them, that is, their religion. But why rely upon a cynical theory to interpret it? The answer is, of course, that Ilahita men themselves do so; a kind of possibility not hitherto discovered in New Guinea. We are reminded of the sage words of Turner, who in writing of a kindred problem faced by the Ndembu of Africa within the Mukanda ritual, speculated of the moral ontology of its practice in individuals: "If one could have access to the private opinions of the ritual participants, it could probably be inferred that ideals and selfish motives confronted one another in each psyche before almost every act" (1968: 143).

Why must we recognize the "reality" (metaphysically) of the Tambaran, using the terms of Tuzin's account, but refer to it as a "fiction" or a "lie," as Tuzin does? Such has occurred in other ethnographies, as we have seen. Tuzin supplies the answer by telling us that he asked for "the truth" about the spirit; the procedure of interviewing his informants led him to a critical moment in understanding what the secret ontology meant. Yet by doing so, he unwittingly shifted narrative frames, so to speak, transforming what was the heightened social consciousness of a specially designed intentional secrecy, signifying itself, but almost totally unaware of the other, or the other's ontology. He shifts, then, to a secularizing and rationalized mode of question and self-examination, outside-looking-in, those precious moments shared with the ethnographer. It is precisely this frame shift that opens unawareness to awareness, and lays bare the open contradictions previously hidden in the secret faith. At such a moment, we are keenly aware that it is not what people believe in, but what they doubt, that moves their ritual secrecy.

Thus, the men can realize and express skepticism about the cultural reality of the Tambaran society, indeed, about the god himself, by taking the ethnographer's perspective. Note the avalanche of historical change filtering through the Sepik for decades prior, suggesting that moments of such kind were long dormant in their system. That Ilahita men could interpret their rule and uphold masculinity in these ways suggests that their system of secrecy was ontologically "leaking" already, born of a historical transformation—social change—that would sweep away the Tambaran gatekeeper.

Let us interpret the Ilahita secret collective, not as unique, nor as artifact of a particular ethnography, but rather as an exemplar of social change in many areas and cultures of ritual secrecy. I suggest that Tuzin's ethnographic description is insightful and largely accurate, yet I would interpret its form slightly differently, casting some doubt on the cynical theory of course, and drawing greater attention to the discrepancy between Ilahita ritual and domestic ontologies, which I believe to have been the underlying structural cause of guilt, shame, and the comparisons Tuzin had reflected back to him by his male informants.

Ilahita traditionally had two separate realities, male and female, which corresponded to distinct spheres of social life, Tambaran cult and domestic household. These were fundamentally distinctive historical formations, and to refer to them as "ideologies" or "spheres" is mechanical. Among the Ilahita, these two ontologies were in uneasy and unstable relationship, mediated by a dualistic organization, warfare prerogatives, and later the problems of intertribal competition throughout the region. The divisions of society and culture created by ritual secrecy express conflicting and divided loyalties of actors, discrepant and discontinuous desires and intentions, which compete against each other. Thus, the reason that the Ilahita old men are simultaneously leaders of the secret cult and leaders of society is that they participate in two different modes of social cognition, requiring divergent constructions of reality. These are, basically, men's feelings and loyalties as fathers and husbands, versus their loyalties as clansmen. Increasing awareness of outside social formations cut to the heart of the Sepik River societies (Gewertz 1983). Secrecy maintained them in a hierarchical relationship; but its historical nature was poorly integrated, gradually undercut by village endogamy and a widening social landscape of external influences, government, and tourism. Secrecy was a means of maintaining the integrity of these different "worlds," with "moral badness" a cynical consequence of the gradual breakdown of differentiation between the sexes, and solidarity within the Tambaran cult. It will be obvious that each of these conditions created differences in male agency and different forms of masculinity among the Ilahita.

Thus I suspect that an unparalleled problem entered into Ilahita reality: the jural individual began to experience his secret reality no longer as "natural" or as the Voice of the Tambaran, but rather as "convention" agreed upon by men. It is a brutal insight. The difference in intentional realities is great, and while at first the changing reality may not have impacted the men's individual motivations or will, eventually it could only lead to conflict and intergenerational disruption. Conditional masculinity, dependent upon ritual secrecy, broke down. Where all traditions of ritual secrecy we have previously observed in New Guinea have had to cope with keeping at bay the public and "polluting world" of the village, the Ilahita are illustrative of a different order of ontology—psychological transformation. Ritual secrecy in such a changing reality represents a subjectivity that is not about how to repel or ward off the intrusions of ordinary pollution into the men's house. It represents a new threat; how to keep oneself from unbelieving—losing faith, and shattering the received collective sociality of male secrecy.

The notion that the elders can propound the Tambaran customs as "what men do" is to suggest that the faith required of believing in divine and omniscient *Nggwal* had eroded to individual, even selfish agreements of self-interest, to hoard the pig meat and sometimes "lie" to women. That is what contractual secrecy is all about; men no longer privilege the physical body and the rituals to protect it, but rather, they privilege personal exchanges in secret that further the goals and aims of the actor. The problem became how to give the increasingly secularizing actor—more a private self and less the Ideal Man, a glorified collective masculinity—something in which to have faith and upon which to depend while confronted with the decline of the Tambaran. This is the step from collective to private experience: the dissolution of collective ritual consciousness into alienation.

When the jural individual becomes incipient in such a cultural system, it opens up far-reaching and nearly impossible demands that burden the person and ultimately discredit performances. If there are two competing realities, public and secret, the person can pick and choose from either. But which to choose, and when is best? Once the formula of ritual is removed, agency devolves; individualistic agency pursues, not conditional masculinity, but absolute and universal ends. The internal questioning leads to uncertainty. But the ability to seamlessly perform the acts necessary of the secret-sharer is a function of a heightened self-consciousness, as Simmel suggested, combined with a degree of unconsciousness that never flinches from the premises and contradictions of secrecy. Insight or soul-searching are virtual negations of secret ontologies for this reason. Thus, secret belief and a public conviction compose parts of a larger system of "common sense" cultural reality (Geertz 1984b), which are not rational-logical in the sense that rationality reflects a linear entrance into the time and space world. We have long known that the social and cultural constitution of the self or self-awareness can be heavily fractured and fragmented, as psychologists since Freud and William James have been wont to show (Bellah et al. 1985). Ehrenreich has drawn attention to the concept of "dissembling" in this regard—of the ability of the self to "hide under a false appearance"

(1984: 28). The ethnodifferentiations of ritual secrecy in New Guinea impose sensibilities that are divisive or oppositional in the body and subjectivity of the person, but without "mentation" in the sense of internal suffering or conflict. This is a special case of an intentional reality, resting upon cultural learning and displacements of energy, that defies reality postulates and ontological propositions of a logical kind (Shweder 1990).

What the women learned upon the collapse of the Tambaran is worth hearing from the latest account:

> Women were now at liberty to admit to us, and to concur among themselves, that they had always assumed that the men were lying when they spoke of gigantic people-eating monsters, adolescent initiates being turned into flying foxes, and other improbabilities; it is just that they did not know, and did not particularly care, what the truth was beyond the men's fictions. Finding out what had actually been going on excited them about as little as being shown a urinal would excite a grown woman in our society: a male thing, a male "secret"—so what? (Tuzin 1997: 161)

The "so what" suggests a complete change in cultural reality, a totalizing cynicism expressed through American tropes, sufficient to confirm: these are not the Ilahita who experienced war and conditional masculinity and sacred ritual all those years before. This plaintive cry recalls K. E. Read's final account of the Gahuku-Gama. Both traditional cultures are gone. In what sense, then, can it be asserted that the women's subjectivities were uninterested in ritual secrecy or viewed the men's performances as fictions? These are the destabilizing images of a new social order that bears only a dim resemblance to the preceding one.

As Tuzin implies, the presence of "guilt" is certainly a complex subjectivity; it signifies the intrusion of an unwanted self-consciousness that was formerly alien to the ontology of ritual secrecy. What was once a virtually automatic and easy performance of these things is now thrown into turmoil, which spells sudden death to the near-perfect timing required of a secret performer. "Guilt," one realizes, is a double-edged sword; it may be the expression of moral regret over a conflict concerning one's actions; but it may also express the failure of nerve that once meant confidence and success in the face of disrupted sociality. The latter is what conditional masculinity was all about. For the first time, jural individuals are faced with splitting up "natural reality" into "genuine" and "false" motives, which were previously unconscious or unthinkable; the problem of the so-called true and false self pervasive to Western ethno-psychology now enters into the narrative on self/other relations (Winnicott 1971). Much of Goffman's (1963) brilliant theorizing on secrecy and passing (as normal) was devoted to precisely this problem of protecting the socially esteemed self from this kind of moral discredit. Yet, as the structural-functional sociologist understood so well, this is not simply the result of an internal psychology or some computer chips that failed to ignite masculine identity. Guilt is a token of stigma, the torment of unsuspected social doubt. The Tambaran, however, is exacting, and he requires much more certainty of male rule than implied by this muddled performance. And the male actor knows it. He surrenders to a sense of incoherence; that one can never know the perfection of before, which secrecy could secure. That is utopia. And mercifully, the traditional male actor could not read the mind of *Nggwal*. "As to the gods," Protagoras offered, "I have no means of knowing that they exist or that they do not exist. For many are the obstacles that impede knowledge, both the obscurity of the question and the shortness of human life" (Stone 1989: 237).

The shattering of secrecy is the inevitable consequence of social change. The cultural productivity of the Tambaran involved a gigantic and rich medley of sacred music and symbolic play, in the precolonial system, along with fabrications and a blustering social performance in the face of self-doubt in the modernizing one. This realization overburdens the self, which is an intolerable situation. It effectively locates secrecy inside the lone person, who now must accept the system of secret desires and objects as juridical "convention," not natural "reality." This step privatizes secrecy, locking it into the reaches of the hidden mind that Freud was to rediscover as the "unconscious," a rationalizing step toward the Simmelian conception of secrecy that protects the self but can also be "moral badness." The outcome is a different kind of conditional masculinity, not unlike the Victorian world outlined in chapter 1.

Under those circumstances, it was only a matter of time before the Tambaran cult would collapse, as it did in 1984 (Tuzin 1997). Among the neighboring Kwanga, the process occurred earlier and reminds us of Williams's intriguing account of the Vailala Madness among the Orokolo, nearly fifty years before: "Revelation of cult secrets in a Christian revival movement and general disinterest have severely undermined the cult and many believe that it will never be performed again" (Brison 1992: 40). Yes, the Tambaran is dead now, swept away by a messianic Christian religious movement that promises salvation instead of guilt, remorse, or ritual violence—at least for the time being, till someone realizes that it, too, is an imperfect society (Tuzin 1989: 206).

In a sensitive portrait of an Ilahita prophet, Samuel, a previously disparaged man who was rehabilitated and has become a luminary of the change at the apex of Christian revival, Tuzin provides a case study of these transformations. As an Ilahita ritual performer he was a failure. But after the death of his father and a kind of characteristic life-crisis rebirth, the man renamed himself after the prophet and was acclaimed as a leader of great proportion. This in itself was a sweeping change from the past, since Tuzin (1980: 304) informs us from his prior study that the Tambaran system could not tolerate prophets. Tuzin is scrupulous in showing the interpenetrating of a whole way of life with an ontology that dictated this contradiction. His careful and fascinating account of the prophet Samuel shows the difficulties that faced a man who had lost his father and could not live up to the high ideals of the Tambaran, ironically becoming a fundamentalist Christian in the aftermath of the collapse of the cult. Was Samuel forced to become a jural individual through his discredited social self? His psychological and medical problems led to the proverbial visions and spirit supports we know all too well from centuries of millenarianism and later cargo cults. A new intentional reality is created out of the problems and prospects of colonial life, especially, among the Ilahita and the many New Guinea peoples reviewed in this book, the promise of change in gender and age inequalities. "A prophet offers both sexes a wider and more satisfying redemption, and his sexual attractions and virility suggest an awareness of new babies as well as new men: total rebirth, a new community" (Burridge 1969: 161).

We are reminded of the incursion of missionaries among the Yagwoia in chapter 3, which resulted in the compromise of the younger men's souls and ritual knowledge. Their ritual torment was also a personal suffering in the loss of secret reality. We saw that the Yagwoia elders felt they had no choice but to hide all of their ritual practices and desires from the younger generation, once they had lost control of the ability to stage initiations at will and to regulate the process of secret socialization. That was the price suffered under colonial rule. War was gone. There was no way to control the young men and women without that imperative, and the colonial authorities had taken it away. You cannot undertake the necessary control of reality in such unstable conditions; you go off on your own, or resort to a utopian vision, leading to the promised land, or to failed promises, whatever the case (Wallace 1965). Have the Yagwoia and the Arapesh contracted for a new kind of personal being, of individual and private selfhood, in exchange for a Christian soul? Or as a part of the purchase of middle-class life in a developing nation such as Papua New Guinea (Gewertz and Errington 1999)? They may no longer be full of doubts and speculations, and no longer have faith in a Tambaran, but have contracted perhaps instead with a Christian God. Whatever the case, the resolution must make the transformation complete. "In such circumstances the *We—They* opposition inherent in a colonial situation must resolve itself in *Us:* a single and synthesized total community" (Burridge 1969: 56).

All or nothing: that is the way of ritual secrecy. Its effort to define and control reality and deal with the threat of war can never be halfhearted, because the project of building trust and sociality among men—and most important, of creating reality out of secrecy—is all or nothing. That is what the studies in many times and places of cults and prophecies show: When the prophecy of millennium and apocalypse fails, then the cultural reality as previously believed in and acted upon must fall, making way for a new order to come (Wallace 1972). The production of ritual secrecy is the means of producing culture in these faraway places, and when these colonial challenges and intermittent failures are introduced into it we are caught in the transformation from ritual secrecy to civil society.

Afterword: Secrecy & Cultural Relativism

❋

BETWEEN THE PREMODERN ABSOLUTISM of ritual secrecy, coded in utopian and millennial worldviews, and the neoliberal democracy that invented cultural relativism, there is the voice of anthropology. In the modern period, this voice was reflective of the intellectual promotion of relativism—the cherishing of cultures as contextual systems of beliefs and practices, each having its own integrity and dignity, worthy of respect wherever they are found. Though many challenges to this modernist paradigm have emerged over the decades, none has been more misunderstood in anthropology than the meaning and practice of secrecy. What of the absolutist side?

All-or-nothing initiation means to rule and share in secret reality—or else to be excluded and die: ritual secrecy is such a totalizing social strategy. That is the cultural lesson of these comparative ethnographies. Men employ threats and war to rule a society at war, through the production of an alternative cultural reality of initiation rituals in the nerve center of the men's house. Such a rule is not just or democratic; it has nothing to do with the law in the neoliberal sense. It is fragile and tenuous, this hold; and so it lasted only as long as the warfare; and when colonial agents entered Melanesia these secret systems were challenged and began to dissolve through pacification, missionization, and external hegemony.

Cultural relativism was vital to anthropology's scientific idealization of secrecy in the comparative ethnography of New Guinea societies. The contradictions in the ways that secrecy was suspect but promoted in American government and culture as hegemonic to the cold war, the issue of being a male ethnographer studying conditional masculinity that depended upon ritual secrecy in societies such as precolonial New Guinea, the social inequalities that typified these societies before and after colonialism, and the omission of sexuality, homosociality, and a concept of male desire from these ethnographies merit reflection in this Afterword.

Surely at the heart of the neoliberal worldview against secrecy is the pervasive historical attitude that secrecy is opposed to democracy, that it harbors selfish, subversive, or antisocial interests in opposition to the collective good. Let us review the main reasons for these negative attitudes of Western bourgeois society. First, there is the libertarian attitude: the individualism of privacy is sacred, whereas the collective form of secrecy is perceived as a cabal that undermines free expression of individual rights and thus goes against democracy. Hence, privacy is good, secrecy bad. Second, the civilizing process can never be supported by privacy, much less secrecy; culture is public (i.e., rational), ritual is secret (i.e., irrational); therefore secrecy cannot be the basis for society or culture. Third, secrecy is a ruthless and anticivilized form of power; it is strongly associated with the "primitive" and the "unconscious," and is thus disruptive of democracy (see chap. 2). Fourth, in science as well, where hypotheses are falsifiable, method is public, and truth is a primary aim, "secrecy has no permanent place in this form of scientific enterprise" (Mitchell 1993: 31). Democracy and civic life, in this modernist project, must be open and married to the rule of law—all that is unsecret.

It is no coincidence that cultural anthropology in the United States, following the influence of its institutional founder, Franz Boas, and his illustrious protégés Kroeber, Sapir, Benedict, Lowie, and Mead, created a discipline committed to the ideals, if not in fact the practice, of democracy. Generally these great scholars were opposed to racism and critiqued prejudice. Of course, like all the social sciences of the times, anthropology harbored its own blind spots and elitist tendencies, including heterosexism and homophobia (Weston 1993), standard for the times. In this early-twentieth-century scientific worldview, democracy and freedom were thought to be foundational and transparent; secrecy should not play a part in any of them. The social reality was more complex. Moreover, anthropologists had staked a claim on the "culture concept," one of the greatest orienting ideas of twentieth-century social study; and all through the period up to the end of the cold war, anthropology advanced the cause of culture as a "good thing" that was open and served as counterpoint to the "bad things" of the cold war itself—the culture of secrecy created through East/West antagonism in society, science, and art (Moynihan 1998). It must be noted, again, that certain anthropologists worked for military or secret government organizations, typically unknown to their colleagues (di Leonardo 1998). Was this a kind of conditional anthropology?

Furthermore, it was this secret and nefarious activity by researchers, anthropologists included, that had gotten the Academy into trouble during the high imperialism following World War II that was to include Project Camelot in Latin America, counterinsurgency work in Thailand, and a variety of questionable undertakings related to the Vietnam War (di Leonardo 1998: 237). For myself, it was unthinkable in the early 1970s that I would work as an anthropologist in a totalitarian or repressive regime, such as Irian Jaya under the colonial occupation of the Indonesian army, an occupation supported initially by the United Nations and implicitly warranted by the United States. However, I was thrilled by the idea of working in a Papua New Guinea men's secret society of the kind my professor, Kenneth E. Read, had lectured about in class. The seeming contradiction between the refusal to work in oppressive states and the enthusiasm of working in a traditional secret society did not present itself, nor did we see the apparent contradictions between the condemnation of secrecy in cold war State policies and the participation in premodern ritual secret societies. These systems were perceived to be radically divergent realities: the one was a regime of terror and state oppression, all too familiar as American military actions in Vietnam; the other strange and exotic, its rituals marginal to these larger global conflicts, having little or no resemblance to contemporary neoliberal society. Understanding these contradictions and their permutations in anthropology and social study has motivated this book.

Secrecy is a mode of sociality—a particular kind of social relations that creates and reproduces an order of rule of men over women and children in public and a means of reality-making by men with men in secret. The subjectivity of this sociality creates alternative shared reality precepts and concepts, even hidden objects of desire—the ontology of the men's house in certain areas of Melanesia. Secret cultural reality is therefore a critical political project, not unlike utopian movements of the modern period, albeit restricted, premodern, and prestate. Why then have anthropologists, especially male European anthropologists, so often typified these formations in pejorative ways?

Seen as a totalizing system, folding into itself the inequalities and injustices of a closed, nontransparent hierarchy, male rule through ritual secrecy in precolonial Papua New Guinea societies was tenuous but fierce in its proclamations of reality and utopian power. After the fall, the obliteration of the men's house, its rituals and paraphernalia, with only remnants remaining for the anthropologist to pick up, it is hard, as we have seen illustrated in this book, to understand how such a system could operate effectively. To observe the unraveling of these systems is unnerving; it destabilizes the positionality of White male ethnographers—in the field and in their texts.

Moreover, instead of making "the future" or futurism in a state formation, a.k.a. "nationalism," its raison d'être—emotions and cognition that are closer to the form of performative modern masculinity in the West—the New Guinea men's house took a different direction. Its reasoning, as characterized by Whitehouse, is unlike "the doctrinal mode of religiosity" (1995: 201). Male ritual secrecy was more revelatory in character. It was given to grapple with problems of religion and social life that were inherent in war and the Ideal Man mythology, imported wives, and sons who were mistrusted offspring of these marriages. Masculinity was created through intense ritual male homosociality that assured local rule by men, however tenuous, on the condition that their performances of masculinity conformed unfailingly to the rules of the secret game.

Masculinity was then subtext and pretext, foreground and background, for ritual secrecy—and the kind of conditional secrecy, so tough, so fragile, found in these societies required performances that were specific to context, actors, aims, audiences, and goals. That is, the habitus of masculinity was relational and deconstructed through ritual and then rebuilt through verbal teaching and emotional revelation and dietetics of absolute taboos and renunciations. Eros and desire could not escape this absolutism; initiation means the socialization of secretly taught desires. Even the location of this habitus in the men's house was successful only so long as its emotional climate was reproduced through the continuous threat of external war, the presence of willing warriors with human desires that included sexual outlets, and, among the Sambia and Baruya, the commitment to secure rule through the reproduction of objectified sexual relations with boys and women. In this social formation women were forever excluded and alien from this secret cultural reality, at least ideally, and probably more often than we should like to think, in reality.

Ritual secrecy in New Guinea created one form of subjectivity in secret, and another in public social life, the men's house being the final means of articulation between these two discordant realities for the men. This model implies the precondition of a firm, unshifting male hierarchy, elders and war leaders, ritual experts on top, adult men in the middle, younger men below them, with boy-initiates at the bottom of the totem pole. This model was not secret; it was the ritual knowledge, objectification and subordination, and, in the instance of societies such as the Sambia, the sexual relations between older and younger males that were hidden absolutely from public view, and whence derived male rule in public. In societies that had neither substantial material differences nor strong "egalitarian" ethics, this was no mean achievement. Men's ability to cooperate in the public domain (which included domestic spheres, such as the women's houses, where women and children resided) was all-important. Their ability to manipulate their secret knowledge, to do performances for public consumption, to be able to exercise through secret subjectivity tactics and stratagems of control over women and other men who were key players in the men's house—all of this reproduced the social order through the shared project of ritual secrecy.

The contradictions and moral dilemmas of the men operating in dualistic worlds now seem obvious—though they were not to the anthropologists of a generation ago. However, Burridge had it right: Moral dilemmas implied "dissonances in basic assumptions in power. These, in turn, can be seen in stresses and strains in social relations, and are particularly expressed in the prestige system in terms of which the worth of man is measured, integrity earned, and redemption gained" (1969: 163).

Imagine other social worlds in which the measure of a man is the esteem of his mates in the pub, the Elks Club, the clique of hunting cronies who once a year go to the woods of Maine to recapture childhood dreams; or those who kneel and pray in a circle of sacred reverie; and another that seeks solace in a Victorian club of Greek-admiring practices, made up from the bricolage of Indian rituals and half-forgotten legends like those of Morgan's invented society. Now when you add war to the mix, as was the case in New Guinea—the life and death struggle to rule in shifting sands of uncertain allies and enemies—you begin to understand how vital, how necessary, how burdensome, and ultimately how fragile ritual secrecy was the achievement of this fierce masculinity out of the circumstances of ordinary men (Mead 1935).

In his final work on the Ilahita, *Revenge of the Cassowary*, Tuzin (1997) refers to the utopian project of conditional masculinity by the metaphor of a "haven" of protection. I will not quibble with this characterization; surely it applies to the social circumstances of Morgan and his male cronies in American society long ago, as it also pertains to the Iron Johns of today. But I would add that the stakes are high in war, and they go up when war is the final arbiter of life and death; the middle-class language of choice and nicety connoted by the term *haven* seems weak and insufficient to convey the deadly resolve of a society in which the constant sense is that "a war is going on" (Herdt 1987a).

Indeed, in the Middle East today, in a country such as Israel that feels itself besieged, the kind of masculinity and the kind of extraordinary measure called for make secrecy almost a certainty—a means of promoting trust to feel protected against enemies, inside and out. That surely is one lesson that follows from the horrible impact of September 11 and the terrorist destruction in New York—a new cold war and secrecy have followed in its wake. Conditional masculinity is the product of such dreadful disasters—a deep, floundering sense of dis-ease in the land. Secrecy was the artifice in New Guinea, but not necessarily by choice; whatever pleasure men derived from the excitements of secrecy and the incitement to perform its rituals, ritual secrecy reflected their uncertainty, fear, and unfaith in male rule in public affairs, or the hegemony of their particular men's house in local struggles. This utopianism represents their yearning for a hidden, pure, fundamentalism of shared certainty.

The human suffering of these end games of war thus precipitated the classic rituals of birth and rebirth of manliness and servile masculinity, known from decades of study since Van Gennep (1960) and anthropologists who were to follow in this tradition. One form involved boy-inseminating rituals; the other did not. These traditions were the product of vast historical and material forces, ultimately disruptive of the social order; the rituals were an attempt to tidy up. The insemination of boys, clearly a practice found in only a small number of the thousand and more Melanesian societies, was, however, emblematic of the homosociality and high phallic reverence for the male organ, itself iconic of the Ideal Man—incomplete and vulnerable without the dietetics and semen of older men.

Review of the Lessons of Ritual Secrecy

The cultural lessons of ritual secrecy are revealed through the case studies examined in this book. Sambia men faced the dilemma of the potential betrayal of their sons, which they handled by universal conscription and brutal ordeals to sanction secrecy, ultimately bending the mind of the boy through insemination, bonding his substance to the secrecy of ritual. The Yagwoia men were humiliated by the loss of their sons and their empire to colonizers and missionaries, and had made ritual secrecy a secret from their progeny. And the Gahuku-Gama in their attempt to reproduce a "*nama* cult"—a social construction of K. E. Read's anthropology—found themselves the objects of their spirits, not the free agents that they promoted in their rhetoric to women and children. The Baktaman constructed their ritual secrecy as described by F. Barth through the metaphor of numerous nested Chinese boxes that fade into empty or meaningless practice, completing a circle of failed or lost truth, out of the fear that the truth will be discovered by women, making them too powerful. And then there is M. Godelier's certainty that the Baruya could never do without their semen rituals in the quest to arrange material domination over women and boys, though the men still cannot escape the terrible fear that they shall be betrayed. Finally there was the lesson of the Ilahita, the discovery, witnessed by ethnographer D. Tuzin, that ritual secrecy is performative only—it is "what men do"—not the invention of a high god but an artifice of greed and lust by those who prey upon their own families while masked to impersonate this sham god. Such are the political and moral dilemmas of sociality in a particular civilization. In short, these societies had their own spoiled social relations, internal contradictions that produced bad faith, and desperate counterhegemonic fundamentalism determined to survive in the turmoil of relentless, pounding warfare. Such themes are all too familiar in human history, even if the ritual secrecy is not.

That was the precolonial pattern. The advent of the colonial powers ushered in a brave new world. It was not devoid of secrecy, local peoples thought, as they attempted through cargo cult beliefs and practices to interpret the "unintelligible foreign morality" (Whitehouse 1995: 26) and actions of Dutch and German, Australian and British rulers. These White men seemed to have their own secret means and clubs, their own warriorhoods with more powerful, indeed awesome, technology, and seemingly unlimited material wealth at their disposal. As Lattas has so cogently written: "Whites here are rendered as running their own men's house cult, the secrets of which serve to masculinize them while feminizing Melanesian men" (1999: 73). From Governor-General Van Baal on down to the common barracks policeman, a bond of homosociality connected the Whites, and while New Guineans could never know the fragile quality of this frontier life and its slight hold on civilized masculinity in the heart of darkness, so, too, the foreign rulers feared uprisings and the contagion of "savagery," driving them to destroy ritual temples and icons, to jail cult leaders, and to preemptively strike at locals who resisted making the land safe for missionaries (Keesing 1992).

Viewed in historical perspective, such accounts exoticized and thus removed the study of secrecy from the realm of self-reflection that is the hallmark of ethnography. The exoticization of New Guinea cults (e.g., *The Island of Menstruating Men*, Hogbin 1970) was a means of removing secrecy from serious analysis and comparative study, and thus ultimately from cultural critique. To interpret ritual secrecy as a lie or hoax, or primarily as a sham or game, was to underrate the wonderfully terrifying complexities of Melanesian precolonial life. A kindred point can be taken from cargo cult studies: Western anthropologists who were unable to accept the desire for materialism per se may have been prone to interpret cargo beliefs as morality plays in the manner more acceptable to Western views (Lindstrom 1993). Likewise, by underanalyzing ritual secrecy, or by treating it as individual or contractual, ethnographers may have ignored the social contradictions of these sociocultural systems, so rich and intricately layered in public and secret subjectivities and practices. Moreover, in the cases of Hogbin and K. E. Read, the dynamics of male secrecy and sexuality, that is, the homosexuality (and/or heterosexuality) of the ethnographer in a colonial period of disrupted local rule and compromised masculinity, remained hidden from the text. How could it have been otherwise? As sociologist Connell has suggested of my work and other similar New Guinea studies, the construction of masculinity through boy-inseminating practices disrupted the very notion of homosexuality as unmasculine (1995: 31–32ff.). To interpret the result primarily as a gender game or "war of the sexes," in the cliché of the times, was only partially correct when viewed against local idiom (Herdt and Poole 1982). Even in the world of Lewis Henry Morgan, as we have seen, the veil of ritual secrecy was a social barrier invoked by men, indeed, enjoyed by them, in their tenuous extension of rule.

Conditional masculinity, as I have iterated, relies upon initiation ceremonies, hierarchy, embodiment, and male solidarity, to operate social relations in public successfully. "Success," in this formulaic, means the ability to rule through the exigencies of a secret order to meet the challenges of war and enemies, inside and outside the polity. Treachery, for example, as

Godelier (1989) has well written, was such a constant threat that only the culture of secrecy could succeed as a general weapon to counter it, the men thought. Of course on the side of cultural richness the rituals and secrecy of initiation and its revelations continually invoked all throughout the life cycle of men added a measure of grandeur to these stark realities.

But how is masculinity connected to secrecy in this model? An important clue to this question comes from K. E. Read's (1955) classic formulation of "morality" in Melanesia, which influenced an earlier generation of thinking about comparative morality and ethical relativism in anthropology and religion. The discussion of universalism and relativism by Read, via detailed comparisons of Gahuku-Gama and "Western" moral categories, was couched almost exclusively in the male-centered language and masculinist imagery of his day. Unfortunately Read did not explicitly deal with the link between masculinity and ritual secrecy. Instead, ritual was treated as but one of myriad social and relational attachments that made the category of the person and "his" conduct situational or context-specific. On one occasion Read discusses "unmanly" conduct in relation to "appropriate" behavior for Gahuku men, saying that while there are rules, the Gahuku expressed a "continually changing moral perspective" (1955: 261). Even homosexuality, Read suggested, was treated as "foolish rather than immoral."

Moreover I do not think that Read or his generation, including his friend Margaret Mead, for instance, as expressed in her brilliant meditation on gender, *Male and Female* (1949), ever made the connection between secrecy, masculinity, and male rule writ large. Morality was morality—a *man's* responsibility, whether applied to men or women—and never mind that the tropes and measures of rhetoric about moral development were construed through masculine or heterosexist frameworks (Gilligan 1982). That was not how gender was understood, when it was thought about; as a prefeminist or pre–gender relations analysis of the issues showed, masculinity was more physical and material.

But why secrecy? To return to the rhetoric of chapter 2, by deconstructing masculinity as less of a thing and more of a relationship, with power embedded in ritual bonds, it was then possible to imagine two kinds of masculinity—the public and the secret—or what Lattas has referred to as "the lived experience of a double existence created from living secret worlds of underground meanings" (1998: 289).

Lewis Henry Morgan, the scholar who pioneered these studies, again provides a lead case. Now it seems more obvious that Morgan and the men of his age faced the dilemma of their own desires in the creation of men's secret societies. Clearly, Morgan was in search of another kind of society or fraternity, through a higher, purer, finer, and more elemental sort of social manhood provided for by his own cultural age. *Utopian* is the proper word for that higher state on earth. We know little of his wife or family relations, and Lewis Henry Morgan was later to remain silent about his experience of ritual and adoption among the Iroquois. His reflections were never published; he seems never to have reconciled his young manly desire for secret homosocial fraternity with male American peers, or to have explained his later adoption by the Indian tribe. We can only speculate that his ventures first into pseudo-Greek ideals and then into the Iroquois initiation lodge left him with an increasing sense of existential ennui, or perhaps alienation. Still, he persisted with his ethnology and the extraordinary effort to do justice to the cultural ways of the Iroquois, while remaining a member of the cultural world of frontier America.

Then something shifted in Morgan, as if having realized a dream or desire, an equally strong pulse to deny it or to leave it behind seized him. The impulse momentarily leads him to belittle his own cultural production, the Order of the Iroquois, as a "boyish" thing. Perhaps having felt closer for a moment to the rituals of the Iroquois, though purchased, and make-believe, the disingenuousness of the white male practices or his fantasies about them shone through and disturbed him. Perhaps Morgan's "gift" of secret societies to his peers alienated the owner from it. Nonetheless, this sudden alteration of desires was accompanied by a newfound intellectual interest to write about the Indians as a substitution for living among them. Morgan's intellectual interest in the Indian came to fruition in his grand book *The League of the Iroquois* (1851), and while Morgan became a public intellectual, his role in building secret societies became a secret.

Morgan was the quintessential Victorian in this double and compartmentalized existence. Ironically, he was also a lawyer—that most cunning of market-driven creatures, whose exploitation of the growing political economy of what I have called contractual secrets, or some would call legal secrets, must not go unnoticed. Indeed, legal studies define secrecy as the intentional withholding of information from another person, to their disadvantage, with the result of "bringing some people together while pushing others apart" (Scheppele 1988: 16). Thus, this eminently intelligent man became cynical of his own youthful dreams and even dismissive of secrecy thereafter. Men such as Morgan were aspiring not only to cast aside the remnants of the premodern era, including religion; they were, as Maurice Godelier (personal communication) has reminded me, attempting to assert science and anthropology as the very zenith of human civilization and, as Freud liked to say of psychoanalysis, the pinnacle of reality-making. Morgan's contributions and his interest in secrecy only enlarge the distinctively American qualities of this great man. His work presaged the challenges and compromises experienced by many anthropologists in the next century—and in this sense his life anticipated the moral dilemmas of anthropology. The humanity of Morgan is enlarged, not diminished, by this history.

I hope that by now it is obvious that men and women in the precolonial era of New Guinea societies typically did not construe secret rituals the way that the modernists who succeeded Morgan did: as fraud, lies, fakes, or simply as a grab for or abuse of power, and hence, moral corruption. Gender relations must of course condition such a claim, for as we have repeatedly seen, the interests and power of men and women differ in these societies. This antirelativist theme in the interpretation of ritual secrecy folded into its persuasion old colonial critiques of traditionalism and custom with postcolonial critiques of Christianity and its missionization (Lattas 1998). The United States and Western Europe have more recently viewed secrecy in the light of cold war and state secrets on the international plane, and as a problem in moral contracts (more precisely the failure to keep contracts secret), contracts defined as the forerunner to commercial agreements, created between lawyers and clients or doctors and patients, tolerated but not celebrated by neoliberal society. In general, Americans are wary and mistrustful of the use of secrecy, especially when illegal or antisocial ends are suspected, whether by criminals or the CIA (Moynihan 1998). Surely conspiracy theories would not be so popular otherwise. As Roland Merullo has cautioned about America's "secret culture," however, we are too big to be "encapsulated in a sketch of Uncle Sam: We are something more than a capitalist demon and something less than the Statue of Liberty" (2002: 19).

A General Theory of Secrecy

Throughout this book I have proposed a general theory of secrecy that posits the creation of cultural reality, or alternative conceptions of reality, as the central and driving force behind the institutionalization of ritual practices in small-scale societies over historical time. I have suggested that we reflect upon our own Western notions of secrecy, which are largely negative and cynical, being the manifestations of liberal democracy and other views of individualism and collectivism, which assume full disclosure of all aspects of personal and social life. A reexamination of the role of secrecy in precolonial New Guinea societies reveals the need to value the uniqueness of cultures in the tradition of cultural relativism, while also understanding the fundamental dilemma of individual actors' lived experience in a secret tradition marked by contradictions on the cultural level and conflicts on the interpersonal one.

This is true in a general way, but what of its practice in anthropological fieldwork? The fact is, secrecy presents a special challenge to cultural relativism and the epistemology of anthropology, particularly as this is understood in other cultures. Some skeptics will wonder if my emphasis upon the cultural functions of secrecy amounts to an apology for the abuses of secrecy, whenever or wherever they occur. Is this but another instance of anthropology's failure to take ethical positions in their ethnographies of other cultures (and possibly their own)? No, I do not think so.

The historical survey of theories of secrecy (chap. 2) found both positive and negative meanings of secrecy in social study, but it is the Machiavellian view of secrecy that haunts anthropology. Like Simmel, I do not entirely disagree with it. Rather, I find its logic and images incomplete, as in fact Simmel did: aside from the potential for power, he saw the solidarity-enhancing potential for the group and protective functions of secrecy for the individual, even though he also understood that secrecy "de-individualizes" the person. Secret practitioners, according to the folk model, actually enjoy the terrorism and brutality of secret human organizations. Such a historical legacy makes the anthropologist extremely wary of the premises of secrecy for fear of being charged with ethnocentrism (or worse), a professional hazard of all scholars of secrecy. A few anthropologists, such as Eric Schwimmer (1980) and Simon Ottenberg (1989), have diverged from the conventional moralistic view, suggesting that ritual secrecy has its own cultural purpose and culture-creating meanings.

In thinking of the legacy of anthropology, and the lessons of Lewis Henry Morgan's work in particular, one is struck by how often anthropologists have rebelled against the Enlightenment and rationality ideologies in the narrow sense to espouse cultural relativism as it has come down to us from Boasian cultural anthropology (Shweder 1984; Stocking 1997). The cultural relativist epistemology has been substituted for evolutionary and moralistic readings of cultural and social phenomena, even in the face of Western contradictions and utilitarian practicalities (Geertz 1984a; Spiro 1986). Skeptics are all too quick to point out the limitations of antirelativist positions. However, there is one area in which anthropologists have generally forsaken cultural relativism, and the study of New Guinea ritual secrecy provides a textbook example. Why in this one area—secrecy—did anthropologists resist the acceptance of a social practice as part of cultural reality?

Anthropology's epistemological rebellion against the rationality of the Enlightenment widely embraced much that was strange, exotic, but human in the domain of customs and their cultural logic; and yet when it came to the practice of anthropology its professionals demurred, failing to accept secrecy as part of the positive and relativistic Science of Culture. There were other exceptions to this general trend, of course; certain notions of racism, homosexuality, and a few other forms of social inequality were pathologized with the result that the social oppression was maintained (Herdt 1991a). But in the arena of secrecy the conditions that thwarted relativism may be summarized as follows: (1) The field-workers in question were all men, or honorary men (e.g., Margaret Mead). (2) These ethnographers had little or no self-conscious experience of collective or ritual secrecy in their personal lives, at least in significant, nontrivial ways; the relevant exception in the instances of Hogbin and Read (homosexuality) was so derided and punished by society that it was virtually impossible for this cultural experience to be reflected upon in the fieldwork, and to do so would have disqualified these professionals, prior to the emergence of "gay and lesbian studies." Most of these men were uncomfortable with the explicit homosociality, and seeming homoerotic aspects, of the men's house in New Guinea. (3) To suggest that a male ethnographer accepted male ritual secrecy in a New Guinea society was to grant the men's separate cultural reality, thus qualifying the "unified concept" of culture then prevalent in anthropology. To take seriously the worlds of ritual secrecy anticipated the diversity studies that followed postcolonial perspectives on contemporary social formations. (4) Furthermore, to accept men's domination of women through the social practice of secrecy as relevant to New Guinea culture increasingly went against the grain of neoliberal democracy tendencies after the advent of second-wave feminism in the 1960s, and the establishment of feminist anthropology in largely White, heterosocial, highly educated, and bourgeois circles. (5) The acceptance of conditional masculinity through ritual secrecy was, in the cold war era of Western civilization at least, counterhegemonic, and would have called into question the essentializing privileges of being White, male, and middle class, in the elite. A male ethnographer who "understood" the subject-desire and positionality of being only a part-agent (like the boy initiated into ritual secrecy in a New Guinea men's house) implied a counterhegemonic developmental subjectivity, whether of being homosexual or effeminate or neuter—or some such imaginal. And since interpretative anthropology had not yet been invented, the notion of agency implied in accepting conditional masculinity would have been suspect—strongly implying that the anthropologist was not a full agent in himself: that he, too, had once been an object (of attraction, desire, manipulation, etc.), rather than having always been a subject throughout life, consistent with Western male ideology right up to near the end of the cold war. (6) And so there emerged a generational difference between older and younger anthropologists who worked in these societies. The younger cohort was to follow up the implications of ritual secrecy as conditional masculinity, where men in public did things for the good of society, while in secret they did things for the good of themselves.

Ironically, of course, some of the male ethnographers of the prior generation (such as the American Robert Murphy) and those to follow in my generation were motivated by the neoliberal tendency to seek equality in gender relations and hence justice in society. This approach, aptly termed prefeminist or protofeminist, might well have been reflected in the cynicism toward male ritual secrecy in period ethnographies of New Guinea, and such a social and philosophical attitude is certainly discernible (Knauft 1995). However, as anthropologists following the lead of Marilyn Strathern have suggested, this paradigm avoided the deeper question of social analysis and political economy: How is male reality and masculinity as its social condition created? If not inherent in muscles and genes, from whence does male agentic power flow? Anthropology in the period of the cold war was not prepared to examine this question; second-wave feminism and gay and lesbian studies would have to be created, and a new generation of field-workers would begin to raise such questions.

However, to examine the protofeminist position, the assumption that men have power, or the ability to express it, assumes that male power is already inherent in nature, culture, or interpersonal relations, rather than being dependent upon secrecy in the men's house, as I think was the case in precolonial Melanesia. As we have seen repeatedly in the comparative ethnography, that men had power did not automatically mean that they could rule; indeed, a strong central tendency in New Guinea cultures dominated by the men's house is that male ideologies emphasize the rhetorical power of men in public and in the social order. There is something almost compensatory in this rhetoric that the great ethnographers, such as K. E. Read, recognized in their fieldwork.

Yet male power as presented in Read's classic ethnographies, as well as the works of his peers, such as Ian Hogbin, and his student L. L. Langness (1974), is described as inherent, insistent, and incorrigible. Read (1965), as I have pointed out before (Herdt 1982a), understood the tentativeness or fragility of male identity development, as his beautiful ethnography portrays, but this sensibility was not inflected in his theoretical understanding of male power or the description of ritual secrecy as "hoax." In this view, male agency (the ability to be effective in life, and the subjective sense of being able to carry out goals) is not inherent in anything, except the men's ideology—and that only in public. Ritual secrecy was vital to make this rhetoric work in public. It commanded the socialization and solidarity of the males living in a particular men's house. Ritual secrecy is what made the achievement of male power a matter of praxis. While the evidence will never be untainted, our review of ethnographies (chap. 4) suggests that male ethnographers have consistently misinterpreted the public rhetoric of men as synonymous or isomorphic with secret male discourse and practice, as pointed out long ago (Herdt 1981). Some ethnographers continue to misunderstand how dependent male agency was upon ritual secrecy, as we see from Langness's (1999: 98) assertion that secrecy is a "charade"—some fifty years after Read first made this assertion.

The point is that this model (with its still-prevalent cheerleaders, e.g., Langness) precludes consideration of the more radical ontological position that ritual secrecy in the men's house was a tenuous but often successful effort to create male agency through an idealist or utopian cultural reality outside of public affairs. The men made rule in public and the men's house dependent upon ritual advancement through male secrets; thus all masculinity was qualified through the performance of ritual and secular demonstrations of "masculine" domains, such as hunting and shooting, ritual rhetoric, sexual prowess, and so forth. The fact that men continued to demonstrate and perform these functions well into old age suggested of course that conditional masculinity is seldom if ever complete, or realized, and certainly was not inherent (Herdt 1982b).

Nevertheless, the men's success at waging war, at parlaying their alliances into larger confederacies of power relationships with other villages and men's houses, and hence at creating social reality or utopian worlds in the service of war-making, exacted a terrible human cost, one that neoliberalism was not willing to pay. It saw a situation where, in addition to the violence and constant stress of warfare, women and children were treated as objects, never as subjects. Moreover, their subjectivity was treated as irrelevant to the social order, and, having been marginalized and scapegoated in this way, it was virtually guaranteed that a vicious psychosocial process of "blame the victim" would ensue, in which women were imagined to be oppositional and destructive to men, their bodies the projective screens onto which the anxieties and dread of these fragile psyches were to direct their fear and hatred.

In taking this feminist critique seriously, however, we should critically examine its premises of victimology and the imagery of who is a victim and who is in power, to pursue an analysis of male power that too has often been overlooked in condemnation of the victimology (Harrison 1993). Finally, such a critique underanalyzes the cultural context of victims, and it too easily resulted in the dismissal of ritual secrecy—demeaning respect for the exigencies of agency and powerlessness in the politicosocial life of these communities. That this one-sided analysis has not struck us as odd is indicative of the great difficulties inherent not only in the study of secrecy but in the challenge to anthropological authority that is posed by it.

Anthropologists are faced with a double standard, as cultural natives of our own tradition, since secrecy at home is generally condemned for such reasons and more. With few exceptions, these attacks and their underside have seldom been adequately analyzed in social or cultural study. When anthropologists work abroad, on the other hand, they are placed in the ethical dilemma of having always to respect and honor the ways of the community, even those which might violate our own code of human conduct or human rights (Mitchell 1993). Sometimes the difficulties inherent in this latter posture lead to a variety of ethical dilemmas, which have been the subject of not a little attention in clinical ethnography, though seldom focused on secrecy as such (Herdt and Stoller 1990).

Past studies assumed that the purpose of the secret was to further the selfish or antisocial interest of individual actors. But with regard to ritual secrecy in New Guinea, this point of view is wrongheaded, implying acts that are meant to exclude others, or to preclude social relations with them (those kept out of the secret), in favor of contracts that bind two people, lawyer and client, psychiatrist and patient, abuser and victim of abuse, in a hidden society of two. Ritual secrecy, by contrast, opens up social relations to initiated others, just as it forecloses other relations. And whereas contractual secrecy relations are based upon money and litigation, healing, and abuse, again, involving payments, not embodiments and dietetics in the larger sense used in this book, ritual secrecy relations are, to quote Godelier's new rendering of the gift, based upon things people "could neither sell nor give away but which must be kept" (1999: 8). Past interpretations of New Guinea ritual secrecy have conflated these forms with the contractual agreement in Western civilization. Where contractual secrecy surely secures or suggests self-interest, ritual secrecy ensures male agency in communities that have never known Western selfhood and whose collective insecurity makes social relations possible, in their utopian view, only through the reproduction of the men's house. This confusion of ontological forms in accounts of the past, I am convinced, is at the historical root of the romantic-cynical attack on secrecy in all its forms.

But this issue of "judging" or misjudging ritual secrecy as antisocial and even anticivilizational implicitly violates the modernist canon of cultural relativism in anthropology. Societus non-nocere: harm not the culture. Relativist anthropology is particularly troubled by the dark fear of judging other cultures by the values and beliefs of our own. Ritual secrecy, with its representation in past and present ethnography as dark, negative, cynical, selfish, and fraudulent, feeds right into this trouble, as Simmel (1950) might have warned long ago. Surely ritual secrecy must undermine public culture and society as good things in themselves. To recall Sapir's (1949) audacious effort from long ago is to ask what is genuine and worthy about a culture, about Culture for the human species, not only for understanding the human condition, but also in modeling the ideals of high civilization. Culture, Sapir could dare to say, in its most genuine and idealizing utopian mode—freedom loving, individual venerating, creative and inspiring of high art and philosophy as associated with Socratic Greece or Elizabethan England—was a good thing to emulate. This value-laden position was of course a strong challenge to epistemological relativism, and the prior generation of anthropologists, with exceptions (such as Kenneth Read), would not have typically agreed with such a sweeping view. But apart from whether they would agree with such a universal model, it should be clear by now that many of them would not accept secrecy or ritual secrecy as part of this high civilization and idealized culture. This prior generation of anthropologists as members and natives of their own cultural tradition have been predisposed by their training and cultural history to think of secrecy as a bad thing.

Implications for the Position of Male Ethnographers

Here, then, is the historical dilemma: How were anthropologists to describe and interpret a culture that could implement secrecy on purpose, and think of such a culture as a good thing? Certainly relativist anthropology could not accept the creation of cultural reality through ritual secrecy. In what remains I would like to pursue the acute implications of this dilemma for the position of male ethnographers and the masculinist perspective that underscores much of the ethnographic tradition of writing on ritual secrecy in male cults and ceremonies, understanding that recent ethnographies (Harrison 1993; Whitehouse 1992, 1995, 2000; Lattas 1999) have taken a new turn that departs from this anthropological past and theorizes secrecy quite differently.

There is a missing discourse on New Guinea men's secrecy: reflection by European male ethnographers as they attempted to perceive and define, subjectify and interpret divergent realities, that made up sociality in these ritual secrecy–dominated communities, and to "translate" them back into Western discourse. How have male ethnographers typically handled this issue in the past? Largely, of course, by their silence on their positionality, which is true of kindred work in anthropology of the past. The problem goes beyond seeing ritual secrecy as a collective versus an individual problem.

Is it not a conundrum of our epistemology and a paradox of ethnographic methodology that Western male anthropologists confronted by systems of ritual secrecy had so little experience, need, or practical understanding of secrecy in their own developmental subjectivities and social lives? Of course it is true that, in growing up, men may have had the experience on occasion of having something to conceal—a white lie or petty wrong—that was experienced with guilt and was kept hidden. That is the trivial form of subjective contractual secrecy. Even the shared fantasies and erotic experiences of solitary development or shared homosociality for heterosexual men growing up in the United States (Gagnon 1971) do not qualify, in my opinion, as a radical departure from the standard that all social experience of importance is public, not secret, especially following adolescence. Thereafter the actor enters a social world whose moral rules generally provide voluntary privacy as a sacrosanct right, but where secrecy is disapproved of or disliked as a strategy for social development.

However, these rather normative experiences and mundane assignments differ from the universal obligation in New Guinea to be initiated into the men's house, as the condition of being an adult, as the prerequisite of agency in being treated as a whole person struggling with the life and death stakes we have observed in these accounts of precolonial New Guinea. To live with these social and secret subversions and tests of conditional masculinity, and all the dissembling that comes with a double reality in daily life, is a great and even intolerable burden for someone unfamiliar with such matters (see chap. 3).

Only my lived experience of being a gay man, growing up in a hetero-normal society that was predisposed to homophobia and thus the oppression of all signs of sexual variation, enabled me to gain a perspective, however inadequate, on this alternative cultural reality quite at odds with the public culture of Sambia. That I can write of this now in ways that Kenneth Read or Ian Hogbin could not—indeed, would have dreaded to raise in public due to their social upbringing and sense of propriety that absolutely separated their sexuality from society, public from private—is of course the result of incredible historical, cultural, and scientific change. To live as those who were closeted in the former generation had to live (Read 1980) dictated that they could not bring to bear into their ethnography the insights or reflections that might have expanded their interpretation of these conflicting cultural realities. Ritual secrecy as a practice and as power relations requires another mode of understanding that was missed or typically missing from the text: the difference of order between going to the theater to see a play versus writing and acting it every day for the audience. And playwrights, even good ones, suffer burn out.

But back to the mainstream of heteronormal white male anthropologists. Following this logic of social typification, I think that there is nothing surprising or mysterious about the assertion that White heterosexual men would have little experience of secrecy in their adult lives to fall back upon in understanding or reflecting upon the secret cultural realities and compartmentalization of their male friends and informants in New Guinea. Some of the greatest mainstream ethnographers of the past two decades, such as Bruce Knauft, have been able to bridge this gap and achieve remarkable and sensitive descriptions of these issues, including the erotic and social desires of local men as instanced in Gebusi society (Knauft 1986, 1999). Perhaps this is an example of the remarkable power of anthropology to transcend the limitations of one's culture and developmental experience when motivated by theoretical and ethnographic concerns to truly reveal the Other. However, Knauft is rare; I know of no other mainstream example in the corpus of New Guinea. By contrast, there is the more prevalent claim, made iconic by a recent text of Langness (1999: 93) who asserts that "homosexuality . . . as reported by [Godelier, Herdt, and others] is in a sense only one trivial element" of a larger complex in New Guinea. Taken at face value, I would not quibble with that characterization, as I have myself stated elsewhere (Herdt 1993). However, that is not the face of the text, which conveys a deep heteronormativity that defies being punctured by twenty years of ethnography that, to quote Marilyn Strathern (1988: 115) so aptly, tells how "secrecy 'fixes' motivation"—privileging desires and categories of people, excluding others, making the men's claim to power "self fulfilling." This, for example, is why the boy-inseminating traditions of ritual secrecy in Melanesia are not trivial at all, but rather provide a deep insight into the unstable and insecure positionality of men and male agency in these societies.

Consider the element of heteronormativity in this dilemma. What is it? Of the many critiques that might be brought to bear (Herdt 1997a), the one that I would stress in this context is how being heterosexual or assuming that only heterosexual "things" are normal qualifies all relationships—with men and women. Since, according to that canon, "men" can only be "masculine" if they preclude intimate, homoerotic relations with other men, then it follows that to admit of such intimacy is to disrupt the appearance if not in fact the performance of masculinity, for such a man. A canonical heteronormal male, we might posit, must assert that ritual secrecy is a "charade," or if he guesses that it contains hidden and dangerous "fixed motives," such as sexual relations with younger males, it must be declared "trivial" in order to maintain the appearance of respectability, and certainly the mantle of masculinity. Triviality is here a signifier of the parallel problem of conditional masculinity that besets the Sambia and other kindred cultures of male desire reviewed in this book, wherein male agency is achieved through submission to the political and sexual socialization of older males. The contrasts are worth thinking through. Many heterosexual

White women, however, may be somewhat more attuned to noticing the difference between appearance and reality as a product of growing up in male-defined or patriarchal systems (Gilligan 1982). A European gay man or a lesbian who has had to pass as straight in growing up or perhaps through much of their lifetime is perfectly fitted to deconstruct these premises and this canon, as the autobiography of historian Martin Duberman (1991) suggests. Such a process is not without bias, of course; but then, as I long ago suggested, since all science is perspectival and anthropology as well requires the elucidation, not the elimination of bias, this assertion is pro forma of the ethnographic encounter (Herdt and Stoller 1990; see also Weston 1993). Secrecy may indeed be something that many heterosexual men have seldom, if ever, scrutinized: they may never have even pondered its interactional forms in their own society. By contrast, the nineteenth-century social world of men's clubs in which Lewis Henry Morgan found himself was perfectly suited to explore in a more open way the depth of how ritual secrecy could create cultural reality.

Another aspect of the problem concerns the assumptive privileges with which White male anthropologists grow up, feeling comfortable with power and authority, and thus agentic. Here it would seem is the very opposite of what I have been calling the "conditional masculinity" of precolonial New Guinea. As empowered agents whose masculinity is without conditions, EuroNorthAmerican and Australian anthropologists entered into New Guinea societies equipped to employ their power directly to achieve individual ends, including the goals of their research studies. This is reasonable—no news to postcolonial theory. In this model, EuroNorthAmerican male ethnographers might feel, however, comfortable to exercise their power with male contemporaries and consociates in the local moral world, but feel uncomfortable *reflecting* upon what this all means, including the coercive initiation of young males into prescriptive systems of power and sexual subordination in a society that has a system of conditional masculinity designed to operate through the use of ritual secrecy. Would American anthropologists such as Langness, who asserted that power was intrinsic and homosexuality trivial in these systems, feel comfortable investigating the blend of sexual subjectivity and secret contract of these males on the edges of society? It seems doubtful to me; but my point is larger than particular ethnographers. The exploitation of ritual secrecy is so characteristic of male agency in New Guinea societies that some anthropologists may have been led to assume that only duplicity and fabrication, hoaxes and lies for personal gain, could motivate individual men's actions, and they would have been unprepared to reflect upon their own interpretation of these tactics, or the adequacy of such a cynical model in the light of their own discomfort with conditional intimate masculinity. The point is that the cynical view of secrecy often mistakes individual motives for the collective form, conflating contractual with ritual secrecy.

Some heterosexual males may counter, "But we have our own brand of secrecy in the locker room and, based upon the homosocial settings of boarding schools, boy scouts, boot camp, and fraternities—all of that we gave up after marriage!"—whereafter intimate bonding was transferred into the heterosocial-partnered relationship, that exclusive province of modernity for the self. Surely the attitude that attended this change in a prior generation (the generation, by the way, of Kenneth E. Read) was summed up aptly by Robert Graves: *Goodbye to All That!* For the male ethnographers of that generation, then, there was a hiatus, a developmental discontinuity between childhood/adolescence and marriage: after "social maturity," all secrets were set aside for the intimacy and privacy of intense, lifelong, marital bonding—a kind of social relationship relatively recent in human history. Surely the intimate secrecy of homosocial bonding—a pleasure in its own right for many of the actors in New Guinea men's societies, though unknown to some of these male ethnographers, at least after marriage—is a cause of misinterpreting ritual secrecy. I think that Lewis Henry Morgan was better equipped to understand this conundrum in the nineteenth century than later anthropologists because of the social economy and more formal gender relations of his times.

Another and perhaps more cynical view—best known to the Freudians—would have it that male anthropologists have something from their own past to hide, probably unconscious, which the ritual secrecy of a New Guinea men's group has disturbed, resulting in an overdetermined reaction to it, even a phobic relation to homosocial and especially, homoerotic feelings, tilting interpretation. This transference reaction—to overlook secrecy as if winking co-conspirators—again results in a different form of duplicity: condemning these as if they have absolutely no parallel in our own tradition and should not be compared to anything in our own cultural experience. This has a countertendency: to pardon the violation of women and children's lives, in what we in the West would call human rights. In either case, these conflicted interpretations of ritual secrecy depend upon the personal development and agency of the anthropologist, as much as the inherited structures of gender power and political economy in which we operate.

Perhaps some ethnographers have a history of their own secret acts of one kind or another that might embarrass them. If so, they might have felt a vested interest (conscious or unconscious) in colluding with New Guineans—men or women, but usually men—in hiding the darker side of male bonding. This is speculation, of course, but it need not be treated as conspiratorial or malicious to see how, as a result of living in societies that privilege certain positional identities, privileged male actors come to be relatively unaware or even unconscious of their complicity with the compromised ethics of another people. But surely, based upon the work of this book and what is known from sexuality studies at large, sexual orientation is today an important part of the ability to reflect upon male power and the positionality inherent through secrecy. Nonetheless, the insidious denial continues, as observed in the following commentary by Australian anthropologist Jadran Mimica:

> Regarding the issue of the sexual object-choice preference of the ethnographer, contra Herdt and some other gay anthropologists, the self declaration of one's sexual/gendered being (e.g., bi-, homo-, hetero-, third, fourth, n-th, two-spirit, no-spirit, etc.) makes a priori no difference as to the direction and depth of the exercise of self-critical understanding and transcendence as the basis of the project of ethnography. As a self-legitimizing strategy it is exactly that, hence its internal limitations. (2001: 236)

That a heterosexual White male ethnographer would regard sexual "preference" as a "choice" and deny its role in the interpretation of culture is a delicious absurdity.

Historically the reader wonders how such a moral worldview regarded secrecy and exploitation of women. While social solidarity and religion were important factors appealed to by Read's generation of structural-functional theories long ago, even in their day they were insufficient to explain ritual secrecy. What they omitted were the cultural and ontological realities of the genders and generational divide: an element of the ontological creation of reality among males and females in New Guinea village life that cannot be reduced to the neoliberal ethos, which appeals to such concepts as "justice" in the public domain. Indeed, my guess is that for the

Sambia and perhaps other New Guinea peoples, the male self-image is suggestive of the very core of ritual secrecy and embodiment, a utopian Ideal Man imagery (e.g., Godelier's notion of Great Man) that excludes other modalities of being and knowing, hence precluding such a concept as "justice." Here we have manliness as the cultural ideal that was combined—as an internal contradiction—with gendered ontologies of misogyny that stemmed from initiation. This secret discourse displaced the actors; their secret subjectivities made their sense of maleness, of masculinity, of agency conditional, limited, and always vulnerable. In this idealized, secret subjective sense of time, the scripts of the men are frozen in unequal subject/object relationships which displaced themselves as men and replaced them in the discursive frame of the men's house as "boys," thus casting themselves as forever the victim in a timeless social drama that they could not "win" against subversive, sophisticated, and sexy women (Gillison 1993). This is the objectification of the ontology of ritual secrecy; its psychocultural script if you like, as the socialization of secret male development provides for the Ideal Man growing up first in the women's house and later, protected by secret ritual practices, in the men's house. It is not so greatly divergent from the distant echo of American mainstream men today as to be unknowable.

Upon closer inspection, I suspect that it may have been this intimate and manly form of pleasure—here I mean the pleasure of mastery that derives from learning how to produce ritual secrecy—that misled such astute observers as Kenneth Read, Ian Hogbin, L. L. Langness, and others of their cohort to interpret the men's behavior as a hoax; while subsequent ethnographers, such as Barth, found in them a fabled and ill-fated search for Truth. Underlying the ritual secrecy in all these communities is the effort to anchor reality, to seek a means of building trust with one's fellows, in spite of the odds.

These ethnographies also suggest that observers in precolonial New Guinea societies often misunderstood the pleasure that boys and men felt in becoming objects of desire for other men and for women and in learning how to properly perform the rituals, by taking that pleasure to be an inauthentic, bastard form of masculinity. A prior generation, before feminism and the gay movement, reasoned that New Guinea men could not desire each other in these ways. The anthropologist may have misinterpreted that such a desire could only make them into "homosexuals," a category that did not exist in New Guinea precolonial society (Herdt 1993).

And since these men were not effeminate, but rather intensely masculine by the standards of the Western worldview of the cold war period, there must be another explanation: given that these societies lacked "homosexuality," the secrets themselves must therefore be a lie or a farce. But this objection ignored the local theory of desire and made the men's secrecy—the Ideal Man that only the men could know about—into a negation of culture. A totally different, more culturally relative approach would have been to interpret the ritual secrecy as the very means of the production and reproduction of a more contradictory cultural reality than that of their own Western society. In the men's house sexual subjectivity of the Ideal Man, the imagery divides the world along different lines: not public and private, as in the Western frame, but public and ritual secrecy, with objects and their meanings anchored in both spheres, and "truth" a nebulous and shifting discursive frame of memory (Whitehouse 2000). It was easy to misjudge this split between social solidarity of the total society and the deceit of the women and children as "the" split between truth and lie, in a rhetoric of neoliberal democracy alien to these societies and their men's house tradition.

I would not like to be placed in the position of ethically defending the traditional practices and beliefs found in New Guinea; this is not an apology for them, nor is that required of me. I know that contractual secrecy can under certain conditions protect human life. I believe that in order to understand the role of the ethnographer's subjectivity as an element in the interpretation of culture and power, we ought to know about the sexuality of the anthropologist, which is of course far more complex than being either a "choice" or merely a "biological given," as the Mimicas and popular culture might like to think. But I am aware of the terrible human cost exacted by ritual secrecy in New Guinea and contractual secrecy in many arenas today in the United States: although survival for a time can be assured by the protections of secrecy, the cost may be great suffering long afterward.

But while we in Western neoliberal democracies may object to secret rituals, and, indeed, our objections may be well grounded in humanistic and compassionate reason, it is not our right to oppose these customs in their own land. It is too easy to moralize and condemn that part of pre-colonial New Guinea, the more so as secrecy seems so exotic and so much at odds with us—an Otherness that is cruel and grotesque, not at all what Lewis Henry Morgan found in such traditions. Too easy, that is, to collude with the colonial domination of these customs and by critique assume that these customs and their purveyors should be removed or at least reformed (Lattas 1999). But we now know—thanks to the nineteenth-century history of Morgan—that such a view is shortsighted. To admit that our own recent cultural history biases us to chide or dismiss ritual secrecy because we have forgotten this part of our own past—not just anthropology's past, if not indeed a more distant developmental social history—is part of the means by which we should seek to understand, and then if necessary to defend, these non-Western traditions against their detractors from the outside, especially from the attacks of Western agents such as missionaries.

To me, the most important and wonderful gift of ethnography in New Guinea has been to capture that extraordinarily precious and momentary disjunction of time and space when the subjects and objects of ritual secrecy were suddenly inverted and made transparent to the eyewitness. No longer were they simply a part of what is "natural" to the cultural history and conventionality, as we saw so acutely among the Ilahita Arapesh (chap. 5). This critical moment is when actors begin to reflect upon their own objects of ritual action—whether cult practices, ritual masks, Tambaran spirits, boy initiates, or women spectators—either reproducing or becoming cynical, even laughing at their own traditions. A generation later they may become nostalgic over what was lost or, as in the case of the Yagwoia, yearn for an Other to whom to narrate this vanishing tradition. In such examples the ritual secrecy reflects back to a people their contradictions, the public/secret split, the subjectivities hidden in the past—a distant, even forgotten sense of cultural reality. These native observers may become the worst critics of what is now seen no longer as genuine culture but as spurious—as cardboard power. Perhaps they begin to view what was once a matter of absolute faith in the sacred and divine as fake and contrived, or—even worse—as the petty ambitions of what small men do to seem bigger. "People reinvent the civilizing process by making it partly their own, and it is part of their project of making themselves at home in which their identities and their world have both been severely problematized" (Lattas 1999: 314).

It is such a wondrous and dreadful thing to witness, this turn of conventional cultural realities: the sudden and definite realization that a whole way of life lacked the feared sacred power and merit of the gods attributed to it. The rage released by this insight is terrifying and can barely be reckoned with, as shown in the account of the Sambia and Yagwoia narratives (chap. 4). Only the word *pathos* is sufficient to capture the fury and despair of a people after the fall of ritual secrecy. Of all the emotions observed at the time, however, rage and grief are among them, reminding us of Freud's (1913) incredible insight that those who grieve for the dead would also like to attack and destroy the remains of those they once loved. But how is this possible, and how can it be reconciled with the real love once felt for the desired object? Freud's answer, of course, was to understand that humans are often ambivalent, and they press their aggressive tendencies against the object that they feel has abandoned them at their hour of greatest need. Anthropologists, however, are not satisfied with such a psychologistic answer; we understand the shattering of social worlds as complex processes, leaving shards in their wake, the elements of ritual and myth scattered across vast regions in mosaic and disguised cultural forms (Lévi-Strauss 1974).

The rage may take as its object the human objects of action, the boy-initiates and women who were marginal to ritual secrecy. But it may then be directed toward the very objects of desire formerly identified with the cult itself—its masks and paraphernalia, its spirits, even the god Tambaran: that he cheated and failed and died!—and failed to protect the male believers from the antisecrecy rhetoric in the dreadful aftermath. Indeed, the detractors of the men's cult suggest that the Tambaran was feeble enough to be rendered impotent by puny European agents and a handful of missionary zealots. More than a century of cargo cults in this area of the world carry in their history this rage and effort at cultural renewal.

The effort to capture all of this desolation of the human spirit in our ethnographies is a monumental task for anthropology, and many shirk from it, because we are not immortals, either. Hovering over our shoulder all throughout the process is that faint accusation of our long tradition: "This secrecy is a sham." To reflect upon this avalanche of cultural change is daunting, and the anthropologist may experience wanting to walk away from the desolation of it all, much as Lewis Henry Morgan seemed long ago to have walked away from the ritual secrecy projects of his youth. Confronting these contrary impulses in the task of doing and writing ethnography is what is required to deal with the larger social ethics of describing and interpreting the demise of secrecy in these magnificent cultures.

To contest these realities from the Western point of view is problematic, because it threatens to repeat—recapitulate, in another form, and another time—what occurred in the colonial encounter. It is not our right but rather the right of local actors and their communities to work out these historical formations and their contradictions in their own way. We must resist the temptation to place ourselves in the position of the deposed Tambaran and say what is right or wrong about the old ways. It is more ethical for anthropology to respect these complex historical realities and leave it to local communities to find their own Morgans and reformers who will reclaim dignity as they come to define it for themselves.

Notes

✳

1. This text is based on four public talks delivered over the course of two weeks at the University of Rochester in March 1991. I originally formulated the text to be presented in oral form since I tend to be a lyrical writer and enjoy that particular dimension of the spoken word. But lectures do not a book make, and the text proved too unwieldy to be directly translated into book form. As it was, the material included more information than was necessary on substantive domains ranging from ritual secrecy in New Guinea, to gender and sexuality in the transition to the modern age, and on to conceptions of the modern self in literature, social relations, and personal development. For this reason, the original lectures were revised, and the other material, including the historical and cultural emergence of modern sexual and gender categories and identities—especially details concerning the ways in which the epistemology of closeted homosexuality created new secret desires of the sexual citizen and the state—was removed. These other aspects of the lecture series are dealt with elsewhere in my writings. My theory of secrecy has also undergone three transformations on the way to its present form, and at present it is something which I like to call a semi-ontological theory, for it asserts that there are different kinds of secrecy that are grounded in distinctive social problems within varying historical periods, each having divergent social economies of exchange, different realities, and distinct challenges to trust and commitment in the individual.

CHAPTER I

1. Much of the detail surrounding the childhood and family life of Morgan in the following two paragraphs derives from Carnes (1989: 94–98), whose book is recommended.
2. I owe this insight to my friend Raymond Fogelson.
3. Fenton quotes Parker: "The society was to be a most secret one and only for a qualified number. Its meetings were to be held only when the moon was away" (148). Though we cannot be sure, the well-known correspondence between Parker

and Morgan (see Fenton 1941) raises the question of Morgan's own idealized influence upon Parker, and whether the Masonic activities of Parker, which may have been participated in by Morgan, were not in themselves a source of Parker's own romantic ideas regarding the revival of Iroquois ritual practices.

4. Parker's later account of the secret medicine societies and initiations of the Seneca praises Morgan's. Fenton (1987) has objected to Morgan's handling of secrecy in particular, arguing that the kind of secrecy Morgan reports was not traditional, at least in the period before the revivalism of Handsome Lake. But Parker's account of social change and competition within the tribe over the role of Handsome Lake's religion and the rites of the medicine group "performed in secret places" over the years following the prophet is supportive of Morgan's view (Parker 1909: 163).

5. Though he might not have approved of its use, for he meant it to be secret, let us begin the larger investigation to follow by invoking a ceremonial injunction that draws the line between insider and outsider, a necessary condition of all ritual:

> Guard of the Forest, you will see that the outer wicket is securely closed during the burning of the council fire so that no paleface may enter or pry into our secrets. You will permit no member of another Tribe to pass your wicket without giving the proper signal and universal password of the current term.

Thus opened the initiation into the Grand Order of the Iroquois according to the rules of the Kindling of the Fire penned by Morgan himself.

6. In later years the Reverend became a professor of belles lettres at Princeton University and eventually founded the Evelyn College for Women in Princeton in 1887 (White 1959: 202).

CHAPTER 4

1. "The wide differences in gender imagery which we observe in different cosmological sub-traditions arise from clearly identifiable processes. The starting point is provided in a basically shared wide spectrum of male experience and emotions relating to women: sexual drive, lust, repulsion, fear, love, deepness, nurturing" (Barth 1987: 43). Notice the completely unreflective categories, such as sexual drive, which we have long since come to think of as being anything but "natural" or "raw," and which are social constructions within our own historical and social tradition (reviewed in Herdt 1991b, 1997a; Knauft 1999: 167).

2. "Le secret des hommes, c'est de devoir, pour atteindre leur masculinité, agir selon le modèle de la procréation, où la femme a le rôle majeur. Mais, par définition, le contenu d'un secret—ici, à la fois l'imitation des pouvoirs nourriciers féminins et les différentes opérations de déféminisation—ne peut en lui-même constituer ce qui met l'autre, ici la communauté des femmes, dans un état d'inferiorité" (Bonnemere 1996: 375).

CHAPTER 5

1. So many cultural complexities and discrepant sources of information surrounded Marind-anim ritual and religion, provided by an army of reporters, many of them letters from missionaries, that after a thousand pages of that extraordinary and maddeningly multilayered work, *Dema* (1966), Van Baal would in the end throw up his hands at the apparent "contradictions" of Marind-anim belief and mythology, allowing that a "phallic" religion must reside ultimately in the inscrutable mysteries of the archaic human mind. We have come across the notion before in the nineteenth-century armchair evolutionary view.

2. Margaret Mead's Preface to D. F. Tuzin's (1976) first book praised its careful attention to the larger themes of Arapesh culture.

References

Adam, B., et al. 1999. *The Global Emergence of Gay and Lesbian Politics*. Philadelphia: Temple University Press.

Allen, M. R. 1967. *Male Cults and Secret Initiations in Melanesia*. Melbourne, Australia: Melbourne University Press.

———. 1984. Homosexuality, Male Power, and Political Organization in North Vanuatu: A Comparative Analysis. In G. Herdt, ed., *Ritualized Homosexuality in Melanesia*, 83–127. Berkeley: University of California Press.

———. 1998. Male Cults Revisited: The Politics of Blood versus Semen. *Oceania* 68:189–99.

Andrew, C., and V. Mitrokhin. 2001. *The Sword and the Shield: The Mirokhin Archive and the Secret History of the KGB*. New York: Basic Books.

Apter, E. S. 1991. *Feminizing the Fetish: Psychoanalysis and Narrative Obsession in Turn-of-the-Century France*. Ithaca: Cornell University Press.

Baran, A., and R. Pannor. 1989. *Lethal Secrets: The Psychology of Donor Insemination*. New York: Amistad.

Barker, J. 1990. *Christianity on Oceania: Ethnographic Perspectives*. Lanham, MD: University Press of America.

Barnes, J. A. 1962. African Models in the New Guinea Highlands. *Man* 62:5–9.

Barth, F. 1971. Tribes and Inter-tribal Relations in the Fly Headwaters. *Oceania* 41:171–91.

———. 1975. *Ritual and Knowledge among the Baktaman of New Guinea*. New Haven: Yale University Press.

———. 1987. *Cosmologies in the Making: A Generative Approach to Cultural Variation in Inner New Guinea*. New York: Cambridge University Press.

———. 1990. The Guru and the Conjurer: Transactions in Knowledge and the Shaping of Culture in Southeast Asia and Melanesia. *Man* 25:640–53.

Bateson, G. 1932. Social Structure of the Iatmul People of the Sepik. *Oceania* 2:245–91, 401–53.

———. 1958. *Naven: A Survey of the Problems Suggested by a Composite Picture of a New Guinea Tribe Drawn from Three Points of View*. 2d ed. Stanford: Stanford University Press.

———. 1972. *Steps to an Ecology of Mind*. Scranton, PA: Chandler.

Bech, H. 1997. *When Men Meet: Homosexuality and Modernity*. Chicago: University of Chicago Press.

Bellah, R., et al. 1985. *Habits of the Heart*. Berkeley: University of California Press.

Bellman, B. L. 1984. *The Language of Secrecy: Symbols and Metaphors in Poro Ritual*. New Brunswick, NJ: Rutgers University Press.

Bercovitch, E. 1989a. Mortal Insights: Victim and Witch in the Nalumin Imagination. In G. Herdt and M. Stephen, eds., *Varieties of the Religious Imagination in New Guinea*, 122–59. New Brunswick, NJ: Rutgers University Press.

———. 1989b. Disclosure and Concealment: A Study of Secrecy among the Nalumin People of Papua New Guinea. Doctoral dissertation, Stanford University.

———. N.d. No Right Way to Live: Hidden Exchange and Agency in Inner New Guinea. Manuscript, University of Chicago.

Berger, P. L. 1963. *Invitation to Sociology: A Humanistic Perspective*. New York: Doubleday Anchor.

———. 1969. *The Sacred Canopy: Elements of a Sociological Theory of Religion*. New York: Doubleday Anchor.

Berndt, R. M., and C. H. Berndt. 1962. *Sexual Behavior in Western Arnhem Land*. New York: Viking Fund Publication no. 16.

Berndt, R. M., and P. Lawrence, eds. 1971. *Politics in New Guinea*. Nedlands, Australia: University of Western Australia Press.

Bettelheim, B. 1955. *Symbolic Wounds: Puberty Rites and the Envious Male*. New York: Collier.

Biersack, A. 1982. Ginger Gardens for the Ginger Woman: Rites and Passages in a Melanesian Society. *Man* 17:239–58.

———, ed. 1991. *Clio in Oceania: Toward a Historical Anthropology*. Washington, DC: Smithsonian Institution Press.

Blok, A. 1974. *The Mafia of a Sicilian Village, 1886–1960: A Study of Violent Peasant Entrepreneurs*. Prospect Heights, IL: Waveland Press.

Bok, S. 1982. *Secrets*. New York: Oxford University Press.

Bonnemere, P. 1996. *Le Pandanus Rouge: Corps, Différence Des Sexes et Parente Chez les Ankave-Anga*. Paris: CNRS Editions.

Bram, C. 2000. *The Notorious Dr. August: His Real Life and Times*. New York: Perennial Books.

Braude, A. 1989. *Radical Spirits: Spiritualism and Women's Rights in Nineteenth-Century America*. Boston: Beacon Press.

Brison, K. J. 1992. *Just Talk: Gossip, Meetings, and Power in a Papua New Guinea Village*. Berkeley: University of California Press.

Brown, P. 1978. *Highland Peoples of New Guinea*. New York: Cambridge University Press.

———. 1995. *Beyond a Mountain Valley: The Simbu of Papua New Guinea*. Honolulu: University of Hawaii Press.

Brown, P., and G. Buchbinder, eds. 1976. *Man and Woman in the New Guinea Highlands*. Washington, DC: American Anthropological Association.

Burridge, K. 1969. *New Heaven, New Earth: A Study of Millenarian Activities*. London: Basil Blackwell.

Carnes, M. C. 1989. *Secret Ritual and Manhood in Victorian America.* New Haven and London: Yale University Press.

———. 1990. Middle-Class Men and the Solace of Fraternal Ritual. In M. C. Carnes and C. Griffen, eds., *Meanings for Manhood: Constructions of Masculinity in Victorian America,* 37–66. Chicago: University of Chicago Press.

Carrier, J. G., ed. 1992. *History and Tradition in Melanesian Anthropology.* Berkeley: University of California Press.

Carrier, J. G., and A. H. Carrier. 1989. *Wage, Trade, and Exchange in Melanesia: A Manus Society in the Modern State.* Berkeley: University of California Press.

Chodorow, N. J. 1978. *The Reproduction of Mothering.* Berkeley: University of California Press.

Codrington, R. H. 1891. *The Melanesians.* Oxford: Clarendon Press.

Comaroff, J., and J. L. Comaroff. 1991. *Of Revelation and Revolution.* Chicago: University of Chicago Press.

Connell, R. W. 1995. *Masculinities.* Berkeley: University of California Press.

Corber, R. J. 1997. *Homosexuality in Cold War America: Resistance and the Crisis of Masculinity.* Durham, NC: Duke University Press.

Deacon, A. B. 1934. *Malekula: A Vanishing People in the New Hebrides.* London: George Routledge.

D'Emilio, J. 1983. *Sexual Politics, Sexual Communities.* Chicago: University of Chicago Press.

D'Emilio, J. D., and E. B. Freedman. 1988. *Intimate Matters: A History of Sexuality in America.* New York: Harper and Row.

di Leonardo, M. 1998. *Exotics at Home.* Chicago: University of Chicago Press.

Dover, K. 1978. *Greek Homosexuality.* New York: Cambridge University Press.

Duberman, M. 1991. *Cures.* New York: Dutton.

Durkheim, E. 1914. The Dualism of Human Nature and Its Social Conditions. Trans. C. Blend. In K. H. Wolff, ed., *Essays on Sociology and Philosophy,* 325–39. New York: Harper Torchbooks.

———. 1915. *The Elementary Forms of the Religious Life.* Glencoe, IL: Free Press.

Ehrenreich, J. 1984. Isolation, Retreat, and Secrecy: Dissembling Behavior among the Coaiquer Indians of Ecuador. In J. Ehrenreich, ed., *Political Anthropology in Ecuador: Perspectives from Indigenous Cultures,* 25–57. Albany, NY: Society for Latin American Anthropology.

Engels, F. 1972 [1884]. *The Origin of the Family, Private Property, and the State.* London: Lawrence and Wishart.

Evans-Pritchard, E. E. 1964. *Theories of Primitive Religion.* Oxford: Clarendon Press.

Fabian, J. 1983. *Time and the Other: How Anthropology Makes Its Object.* New York: Columbia University Press.

———. 1991. *Language and Colonial Power.* Berkeley: University of California Press.

Faderman, L. 1981. *Surpassing the Love of Men: Romantic Friendship and Love between Women from the Renaissance to the Present.* New York: Morrow.

———. 1999. *To Believe in Women.* New York: Houghton Mifflin.

Faithorn, E. 1975. The Concept of Pollution among the Kafe of Papua New

Guinea. In R. R. Reiter, ed., *Toward an Anthropology of Women*, 127–40. New York: Monthly Review Press.

Fajans, J. 1997. *They Make Themselves: Work and Play among the Baining of Papua New Guinea*. Chicago: University of Chicago Press.

Favret-Saada, J. 1980. *Deadly Words: Witchcraft in the Bocage*. Trans. C. Cullen. Cambridge: Cambridge University Press.

Feil, D. K. 1978. Women and Men in the Enga Tee. *American Ethnologist* 5:263–79.

———. 1987. *The Evolution of Highland Papua New Guinea Societies*. Cambridge: Cambridge University Press.

Fenton, W. N. 1941. Tonawanda Longhouse Ceremonies: Ninety Years after Lewis Henry Morgan. *Anthropological Papers*, (15). *Bureau of American Ethnology Bulletin* 128:140–66. Washington, DC: U.S. Government Printing Office.

———. 1987. *The False Faces of the Iroquois*. Norman: University of Oklahoma Press.

Flanagan, J. G. 1989. Hierarchy in Simple "Egalitarian" Societies. *Annual Review of Anthropology* 18:245–66.

Foder, N. 1984. *Ages in Conflict: A Cross-Cultural Perspective on Inequality between Old and Young*. New York: Columbia University Press.

Forge, A. 1966. Art and Environment in the Sepik. *Proceedings of the Royal Anthropological Institute of Great Britain and North Ireland* 1965:25–31.

———. 1970. Prestige, Influence, and Sorcery: A New Guinea Example. In M. Douglas, ed., *Witchcraft Confessions and Accusations*, 257–75. London: Tavistock.

———. 1972. The Golden Fleece. *Man* 7:527–40.

———. 1979. Style and Meaning in Sepik Art. In A. Forge, ed., *Primitive Art and Society*, 170–92. London: Oxford University Press.

———. 1990. The Power of Culture and the Culture of Power. In N. Lutkehaus et al., eds., *Sepik Heritage: Tradition and Change in Papua New Guinea*, 160–70. Durham, NC: Carolina Academic Press.

Fortes, M. 1969. *Kinship and the Social Order*. Chicago: Aldine.

Foster, R. J., ed. 1995. *Nation Making: Emergent Identities in Postcolonial Melanesia*. Ann Arbor: University of Michigan Press.

Foucault, M. 1973. *The Birth of the Clinic*. Trans. A. M. S. Smith. New York: Pantheon.

———. 1980. *The History of Sexuality*. Trans. R. Hurley. New York: Viking.

———. 1986. *The Uses of Pleasure*. Trans. R. Hurley. New York: Viking.

Freud, S. 1913. Totem and Taboo. *Standard Edition* 13: x–162.

———. 1923. The Ego and the Id. *Standard Edition* 19:12–59. London: Hogarth Press.

———. 1960 [1916]. *Group Psychology and the Analysis of the Ego*. New York: Bantam.

———. 1961 [1925]. Some Physical Consequences of the Anatomical Distinction between the Sexes. *Standard Edition* 19:423–58. London: Hogarth Press.

Gagnon, J. 1971. The Creation of the Sexual in Adolescence. In J. Kagan and R. Coles, eds., *Twelve to Sixteen: Early Adolescence*, 231–57. New York: W. W. Norton.

Gay, P. 1986. *The Bourgeois Experience—Victoria to Freud*. Vol. 2, *The Tender Passion*. New York: Oxford University Press.

Geertz, C. 1966. Religion as a Cultural System. In M. Banton, ed., *Anthropological Approaches to the Study of Religion*. London: Athlone.

———. 1973. *The Interpretation of Cultures*. New York: Basic Books.

———. 1984a. Anti Anti-Relativism. *American Anthropologist* 86:263–78.

———. 1984b. Common Sense as a Cultural System. In C. Geertz, *Local Knowledge*. New York: Basic Books.

———. 1988. *Works and Lives: The Anthropologist as Author*. Stanford: Stanford University Press.

———. 2001. Life among the Anthros. *New York Review of Books* 48:18–22.

Gell, A. 1975. *Metamorphosis of the Cassowaries*. London: Athlone Press.

Gellner, E. 1992. *Postmodernism, Reason and Religion*. New York: Routledge.

Gewertz, D. 1981. An Historical Reconstruction of Female Dominance among the Chambri of Papua New Guinea. *American Ethnologist* 8:94–106.

———. 1982. The Father Who Bore Me: The Role of the Tsambunwuro during Chambri Initiation Ceremonies. In G. Herdt, ed., *Rituals of Manhood: Male Initiation in Papua New Guinea*, 286–320. Berkeley: University of California Press.

———. 1983. *Sepik River Societies*. New Haven: Yale University Press.

———. 1984. The View of Persons: A Critique of Individualism in the Works of Mead and Chodorow. *American Anthropologist* 86:615–29.

Gewertz, D. B., and F. K. Errington. 1999. *Emerging Class in Papua New Guinea: The Telling of Difference*. New York: Cambridge University Press.

Giddens, A. 1990. *The Consequences of Modernity*. Stanford: Stanford University Press.

Gilligan, C. 1982. *In a Different Voice*. Cambridge: Harvard University Press.

Gillison, G. 1980. Images of Nature in Gimi Thought. In C. MacCormack and M. Strathern, eds., *Nature, Culture, and Gender*, 143–73. Cambridge: Cambridge University Press.

———. 1993. *Between Culture and Fantasy: A New Guinea Highlands Mythology*. Chicago: University of Chicago Press.

Godelier, M. 1971. Salt Currency and the Circulation of Commodities among the Baruya of New Guinea. In *The Social Dynamics of Economic Innovation: Studies in Economic Anthropology*, 53–73. Washington, DC: American Anthropological Association.

———. 1973. Outils de pierre, outils d'acier chez les Baruya de Nouvelle-Guinée. *L'Homme* 13:187–220.

———. 1982. Social Hierarchies among the Baruya of New Guinea. In A. Strathern, ed., *Inequality in New Guinea*, 3–34. New York: Cambridge University Press.

———. 1986. *The Production of Great Men: Male Domination and Power among the New Guinea Baruya*. New York: Cambridge University Press.

———. 1989. Betrayal: The Case of the New Guinea Baruya. *Oceania* 59 (3): 165–80.

———. 1995. Sexualité et société: Propose d'un anthropologue. In N. Bajos et al., eds., *Sexualité et Sida*. Paris: ANRS.

———. 1999. *The Enigma of the Gift*. Trans. N. Scott. Chicago: University of Chicago Press.

Godelier, M., and A. Strathern. 1991. *Big Men and Great Men: Personifications of Power in Melanesia*. Cambridge: Cambridge University Press.

Goffman, E. 1959. *The Presentation of Self*. New York: Doubleday.

———. 1963. *Stigma: Notes on the Management of Spoiled Identity*. Englewood Cliffs, NJ: Prentice-Hall.

Gregor, T. 1985. *Anxious Pleasures. The Sexual Lives of an Amazonian People*. Chicago: University of Chicago Press.

Gregor, T., and D. F. Tuzin. 2001. *Gender in Amazonia and Melanesia: An Exploration of the Comparative Method*. Berkeley: University of California Press.

Gregory, C. A. 1982. *Gifts and Commodities*. London: Academic Press.

Haddon, A. C. 1917. New Guinea. In *Hastings' Encyclopaedia of Religion and Ethics* 9:339–52.

———. 1920. Migrations of Cultures in British New Guinea. *Journal of the Royal Anthropological Institute* 50:234–80.

———. 1924. Introduction. In J. H. Holmes, ed., *In Primitive New Guinea*, i–xii. New York: G. P. Putnam and Sons.

Halperin, D. 1990. *One Hundred Years of Homosexuality*. New York: Routledge.

Harrison, S. 1993. *The Mask of War: Violence, Ritual, and the Self in Melanesia*. Manchester, UK: Manchester University Press.

Hauser-Schaublin, B. 1989. The Fallacy of "Real" and "Pseudo" Procreation. *Zeitschrift für Ethnologie* 114:179–84.

Hays, T. E. 1992. A Historical Background to Anthropology in the Papua New Guinea Highlands. In T. E. Hays, ed., *Ethnographic Presents*, 1–36. Berkeley: University of California Press.

Hays, T. E., and P. Hays. 1982. Opposition and Complementarity of the Sexes in Nduma Initiations. In G. Herdt, ed., *Male Initiation in New Guinea*. Berkeley: University of California Press.

Herdt, G. 1981. *Guardians of the Flutes: Idioms of Masculinity*. New York: McGraw-Hill.

———, ed. 1982a. *Rituals of Manhood: Male Initiation in Papua New Guinea*. Berkeley: University of California Press.

———. 1982b. Fetish and Fantasy in Sambia Initiation. In G. Herdt, ed., *Rituals of Manhood: Male Initiation in Papua New Guinea*, 44–98. Berkeley: University of California Press.

———. 1982c. Sambia Nose-Bleeding Rites and Male Proximity to Women. *Ethos* 10 (3): 189–231.

———. 1984a. Ritualized Homosexuality in the Male Cults of Melanesia, 1862–1982: An Introduction. In G. Herdt, ed., *Ritualized Homosexuality in Melanesia*, 1–81. Berkeley: University of California Press.

———, ed. 1984b. *Ritualized Homosexuality in Melanesia*. Berkeley: University of California Press.

———. 1987a. *The Sambia: Ritual and Gender in New Guinea*. New York: Holt, Rinehart and Winston.

———. 1987b. The Accountability of Sambia Initiates. In L. L. Langness and

T. E. Hays, eds., *Anthropology in the High Valleys: Essays in Honor of K. E. Read*, 82. Novato, CA: Chandler and Sharp.

———. 1987c. Selfhood and Discourse in Sambia Dream Sharing. In B. Tedlock, ed., *Dreaming: The Anthropology and Psychology of the Imaginal*, 55–85. New York: Cambridge University Press.

———. 1987d. Transitional Objects in Sambia Culture. *Ethos* 15:40–57.

———. 1989a. Self and Culture: Contexts of Religious Experience in Melanesia. In G. Herdt and M. Stephen, eds., *Varieties of the Religious Imagination in New Guinea*, 15–40. New Brunswick, NJ: Rutgers University Press.

———. 1989b. Spirit Familiars in the Religious Imagination of Sambia Shamans. In G. Herdt and M. Stephen, eds., *Varieties of the Religious Imagination in New Guinea*, 99–121. New Brunswick, NJ: Rutgers University Press.

———. 1989c. Father Presence and Masculine Development: The Case of Paternal Deprivation and Ritual Homosexuality Reconsidered. *Ethos* 18:326–70.

———. 1990. Secret Societies and Secret Collectives. *Oceania* 60:361–81.

———. 1991a. Representations of Homosexuality in Traditional Societies: An Essay on Cultural Ontology and Historical Comparison, Part I. *Journal of the History of Sexuality* 1 (1): 481–504.

———. 1991b. Representations of Homosexuality in Traditional Societies: An Essay on Cultural Ontology and Historical Comparison, Part II. *Journal of the History of Sexuality* 2 (2): 603–32.

———. 1992. Sexual Repression, Social Control, and Gender Hierarchy in Sambia Culture. In B. Miller, ed., *Gender Hierarchies*, 121–35. New York: Cambridge University Press.

———. 1993. Introduction. In G. Herdt, ed., *Ritualized Homosexuality in Melanesia* (rev. ed.), vii–xliv. Berkeley: University of California Press.

———, ed. 1994a. *Third Sex, Third Gender: Beyond Sexual Dimorphism in Culture and History*. New York: Zone Books.

———. 1994b. Mistaken Sex: Culture, Biology, and the Third Sex in New Guinea. In G. Herdt, ed., *Third Sex, Third Gender: Beyond Sexual Dimorphism in Culture and History*, 419–46. New York: Zone Books.

———. 1997a. *Same Sex, Different Cultures: Perspectives on Gay and Lesbian Lives*. New York: Westview Press.

———. 1997b. Sexual Cultures and Population Movement: Implications for HIV/STDs. In G. Herdt, ed., *Sexual Cultures and Migration in the Era of AIDS: Anthropological and Demographic Perspectives*, 3–22. New York: Oxford University Press.

———. 1999a. Sexual Cultures, Strange and Familiar: Introduction. In G. Herdt, *Sambia Sexual Cultures: Essays from the Field*, 1–28. Chicago: University of Chicago Press.

———. 1999b. Sexing Anthropology: Rethinking Sexual Culture, Subjectivity, and the Method of Anthropological Participant Observation. In D. N. Suggs and A. M. Miracle, eds., *Culture, Biology, and Sexuality*, 17–32. Athens: University of Georgia Press.

Herdt, G., and A. Boxer. 1993. *Children of Horizons*. Boston: Beacon.

———. 1995. Toward a Theory of Bisexuality. In R. G. Parker and J. H. Gagnon, eds., *Conceiving Sexuality: Approaches to Sex Research in a Postmodern World*, 69–84. New York: Routledge.

Herdt, G., and B. Koff. 2000. *Something to Tell You: The Road Families Travel When a Child Is Gay*. New York: Columbia University Press.

Herdt, G., and F. J. P. Poole. 1982. Sexual Antagonism: The Intellectual History of a Concept in the Anthropology of New Guinea. *Social Analysis* 12:3–28.

Herdt, G., and M. Stephen, eds. 1989. *Varieties of the Religious Imagination in New Guinea*, 99–121. New Brunswick, NJ: Rutgers University Press.

Herdt, G., and R. J. Stoller. 1990. *Intimate Communications: Erotics and the Study of Culture*. New York: Columbia University Press.

Herman, D. 1997. The *Antigay Agenda: Orthodox Vision and the Christian Right*. Chicago: University of Chicago Press.

Hogbin, I. 1970. *The Island of Menstruating Men*. Scranton, PA: Chandler.

Horton, R. 1972. Stateless Societies in the History of West Africa. In J. F. A. Ajayi and M. Crowder, eds., *History of West Africa*, 78–119. New York: Columbia University Press.

Jacobs, S. E., W. Thomas, and S. Lang, eds. 1997. *Two-Spirit People: Native American Gender Identity, Sexuality, and Spirituality*. Urbana: University of Illinois Press.

Jay, N. 1992. *Throughout Your Generations Forever: Sacrifice, Religion, and Paternity*. Chicago: University of Chicago Press.

Jones, B. 1980. Consuming Society: Food and Illness among the Faiwol. Ph.D dissertation, University of Virginia.

Jorgenson, D. 1978. On Not Knowing in Telefomin. Manuscript.

———. 1996. Regional History and Ethnic Identity in the Hub of New Guinea: The Emergence of the Min. *Oceania* 66:189–210.

Juillerat, B. 1990. *L'Avènement du Père. Rite, Représentation, Fantasme dans un culte Mélanésien*. Paris: CNRS Editions.

Keen, I. 1994. *Knowledge and Secrecy in an Aboriginal Religion*. New York: Oxford University Press.

Keesing, R. M. 1982a. Introduction. In G. Herdt, ed., *Rituals of Manhood: Male Initiation in Papua New Guinea*, 1–42. Berkeley: University of California Press.

———. 1982b. *Kwaio Religion: The Living and the Dead in a Solomon Island Society*. New York: Columbia University Press.

———. 1992. *Custom and Confrontation: The Kwaio Struggle for Cultural Autonomy*. Chicago: University of Chicago Press.

Kelly, R. C. 1976. Witchcraft and Sexual Relations: An Exploration in the Social and Semantic Implications of the Structure of Belief. In P. Brown and G. Buchbinder, eds., *Man and Woman in the New Guinea Highlands*, 36–53. Washington, DC: American Anthropological Association.

———. 1993. *Constructing Inequality: The Fabrication of a Hierarchy of Virtue among the Etoro*. Ann Arbor: University of Michigan Press.

Kertzer, D. I. 1988. *Ritual, Politics and Power*. New Haven: Yale University Press.

Kimmel, M. 1996. *Manhood in America: A Cultural History*. New York: Free Press.

Knauft, B. 1985. *Good Company and Violence: Sorcery and Social Action in Lowland New Guinea Society*. Berkeley: University of California Press.

———. 1986. Text and Social Practice: Narrative "Longing" and Bisexuality among the Gebusi of New Guinea. *Ethos* 14:252–81.

———. 1987. Homosexuality in Melanesia: The Need for a Synthesis of Perspectives. *Journal of Psychoanalytic Anthropology* 10:155–91.

———. 1993. *South Coast New Guinea Cultures.* New York: Cambridge University Press.

———. 1995. Foucault Meets South New Guinea: Knowledge, Power, Sexuality. *Ethos* 22:391–438.

———. 1999. *From Primitive to Postcolonial in Melanesia and Anthropology.* Ann Arbor: University of Michigan Press.

Kon, I. 1995. *The Sexual Revolution in Russia: From the Age of Czars to Today.* New York: Free Press.

Kuper, A. 1991. *The Invention of Primitive Society: Transformations of an Illusion.* London: Routledge.

Kyakas, A., and P. Wiessner. 1992. *From Inside the Women's House: Enga Women's Lives and Traditions.* Buranda, Queensland, Australia: Robert Brown.

Landtman, G. 1917. The Folk Tales of the Kiwai Papuans. *Acta Societatis Scientarum Fennicae.* Helsinki: Printing Office of the Finnish Society of Literature.

Lane, C. 1999. *The Burdens of Intimacy: Psychoanalysis and Victorian Masculinity.* Chicago: University of Chicago Press.

Langness, L. L. 1967. Sexual Antagonism in the New Guinea Highlands: A Bena Bena Example. *Oceania* 37 (3): 161–77.

———. 1974. Ritual Power and Male Domination in the New Guinea Highlands: A Bena Bena Example. *Ethos* 2:189–212.

———. 1990. Oedipus in the New Guinea Highlands? *Ethos* 18:387–406.

———. 1999. *Men and "Woman" in New Guinea.* Novato, CA: Chandler and Sharp.

Lantenari, V. 1959. *The Religions of the Oppressed.* Trans. L. Sergis. New York: Knopf.

Lattas, A. 1999. *Cultures of Secrecy: Reinventing Race in Bush Kaliai Cargo Cults.* Madison: University of Wisconsin Press.

Lawrence, P. 1964. *Road Belong Cargo.* New York: Humanities Press.

———. 1965. The Ngaing of the Rai Coast. In P. Lawrence and M. J. Meggitt, eds., *Gods, Ghosts, and Men in Melanesia,* 198–223. New York: Oxford University Press.

Lawrence, P., and M. J. Meggitt, eds. 1965. *Gods, Ghosts, and Men in Melanesia.* New York: Oxford University Press.

Levine, D. N., ed. 1971. *Georg Simmel: On Individuality and Social Forms.* Chicago: University of Chicago Press.

Lévi-Strauss, C. 1974. *Tristes Tropiques.* Trans. J. Weightman and D. Weightman. New York: Atheneum.

Lewin, E., and W. Leap, eds. 1996. *Out in the Field: Reflections of Lesbian and Gay Anthroplogists.* Urbana: University of Illinois Press.

Lewis, G. 1980. *Day of Shining Red: An Essay on Understanding Ritual.* New York: Cambridge University Press.

Lewis, I. M. 1971. *Ecstatic Religion: An Anthropological Study of Spirit Possession and Shamanism.* Middlesex, UK: Penguin Books.

Lidz, T., and R. Lidz. 1989. *Oedipus in the Stone Age*. Madison, CT: International Universities Press.

Lindenbaum, S. 1984. Variations on a Sociosexual Theme in Melanesia. In G. Herdt, ed., *Ritualized Homosexuality in Melanesia*, 337–61. Berkeley: University of California Press.

Lindstrom, L. 1993. *Cargo Cult: Strange Stories of Desire from Melanesia and Beyond*. Honolulu: University of Hawaii Press.

Lloyd, G. E. R. 1983. *Science, Folklore and Ideology: Studies in the Life Sciences in Ancient Greece*. New York: Cambridge University Press.

Luhrman, T. M. 1989a. *Persuasions of the Witch's Craft: Ritual Magic in Contemporary England*. Cambridge: Cambridge University Press.

———. 1989b. The Magic of Secrecy. *Ethos* 17:131–65.

Lutkehaus, N., and P. B. Roscoe, eds. 1995. *Gender Rituals: Female Initiation in Melanesia*. New York: Routledge.

Makela, K., et al. 1996. *Alcoholics Anonymous as a Mutual Self-Help Movement*. Madison: University of Wisconsin Press.

Malinowski, B. 1922. *Argonauts of the Western Pacific*. New York: Dutton.

———. 1927. *Sex and Repression in Savage Society*. Cleveland: Meridian Books.

———. 1935. *Coral Gardens and Their Magic: A Study of the Methods of Tilling the Soil and of Agricultural Rites in the Trobriand Islands*. Bloomington: Indiana University Press.

———. 1967. *A Diary in the Strict Sense of the Term*. London: Routledge and Kegan Paul.

Manderson, L., and M. Jolly, eds. 1997. *Sites of Desire, Economies of Pleasure: Sexualities in Asia and the Pacific*. Chicago: University of Chicago Press.

Mead, M. 1933. The Marsalai Cult among the Arapesh, with Special Reference to the Rainbow Serpent Beliefs of the Australian Aborigines. *Oceania* 5:37–53.

———. 1935. *Sex and Temperament in Three Primitive Societies*. New York: Dutton.

———. 1940. *The Mountain Arapesh: Supernaturalism*. American Museum of Natural History, *Anthropological Papers* 37 (3): 319–451.

———. 1949. *Male and Female*. New York: Dutton.

———. 1956. *New Lives for Old. Cultural Transformation: Manus 1928–1953*. New York: William Morrow.

———. 1970. Field Work in the Pacific Islands, 1925–1967. In P. Golde, ed., *Women in the Field*, 293–331. Chicago: Aldine.

———. 1972. *Blackberry Winter: My Early Years*. New York: Morrow.

———. 1976. Preface. D. F. Tuzin, *The Ilahita Arapesh*. Berkeley: University of California Press.

———. 1977. Twenty-fourth Annual Karen Horney Lecture: Temperamental Differences and Sexual Dimorphism. *American Journal of Psychoanalysis* 37 (3): 179–92.

———. 1978. The Sepik as a Culture Area: Comment. *Anthropological Quarterly* 51 (1): 69–75.

Meggitt, M. J. 1964. Male-Female Relationships in the Highlands of Australian New Guinea. *American Anthropologist* 66 (4): 204–55.

———. 1971. From Tribesmen to Peasants: The Case of the Mae Enga of New

Guinea. In L. R. Hiatt and C. Jayawardena, eds., *Anthropology in Oceania*, 191–210. Sydney, Australia: Angus and Robertson.

———. 1979. Reflections Occasioned by Continuing Anthropological Field Research among the Enga of Papua New Guinea. In G. M. Foster et al., *Long-Term Field Research in Social Anthropology*, 107–25. New York: Academic Press.

Merullo, R. 2002. America's Secret Culture. *Chronicle of Higher Education*, March 1: B7–9.

Mimica, J. 2001. A Review from the Field. *Australian Journal of Anthropology* 12:225–37.

Mishima. 1958. *Confessions of a Mask*. New York: New Directions.

Mitchell, R. G., Jr. 1993. *Secrecy and Fieldwork*. Newbury Park, CA: Sage.

Moran, J. P. 2000. *Teaching Sex: The Shaping of Adolescence in the Twentieth Century*. Cambridge: Harvard University Press.

Morgan, L. H. 1851. *League of the Iroquois*. Rochester, NY: Sage and Brother.

———. 1877. *Ancient Society*. London: Macmillan.

———. 1901. *League of the Ho-de-no-sau-nee, or Iroquois*, ed. Herbert M. Lloyd. New York: Sage.

———. 1917. Constitution of the Grand Order of the Iroquois Organized at Aurora, New York. Photostat of the original of the handwriting of Morgan, Schoolcraft Papers, Box 24, Library of Congress, Washington, DC.

Moynihan, D. P. 1998. *Secrecy: The American Experience*. New Haven: Yale University Press.

Murphy, R. F. 1959. Social Structure and Sex Antagonism. *Southwestern Journal of Anthropology* 15:89–98.

———. 1971. *The Dialectics of Social Life: Alarms and Excursions in Anthropological Theory*. New York: Columbia University Press.

Obeyesekere, G. 1992. *The Apotheosis of Captain Cook: European Mythmaking in the Pacific*. Princeton: Princeton University Press.

Ottenberg, S. 1989. *Boyhood Rituals in an African Society: An Interpretation*. Seattle: University of Washington Press.

Otto, T. 1991. *The Politics of Tradition in Baluan: Social Change and the Construction of the Past in a Manus Society*. Nijmegen, The Netherlands: Centre for Pacific Studies.

Parker, A. C. 1909. Secret Medicine Societies of the Seneca. *American Anthropologist* 11:161–85.

Patterson, Thomas C. 2001. *A Social History of Anthropology in the United States*. Oxford: Berg.

Persico, Joseph E. 2001. *Roosevelt's Secret War: FDR and World War II Espionage*. New York: Random House.

Pincus, L., and C. Dare. 1978. *Secrets in the Family*. New York: Pantheon.

Plummer, K. 1995. *Telling Sexual Stories*. New York: Routledge.

Polanyi, M. 1966. *The Tacit Dimension*. New York: Doubleday Anchor.

Poole, F. J. P. 1981. Transforming "Natural" Women: Female Ritual Leaders and Gender Ideology among Bimin-Kuskusmin. In S. B. Ortner and H. Whitehead, eds., *Sexual Meanings: The Cultural Construction of Gender and Sexuality*, 1–93. New York: Cambridge University Press.

———. 1982. The Ritual Forging of Identity: Aspects of Person and Self in Bimin-Kuskusmin Male Initiation. In G. Herdt, ed., *Rituals of Manhood: Male Initiation in Papua New Guinea*, 100–154. Berkeley: University of California Press.

———. 1985. Coming into Social Being: Cultural Images of Infants in Bimin-Kuskusmin Folk Psychology. In G. M. White and J. Kirkpatrick, eds., *Person, Self, and Experience: Exploring Pacific Ethnopsychologies*, 183–242. Berkeley: University of California Press.

———. 1986. Personal Control, Social Responsibility, and Image of Person and Self among the Bimin-Kuskusmin of Papua New Guinea. *International Journal of Law and Psychiatry* 9:225–319.

Prados, J. 1996. *Presidents' Secret Wars*. Chicago: Ivan R. Dee Publishers.

Rappaport, Roy A. 1979. *Ecology, Meaning and Religion*. Richmond, CA: North Atlantic Books.

Read, K. E. 1951. The Gahuku-Gama of the Central Highlands. *South Pacific* 5 (8): 154–64.

———. 1952. Nama Cult of the Central Highlands, New Guinea. *Oceania* 23 (1): 1–25.

———. 1954. Cultures of the Central Highlands, New Guinea. *Southwestern Journal of Anthropology* 10 (1): 1–43.

———. 1955. Morality and the Concept of Person among the Gahuku-Gama, Eastern Highlands, New Guinea. *Oceania* 25 (4): 233–82.

———. 1959. Leadership and Consensus in a New Guinea Society. *American Anthropologist* 61 (3): 425–36.

———. 1965. *The High Valley*. London: Allen and Unwin.

———. 1980. *Other Voices*. Novato, CA: Chandler and Sharp.

———. 1984. The Nama Cult Recalled. In G. Herdt, ed., *Ritualized Homosexuality in Melanesia*, 211–47. Berkeley: University of California Press.

———. 1986. *Return to the High Valley*. Berkeley: University of California Press.

Reay, M. 1959. *The Kuma*. Melbourne, Australia: Melbourne University Press.

———. 1992. An Innocent in the Garden of Eden. In T. E. Hays, ed., *Ethnographic Presents: Pioneering Anthropologists in the Papua New Guinea Highlands*, 137–66. Berkeley: University of California Press.

Resek, C. 1960. *Lewis Henry Morgan: American Scholar*. Chicago: University of Chicago Press.

Rivers, W. H. R. 1917. Dreams and Primitive Culture. *Bulletin of the John Rylands Library* 4:387–410.

———. 1922. *Essays on the Depopulation of Melanesia*. Cambridge: Cambridge University Press.

Robin, R. W. 1982. Revival Movements in the Southern Highlands Province of Papua New Guinea. *Oceania* 52:320–43.

Robinson, J. J. 1989. *Born in Blood: The Lost Secrets of Freemasonry*. New York: M. Evans.

Roscoe, P. 1995. In the Shadow of the Tambaran: Female Initiation among the Du of the Sepik Basin. In N. C. Lutkehaus and P. B. Roscoe, eds., *Gender Rituals: Female Initiation in Melanesia*, 55–82. New York: Routledge.

Roscoe, P., and R. Scaglion. 1990. Male Initiation and European Intrusion in the

Sepik: A Preliminary Analysis. In *Sepik Heritage: Tradition and Change in Papua New Guinea*, ed. N. Lutkehaus et al., 14–23. Durham: Carolina Academic Press.

Sanday, P. 1981. *Female Power and Male Dominance*. Cambridge: Cambridge University Press.

Sapir, E. 1949. *Selected Writings of Edward Sapir in Language, Culture and Personality*. Ed. D. G. Mandelbaum. Berkeley: University of California Press.

Scaglion, R. 1986. Sexual Segregation and Ritual Pollution in Abelam Society. In *Self, Sex, and Gender in Cross-Cultural Fieldwork*, ed. T. L. Whitehead and M. E. Conaway, 151–63. Urbana: University of Illinois Press.

Scheppele, K. L. 1988. *Legal Secrets: Equality and Efficiency in the Common Law*. Chicago: University of Chicago Press.

Schieffelin, E. L. 1976. *The Sorrow of the Lonely and the Burning of the Dancers*. New York: St. Martin's Press.

———. 1978. The End of Traditional Music, Dance, and Body Decoration in Bosavi, Papua New Guinea. Discussion paper presented at the Institute of Papua New Guinea Studies, Boroko, Papua New Guinea.

———. 1982. The Bau'a Ceremonial Hunting Lodge: An Alternative to Initiation. In G. Herdt, ed., *Rituals of Manhood: Male Initiation in Papua New Guinea*, 155–200. Berkeley: University of California Press.

Schieffelin, E. L., and R. Crittenden. 1991. *Like People You See in a Dream*. Stanford: Stanford University Press.

Schwartz, T. 1973. Cult and Context: The Paranoid Ethos in Melanesia. *Ethos* 1:153–74.

Schwimmer, E. 1975. Friendship and Kinship. In E. Leyton, ed., *The Compact*, 49–70. ISER, Memorial University of Newfoundland.

———. 1980. *Power, Silence and Secrecy*. Toronto Semiotic Circle, Monograph No. 2. Toronto: Victoria University.

———. 1984. Male Couples in New Guinea. In G. Herdt, ed., *Ritualized Homosexuality in Melanesia*, 292–317. Berkeley: University of California Press.

Sedgwick, E. K. 1985. *Between Men: English Literature and Male Homosocial Desire*. New York: Columbia University Press.

———. 1990. *Epistemology of the Closet*. Berkeley: University of California Press.

Seligman, A. 1998. Between Public and Private. *Society* 35:28–36.

Shils, Edward A. 1956. *The Torment of Secrecy*. Glencoe, IL: Free Press.

Shweder, R. A. 1984. Anthropology's Romantic Rebellion against the Enlightenment, or There's More to Thinking than Reason and Evidence. In R. A. Shweder and R. A. LeVine, eds., *Culture Theory: Essays on Mind, Self, and Emotion*, 27–66. New York: Cambridge University Press.

———. 1990. Cultural Psychology—What Is It? In J. Stigler, R. Shweder, and G. Herdt, *Cultural Psychology*, 1–46. New York: Cambridge University Press.

Sillitoe, P. 1998. *Melanesia: Culture and Tradition*. New York: Cambridge University Press.

Silverman, E. K. 2001. *Masculinity, Motherhood, and Mockery: Psychoanalyzing Culture and the Iatmul Naven Rite in New Guinea*. Ann Arbor: University of Michigan Press.

Simmel, G. 1950. *The Sociology of Georg Simmel.* Trans. K. H. Wolff. Glencoe, IL: Free Press.

Simon, B. 1977. *Mind and Madness in Ancient Greece.* Ithaca: Cornell University Press.

Smith-Rosenberg, C. 1975. The Female World of Love and Ritual: Relations between Women in Nineteenth Century America. *Signs* 1:1–29.

Sperber, D. 1976. *Rethinking Symbolism.* Trans. A. L. Morton. Cambridge: Cambridge University Press.

Spiro, M. E. 1986. Cultural Relativism and the Future of Anthropology. *Cultural Anthropology* 1:259–86.

———. 1989. On the Strange and the Familiar in Recent Anthropological Thought. In J. Stigler, R. A. Shweder, and G. Herdt, eds., *Cultural Psychology,* 47–64. New York: Cambridge University Press.

Stephen, M. 1994. *A'aisa's Gifts: A Study of Magic and the Self.* Berkeley: University of California Press.

Stern, B. J. 1931. *Lewis Henry Morgan: Social Evolutionist.* Chicago: University of Chicago Press.

Stocking, G. 1987. *Victorian Anthropology.* New York: Free Press.

———. 1997. *Malinowski, Rivers, Benedict, and Others.* Madison: University of Wisconsin Press.

Stoller, R. J., and G. Herdt. 1985. Theories of Origins of Male Homosexuality: A Cross-Cultural Look. *Archives of General Psychiatry* 42 (4): 399–404.

Stone, I. F. 1989. *The Trial of Socrates.* New York: Doubleday Anchor.

Strathern, A. J. 1968. Descent and Alliance in the New Guinea Highlands: Some Problems of Comparison. Royal Anthropological Institute, *Proceedings,* 37–52.

———. 1971. *Rope of Moka: Big-Men and Ceremonial Exchange in Mount Hagen, New Guinea.* Cambridge: Cambridge University Press.

———. 1974. *One Father, One Blood.* Cambridge: Cambridge University Press.

———. 1979. Men's House, Women's House: The Efficacy of Opposition, Reversal, and Pairing in the Melpa Amb Kor Cult. *Journal of Polynesian Sociology* 88:37–51.

Strathern, A. J., and M. Strathern. 1971. *Self-Decoration in Mount Hagen.* London: Gerald Duckworth.

Strathern, M. 1972. *Women in Between.* London: Seminar Press.

———. 1979. The Self in Self-Decoration. *Oceania* 49:241–57.

———, ed. 1987. *Dealing with Inequality: Analyzing Gender Relations in Melanesia and Beyond.* New York: Cambridge University Press.

———. 1988. *The Gender of the Gift.* Berkeley: University of California Press.

———. 1992. *Reproducing the Future: Essays on Anthropology, Kinship, and the New Reproductive Technologies.* New York: Routledge.

Tambiah, S. J. 1990. *Magic, Science, Religion, and the Scope of Rationality.* New York: Cambridge University Press.

Tefft, S. K. 1980. *Secrecy: A Cross-Cultural Perspective.* New York: Human Sciences.

———. 1992. *The Dialectics of Secret Society Power in States.* Atlantic Highlands, NJ: Humanities Press.

Teunis, N. 1996. Homosexuality in Dakar: Is the Bed the Heart of a Sexual Subculture? *Journal of Gay, Lesbian, and Bisexual Identity* 1:153–70.

Tiger, L. 1970. *Men in Groups.* New York: Vintage Books.

Trumbach, R. 1994. London's Sapphists: From Three Sexes to Four Genders in the Making of Modern Culture. In G. Herdt, ed., *Third Sex, Third Gender: Beyond Sexual Dimorphism in Culture and History,* 111–36. New York: Zone Books.

Turner, V. W. 1967. Betwixt and Between: The Liminal Period in *Rites de Passage.* In V. W. Turner, ed., *The Forest of Symbols,* 93–111. Ithaca: Cornell University Press.

———. 1968a. Mukanda: The Politics of a Non-political Ritual. In M. J. Schwartz, ed., *Local-Level Politics,* 135–50. Chicago: Aldine.

———. 1968b. Myth and Symbol. In E. Sills, ed., *International Encyclopedia of the Social Sciences,* vol. 10, 576–82. New York: MacMillan.

———. 1971. *The Ritual Process: Structure and Anti-Structure.* Chicago: Aldine.

Tuzin, D. F. 1972. Yam Symbolism in the Sepik: An Interpretative Account. *Southwestern Journal of Anthropology* 281 (3): 230–54.

———. 1976. *The Ilahita Arapesh.* Berkeley: University of California Press.

———. 1980. *The Voice of the Tambaran: Truth and Illusion in Ilahita Arapesh Religion.* Berkeley: University of California Press.

———. 1982. Ritual Violence among the Ilahita Arapesh: The Dynamics of Moral and Religious Uncertainty. In *Rituals of Manhood: Male Initiation in Papua New Guinea,* 321–55. Berkeley: University of California Press.

———. 1989. Visions, Prophecies, and the Rise of Christian Consciousness. In G. Herdt and M. Stephen, eds., *Varieties of the Religious Imagination in New Guinea,* 187–210. New Brunswick, NJ: Rutgers University Press.

———. 1994. The Forgotten Passion: Sexuality and Anthropology in the Ages of Victoria and Bronislaw. *Journal of the History of the Behavioral Sciences* 30:114–37.

———. 1997. *The Cassowary's Revenge: Women and the Death of Masculinity in a New Guinea Society.* Chicago: University of Chicago Press.

Van Baal, J. 1963. The Cult of the Bull-Roarer in Australia and Southern New Guinea. *Bijdragen tot de Taal-, Land-, en Volkenkunde* 119:201–14.

———. 1966. *Dema: Description and Analysis of Marind-anim Culture.* The Hague: Martinus Nijhoff.

———. 1981. *Man's Quest for Partnership.* Assen, the Netherlands: Van Gorcum.

———. 1984. The Dialectics of Sex in Marind-anim Culture. In G. Herdt, ed., *Ritualized Homosexuality in Melanesia,* 128–66. Berkeley: University of California Press.

Vance, C. S. 1991. Anthropology Rediscovers Sexuality: A Theoretical Comment. *Social Science and Medicine* 33:875–84.

Van der Meer, T. 1994. Sodomy and the Pursuit of a Third Sex in the Early Modern Period. In G. Herdt, ed., *Third Sex, Third Gender: Beyond Sexual Dimorphism in Culture and History,* 137–212. New York: Zone Books.

Van Gennep, A. 1960 [1909]. *The Rites of Passage.* Trans. M. K. Vizedom and G. L. Caffee. Chicago: University of Chicago Press.

Wagner, R. 1967. *The Curse of Souw: Principles of Daribi Clan Definition and Alliance.* Chicago: University of Chicago Press.

———. 1972. *Habu: The Innovation of Meaning in Daribi Religion.* Chicago: University of Chicago Press.

———. 1975. *The Invention of Culture.* Toronto: Prentice-Hall.

———. 2000. Our Very Own Cargo Cult. *Oceania* 70:362–72.

Wallace, A. F. C. 1965. *Religion: An Anthropological View.* New York: Random House.

———. 1972. *The Death and Rebirth of the Seneca.* New York: Vintage Books.

Warren, C., and B. Laslett. 1980. Privacy and Secrecy: A Conceptual Comparison. In S. K. Tefft, ed., *Secrecy: A Cross-Cultural Perspective,* 25–34. New York: Human Sciences.

Watson, J. B. 1965. From Hunting to Horticulture in the New Guinea Highlands. *Ethnology* 4:295–309.

———. 1971. Tairora: The Politics of Despotism in a Small Society. In R. Berndt and P. Lawrence, eds., *Politics in New Guinea,* 224–75. Nedlands, Australia: University of Western Australia Press.

Webster, H. 1932. *Primitive Secret Societies: A Study in Early Politics and Religion.* 2d ed. New York: Macmillan.

Wedgwood, C. H. 1930. The Nature and Functions of Secret Societies. *Oceania* 1:130–45.

Weeks, J. 1985. *Sexuality and Its Discontents.* London: Routledge and Kegan Paul.

Weiner, A. B. 1992. *Inalienable Possessions: The Paradox of Keeping-While-Giving.* Berkeley: University of California Press.

Weiner, J. F. 1988. Durkheim and the Papuan Male Cult: Whitehead's Views on Social Structure and Ritual in New Guinea. *American Ethnologist* 15:567–73.

Weston, K. 1993. Lesbian/Gay Studies in the House of Anthropology. *Annual Review of Anthropology* 22:339–67.

White, L. A. 1959. Lewis Henry Morgan: His Life and His Researches. In Leslie A. White, ed., *Lewis Henry Morgan: The Indian Journals, 1859–1862.* Ann Arbor: University of Michigan Press.

Whitehead, H. 1985. The Varieties of Fertility Cultism in New Guinea, Part I. *American Ethnologist* 13:80–99.

———. 1986. The Varieties of Fertility Cultism in New Guinea, Part II. *American Ethnologist* 14:271–89.

Whitehouse, H. 1992. Memorable Religions: Transmission, Codification, and Change in Divergent Melanesian Contexts. *Man* 27:777–98.

———. 1995. *Inside the Cult: Religious Innovation and Transmission in Papua New Guinea.* Oxford: Clarendon.

———. 1998. From Mission to Movement: The Impact of Christianity on Patterns of Political Association in Papua New Guinea. *Man* 4:43–64.

———. 2000. *Arguments and Icons: Divergent Modes of Religiosity.* New York: Oxford.

Wikan, U. 1990. *Managing Turbulent Hearts: A Balinese Formula for Living.* Chicago: University of Chicago Press.

Williams, F. E. 1924. *The Natives of the Purari Delta.* Port Moresby, Papua New Guinea: Government Printer.

———. 1930. *Orokaiva Society.* London: Oxford University Press.

———. 1936. *Papuans of the Trans-Fly.* Oxford: Clarendon Press.

————. 1940. *Drama of Orokolo.* Oxford: Oxford University Press.

————. 1976. Bull-Roarers in the Papuan Gulf. In E. G. Schwimmer, ed., *The Vailala Madness and Other Essays,* 73–122. Honolulu: University of Hawaii Press.

Winnicott, D. W. 1971. *Playing and Reality.* London: Tavistock.

Wirz, P. 1933. Headhunting Expeditions of the Tugeri into the Western Division of British New Guinea. *Tijdschrift van de Instituut voor Taal-, Land-, en Volkenkunde* 73:105–22.

Worsley, P. 1957. *The Trumpet Shall Sound.* London: Paladin.

————. 1968. *The Three Worlds: Culture and World Development.* Chicago: University of Chicago Press.

Young, M. 1983. *Magicians of Manumanua: Living Myth in Kalauna.* Berkeley: University of California Press.

Index

✳